The Ultimate iOS Interview Playbook

Conquer Swift, frameworks, design patterns, and app architecture for your dream job

Avi Tsadok

BIRMINGHAM—MUMBAI

The Ultimate iOS Interview Playbook

Group Product Manager: Rohit Rajkumar

Publishing Product Manager: Kaustubh Manglurkar

Senior Content Development Editor: Rashi Dubey

Technical Editor: Simran Udasi

Copy Editor: Safis Editing

Project Coordinator: Arul Viveaun S

Proofreader: Safis Editing

Indexer: Manju Arasan

Production Designer: Alishon Mendonca

Marketing Coordinators: Nivedita Pandey and Namita Velgekar

First published: August 2023

Production reference: 050723

Published by Packt Publishing Ltd.

Grosvenor House

11 St Paul's Square

Birmingham

B3 1R, UK.

ISBN 978-1-80324-631-4

www.packtpub.com

Contributors

About the author

Avi Tsadok, a seasoned iOS developer with a 13-year career, has proven his expertise by leading projects for notable companies such as Any.do, a top productivity app, and currently Melio Payments, where he steers the mobile team. Known for his ability to simplify complex tech concepts, Avi has written 4 books and published 40+ tutorials and articles that enlighten and empower aspiring iOS developers. His voice resonates beyond the page, as he's a recognized public speaker and has conducted numerous interviews with fellow iOS professionals, furthering the field's discourse and development.

A heartfelt thank you to my wife, Tammy, for her unwavering support during the tumultuous journey of writing this book. Your patience during my mad writing spells has been nothing short of amazing. I am eternally grateful.

About the reviewer

Francesco Deliro is an experienced and passionate iOS software engineer. With over nine years of experience in the mobile industry, Francesco, currently at Revolut, has worked with several companies and start-ups, including Glovo in Spain and Bestever.AI in the USA.

Francesco's expertise lies in Swift development, UX design, and clean architecture. Throughout his career, Francesco has demonstrated a deep passion for coding and the latest technologies. He has actively contributed to several open source projects, showcasing his commitment to knowledge sharing and collaboration within the developer community.

Table of Contents

3

Developer Branding   41

Part 2: Swift Language and Coding

4

Data Structures and Algorithms   55

Part 3: The Frameworks

7

Building Great User Experiences with UIKit   125

8

SwiftUI and Declarative Programming   153

9

Understanding Persistent Memory 177

10

Libraries Management 197

Part 4: Design and Architecture

11

12

13

Acing the Coding Assessment   265

Preface

It has been many years since Apple introduced its first SDK for iPhone development (which is what iOS used to be called back then), and in that time, the iOS ecosystem has become one of the most powerful ecosystems in the world. With the goal of supporting billions of devices with up-to-date technologies, the demand for iOS developers remains constantly high.

However, things have become much more complex. In 2009, adding a simple table view or a button would have been enough to land a job. However, nowadays, these tasks are not even asked about in interviews. The knowledge spectrum is so wide today that interviewers focus on aspects beyond just basic knowledge.

The complexity of today's iOS development world, combined with strong competition, has created a diverse hiring process that requires more than just building a simple screen. As a result, there is a great need to prepare ourselves in a professional and extensive way.

The Ultimate iOS Interview Playbook is a comprehensive book that guides you from the early basics of interview preparation to Swift, the different frameworks, and even design, architecture, and coding tasks.

Who this book is for

iOS developers at all levels will find this book appealing and useful. However, there are three types of developers who will find it even more valuable:

- **Junior developers seeking their first job**: Finding your first job as an iOS developer can be challenging. While workplaces understand that junior developers may not have extensive experience, they still expect them to possess the minimum skills and knowledge required for the role. *The Ultimate iOS Interview Playbook* can assist inexperienced developers in successfully navigating this difficult task.

- **Experienced developers who feel stuck in their career**: Spending several years in the same workplace or role can have its benefits, but it may also lead to a decline in interview skills and hinder growth in new development areas. Moreover, for experienced developers, it has been a long time since they completed their studies, making it a good opportunity to revisit the basics.

- **Developers looking to advance their careers**: Those who view their specialization as a long-term career path need to take the next step to progress. Seeking a new role is not an easy task, especially while working full-time and trying to build your personal brand.

In summary, the book caters to a wide range of iOS developers, but these particular groups can benefit greatly from *The Ultimate iOS Interview Playbook*.

What this book covers

Chapter 1, Before the Interview, describes the actions we need to take before the interview itself, including company research, resume writing, and interview preparations.

Chapter 2, Going through the Interview Process, provides an overview of the interview process, including its different steps and their goals.

Chapter 3, Developer Branding, covers how to leverage our brand as developers, such as creating impressive GitHub and Stack Overflow accounts, working on personal projects, and authoring.

Chapter 4, Data Structures and Algorithms, explores the building blocks of Swift and coding in general. It delves into topics such as structs, classes, arrays, Codable, dictionaries, and sets. The chapter includes common interview questions and examples.

Chapter 5, The Swift Programming Language, provides an important overview of the Swift language fundamentals. It covers topics such as optionals, access control, closures, protocols, memory management, and generics. The chapter includes code examples and interview questions.

Chapter 6, Managing Your Code, covers a different aspect of being an iOS developer and helps to develop other important skills, such as planning, testing, debugging, and documentation.

Chapter 7, Building Great User Experiences with UIKit, examines one of the most important frameworks in iOS development – UIKit. It includes topics such as Auto Layout, `UIView`, `UIViewController`, `UITableView`, navigation, and animations. The chapter provides full explanations with code examples and interview questions.

Chapter 8, SwiftUI and Declarative Programming, explores the future of iOS development by focusing on SwiftUI and declarative programming. Even if you have no experience in this field, this chapter is crucial. It covers declarative programming, states and observable objects, navigation, SwiftUI life cycles, and Combine.

Chapter 9, Understanding Persistent Memory, covers a less common interview topic. It provides a glimpse into Core Data, `UserDefaults`, `Keychain`, and Files. The main goal of this chapter is to prepare us for advanced stages such as design and architecture interviews.

Chapter 10, Libraries Management, provides an overview of integrating third-party libraries into our projects (a critical skill for developers these days) and also modularizing our project. This chapter includes interview questions and code examples as well.

Chapter 11, Design Patterns to Solve Complex Questions, covers the toolsets needed to have an effective design in our projects. It provides an overview of the most common patterns in iOS development, such as MVC, MVVM, dependency injection, delegation, singleton, and concurrency.

Chapter 12, Drilling into App Architecture, explores what app architecture means and the basic concepts of building great architecture. It includes the separation of concerns principle, app layers, protocol usage, and networking.

Chapter 13, Acing the Coding Assessment, examines the coding part of the interview, including whiteboard and remote tasks. The chapter explains how to prioritize our work, approach a coding interview, and avoid exposing red flags.

To get the most out of this book

There are many short examples in this book provided solely for demonstration purposes, and you do not need to execute them directly to understand. That being said, it is recommended to practice some of the topics discussed in this book using Xcode and a Mac.

Software/hardware covered in the book	Operating system requirements
Xcode	macOS
CocoaPods	

Conventions used

There are a number of text conventions used throughout this book.

`Code in text`: Indicates code words in text, database table names, folder names, filenames, file extensions, pathnames, dummy URLs, user input, and Twitter handles. Here is an example: "Let's see how the function interface looks once we extract it to a `Person` struct."

A block of code is set as follows:

```
struct A {
    var name: String
}

let a = A(name: "Avi")
a.name = "John"
```

When we wish to draw your attention to a particular part of a code block, the relevant lines or items are set in bold:

```
platform :ios, '14.0'

target 'MyApp' do
  use_frameworks!
    pod 'MyFramework', :path => '../MyFramework'
end
```

Bold: Indicates a new term, an important word, or words that you see on screen. For instance, words in menus or dialog boxes appear in **bold**. Here is an example: "Open Xcode and select **File | New | Package** from the menu bar."

> **Tips or important notes**
> Appear like this.

Get in touch

Feedback from our readers is always welcome.

General feedback: If you have questions about any aspect of this book, email us at customercare@ packtpub.com and mention the book title in the subject of your message.

Errata: Although we have taken every care to ensure the accuracy of our content, mistakes do happen. If you have found a mistake in this book, we would be grateful if you would report this to us. Please visit www.packtpub.com/support/errata and fill in the form.

Piracy: If you come across any illegal copies of our works in any form on the internet, we would be grateful if you would provide us with the location address or website name. Please contact us at copyright@packt.com with a link to the material.

If you are interested in becoming an author: If there is a topic that you have expertise in and you are interested in either writing or contributing to a book, please visit authors.packtpub.com.

Download a free PDF copy of this book

Thanks for purchasing this book!

Do you like to read on the go but are unable to carry your print books everywhere?

Is your eBook purchase not compatible with the device of your choice?

Don't worry, now with every Packt book you get a DRM-free PDF version of that book at no cost.

Read anywhere, any place, on any device. Search, copy, and paste code from your favorite technical books directly into your application.

The perks don't stop there, you can get exclusive access to discounts, newsletters, and great free content in your inbox daily

Follow these simple steps to get the benefits:

1. Scan the QR code or visit the link below

https://packt.link/free-ebook/9781803246314

2. Submit your proof of purchase

3. That's it! We'll send your free PDF and other benefits to your email directly

Part 1:
Everything about Interviews

This initial part of the book focuses on the essential steps to take before starting the interview process. It covers various actions, such as finding a suitable company, writing a compelling resume, understanding the interview process, and establishing a strong developer brand. By the end of this section, you will have the necessary tools to succeed in your first interview.

In this part, we have the following chapters:

- *Chapter 1, Before the Interview*
- *Chapter 2, Going through the Interview Process*
- *Chapter 3, Developer Branding*

1
Before the Interview

We consider ourselves good iOS developers. How good? Well, we have done some impressive things in our lives. For example, we built gorgeous animations, implemented Combine, uploaded app versions to the App Store, and debugged complex bugs.

So, what is the problem exactly? Why do we need this book?

Because knowing Swift, UIKit, and Combine are remarkable, and debugging, algorithms, and CI management are all essential skills for an iOS developer. But one skill needs to be added for many developers, and that's *how to be a player in the iOS developers' labor market*. Playing in this market requires us to learn and adapt to new skills that some of us may still need to learn, such as skills in the fields of self-expression, wording, communication, and even marketing.

By the end of this book, we will take our tremendous iOS development knowledge and learn how to use it to develop a new skill: the ability to pass an iOS interview.

So, how do we start?

Lau Tzu (a Chinese philosopher) said:

The journey of a thousand miles begins with one step.

But the question is, what is the first step?

Is answering a Swift question or scribbling a design for an architecture problem the first step? Well, our first step is to understand what *we want* from our workplace, *where* we want to be, and to get ready to conquer it with confidence.

Understanding all this may sound like an easy task. We just send our resume (that we wrote in two minutes) to all the tech companies we know and expect that something will pop up. Unfortunately, it doesn't work like that. We must research the market and adjust our resume according to our needs. Even more important, before we look at the market, we must look inside and understand who we are and what will be good for us.

In this chapter, we will learn how to reach our first interview with a company that suits us in the best condition possible. We will **build a company profile** together and learn about the different types of companies out there. We will also learn what a *good (or bad) resume* is and write a **resume** that fits us and our target workplace. Then, we will learn *how to be prepared* for our first interview in all matters.

To that end, we will cover the following topics in this chapter:

- Performing company research
- Building our resume
- Preparing for the interview

Performing company research

Many candidates may find the next sentence strange, but some fail in iOS interviews, because they lack knowledge about the company they're interviewing for. Do you believe that? The truth is that mastering UIKit or SwiftUI is essential, and being a **Swift** expert is crucial, but the workplace profile is just as important.

Think of working in a company as a long-term relationship and the interview process as the blind-date meeting where it all started. Remember the excitement, the research we did with our friends, or the questions each of you asked during the session. Well, the job interview is your first date. Dress nicely!

A job interview is a bidirectional process. During the interview, we examine the workplace just as much as the workplace examines us.

The primary reason for learning about the company we're interviewing for is apparent: we want to ensure our next workplace fits us like a glove. But there's another reason. It will be constructive during the interview process if we are familiar with the company, its product, and the market.

Before starting the interview process, we should build a company Profile where we can learn everything about its culture, size, working environment, and more. There's official and unofficial information that we can retrieve, and both are essential to our readiness.

Why? Let's find out!

Knowing where you're going is part of the interview

Here's a secret you can find only in this book: many interviewers check our knowledge, not only in **iOS** development but also regarding the *workplace itself*. Sometimes, it can make a difference when comparing candidates with similar coding skills!

Interviewers look for enthusiastic, self-confident candidates who are familiar with the product, the market, and the industry.

The preceding knowledge leads to another side of our personality that we want to show: that we are mature, serious, and conducted comprehensive research before we came to the interview. This side of us tremendously boosts our chances of succeeding in our role, and that's something interviewers look for.

Company profiles affect our answers

Believe it or not, some company characteristics may influence our answers, especially regarding design and architecture questions. And that's something we will learn in the book. In many cases, interviewers want to *see gray colors* in our personality, not just black and white.

I mean that we always need to balance our answers and understand that there are pros and cons to almost any question. Answering a question with the mindset of the company we are interviewing for can really make a difference in how it looks to the person's eye who is interviewing us at the time.

Learning the company characteristics

What are the things we need to look for when doing our research? What builds our company profile?

Generally, the company profile is divided into three parts: **product and industry**, **company details**, and **working environment**. I think that all of them are important in one way or another to start understanding where we are interviewing and if and how the workplace fits our needs.

Let's see how we build each part.

Product and industry

In a job interview, I can't begin to describe what it means to be familiar with the company's product or industry. Let's talk about what it does to us as interviewees.

First, it *increases our self-confidence*. We feel in control when we understand the broad ecosystem around our interview process. When the interviewer talks about the company and its product, we can quickly understand what he is talking about. But moreover, knowing the product will point our answers in the *right direction and context*. There's a big difference between answering an architecture question when interviewing for a social app company and an advertising company building an SDK. In an iOS development world, these are two different creatures. We will go over that in *Chapter 12*.

And second, asking the interviewer intelligent questions about the company shows that *we did our homework* and know what we're talking about. In most places, that counts for a lot.

Retrieving company details

Company details are our company profile's most accessible and shortest section. There are a couple of questions we should ask ourselves before and during the interview process. These questions can give us a clue about whether this company is suitable for our needs.

The questions that we should ask are essential and intertwined:

- What is the company **size**?
- Where is the company currently in its life cycle?
- Is the company **public or private**?

You may not find these questions necessary, but as a matter of fact, they have a tremendous impact on your career as an iOS developer and even beyond that.

Let's discuss each one in detail and start with the first one – company size.

Considering company size

There are three company sizes: small, medium, and large.

In the USA, a small tech company is considered to have fewer than 100 employees, a medium tech company employs under 1,000 employees, and a company with over 1,000 employees is considered to be large.

Even though these definitions are not identical in different countries and industries, in our discussion, it doesn't matter much. What matters is what it means to us as employees.

Small companies allow us to produce a *more significant impact* on the company and its product. It usually means working in small teams; sometimes teams that are one person only(!). And because these companies are small, they also give us an *intimate feeling*, which comes with a *good work/life balance*. Another pro for small companies is the pace – it's *much faster*. The fast pace is mainly because small teams have simplified working flows. Small companies also have downsides. They are mostly *less stable* than bigger companies and have *less room to grow* your career.

Large companies are the opposite. Even though they are much *more stable*, the employee has a much *smaller impact* on the company product and its path. To gain more influence in large companies, we need to move up in the hierarchy, which, unlike small companies, is much easier. Also, the pace of development is *much slower* due to more dependencies between teams and company regulations.

In a way, *medium* companies are like a mix of large and small. They still provide an *intimate family* environment while being more stable than small companies. Therefore, it is not surprising that medium companies are the preferable firms by most tech workers. The combination of stability, a warm environment, and fast development pace fulfill the preferences of most people in the industry.

But looking at company size as the only indication of suitability is perhaps too superficial. As stated earlier in this section, there are more factors you need to take into consideration, for example, where the company is in its life cycle.

Analyzing a company's life cycle

Companies have a **life cycle** like humans and any other living creature. You might ask yourself now, "A living creature?"

Yes! Like humans, companies have an age, DNA, innovations, ideas, and many other characteristics.

The following diagram shows a start-up company's life cycle:

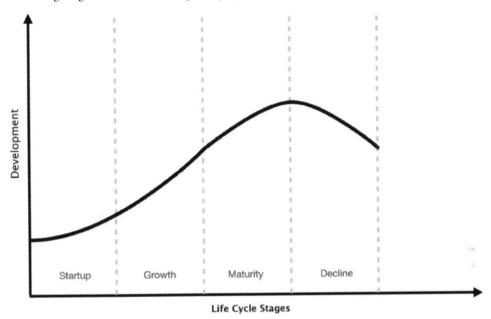

Figure 1.1 – A start-up company's life cycle

Companies are born, and they grow, mature, and sometimes even decline and die. And just like a human, each stage of their life cycle has its own excitement and risks. As a result, when searching for a company, one thing to look at is the stage in its life.

The company's stage may point to the *working atmosphere* we might experience. It can tell us the opportunities and whether the company is at a stage where everything is ticking, or if we need to set up workflows from the ground up.

Another deeper aspect we need to look at is *the life cycle of the mobile team* itself. The company can be mature, but the mobile team was just born. Regardless of the different opportunities a new team may have, there can also be differences in the *technology* it uses, and that's also a critical issue in our interviews.

In many cases, interviewers tend to ask questions about the technology they use or want to use in their projects. For example, if we're talking about a mature mobile team, its developers probably use **UIKit** and might even use **Objective-C** (God forbid!). In this case, expect questions about **UIViews** or **Objective-C** categories and blocks.

Also, in mature teams (and mature products), the project might *contain legacy code,* which can be painful to deal with and sometimes requires refactoring.

When we perform our company's research, we must ask the *right questions* about the company's stage, the team, and the project. The answers we'll get can give us an overview of what we might expect in our interview and the workplace.

Now, notice that the question, "In what stage is the company right now?" is not always a straightforward question, and not all interviewers can answer that easily. You need to dig in a little bit deeper when asking questions and conclude yourself. One of the things we need to consider when analyzing the company's state is whether it is public or private.

Deliberating between public and private

The difference between a public and a private company is pretty simple: its ownership. A private company is owned by one or a few individuals, while a public company is owned by shareholders who have bought stock.

It is difficult to say which type of company is "better" to work for, as this will depend on an individual's personal preferences and career goals. Some developers may prefer the stability and potential for growth that a large public company can offer. In contrast, others may prefer a smaller private company's flexibility and entrepreneurial spirit.

If you are confused between the "public versus private" and the "large versus small" argument, it is not a coincidence. Public companies are generally more prominent. They are more structured, while private companies are considered to be smaller.

But there's much more than just size. The ownership difference has an impact on the company culture. For example, in public companies, the decision-making process is more complex due to the need to consider the interests of the shareholders. That's not the case with a private company with a more agile and faster process.

But I want to clarify this point: we can still find a "start-up" atmosphere in a public company and corporate vibes in a start-up company. Therefore, it is essential to sense the working environment and consider the results.

Let's see what factors we need to look at.

Sensing the working environment

Believe it or not, coding is not everything in life (but I agree it's a lot)!

The product can be excellent, and the team can be super strong. But, if you want to develop not only iOS apps but also your career, you need to work in a supportive environment that can make this happen.

There are several questions we can try to discover about a company's working environment:

- What is the company's *hierarchy*? Is it flat or hierarchical?
- How are the **research and development** (**R&D**) department and the *mobile team built*?

- What is the average working day like? Do we have daily or weekly meetings?
- Are there any **code review** sessions? Who can do code reviews?
- How is the **work/life balance** procedure?
- Is there an option for an iOS developer to write **backend code** and be a full-stack developer?
- Is there *shared knowledge* between the iOS team and the **Android** team?
- What is the *involvement* of the iOS team with other aspects of the company, such as the product?

The primary issue with these questions is the fact that it is hard to get reliable answers from the interviewer. I'm not saying he is a liar! But remember, one of the interviewer's goals is to market the company and the iOS team. However, one of your goals is to get the most authentic answers, and these two goals do not always fit in.

Always take what the interviewer says with a grain of salt and reach for the truth yourself.

So, next, let's talk about obtaining some helpful information and see how we build an unofficial profile.

Building the unofficial company profile

We learned how to perform a basic company profile using basic questions in the *Learning the company characteristics* section.

Now that we made sure the company's "dry details" fit what we need and require, it's time to dive deeper and *collect some unofficial information* about the company. There are three ways of doing that: research, research, and… research!

Analyzing job postings

You can learn a lot from analyzing the job description. Moreover, it doesn't have to be the iOS developer job description, but any other roles in the company. By reading the job description, we can reveal how the company prioritizes its values even though the company probably didn't mean to share that prioritization with us.

For example, if, on the one hand, the job description emphasizes how it's essential to meet deadlines, it shows happy hour events and talks about loyalty. Still, on the other hand, they say nothing about flexibility, it may be a good indication of how the company feels about **work-life balance**. If the job description describes the atmosphere as *dynamic* and *young* but doesn't mention *professional* and *strong*, it may be a good indication of what code reviews will look like.

Remember, nothing is set in stone, but collecting puzzle pieces is vital to see the whole picture.

Looking at social network profiles

Just like job postings, looking at the company's social networks such as LinkedIn, Facebook, Twitter, and Instagram can give us a sense of the *company's ambience*. For instance, we can see how many beach days the company holds versus professional events such as meetups and lectures.

We can open the company page on LinkedIn and see interesting stuff such as **diversity**, **leadership**, and more.

Social networks can provide us with interesting inside information about companies that we won't get in interviews or the company's website.

Another interesting thing is what *employees, customers, or partners share*. Do you feel that they are pleased or unhappy? Do people stay long in this company, or does it look like a revolving door? Do some spy work! It's perfectly legit and helpful.

Browsing the company website

The company website is another excellent place to find additional details about your dream workplace. Besides products, you can discover interesting information, such as company values, leadership, and more.

But you can find even more fascinating information, such as the company **blog** and events. Many companies hold professional blogs where employees can post articles related to their work.

A professional blog maintained by employees can indicate that the company puts developer branding on top of their minds. If that's important to you, a blog can add some points to the equation.

Talking with employees

This is probably the best way to understand what it feels like working in the company you are thinking of applying to.

Today, the world is more connected and linked than ever, and it's effortless to approach almost anyone you want.

LinkedIn's *company page* is probably the simplest way to connect to iOS (or even Android) developers that currently work or worked in this company. Tell them you are considering applying and want to consult with them.

Before the talk, *write questions* about the information that is much more difficult to receive in other channels. This inside information is precious, so prepare seriously for that talk.

Here are some examples for questions:

- What are your *working hours*? Do you work from home as well?

- What *technologies or design patterns* have been added to the project since you started working there?

- Are you doing **tech design** for features? If so, who's writing them?

We should always take what people say with some doubts, so asking direct questions can be tricky. Every person we talk to is different, and each has a different history and experience with their working place. What we do need to do is to listen to what's *not being said* and try to notice any subtext in the conversation.

For example, we can ask them, "What do you like about the company?" Obviously, they will list things, such as company events and perhaps the people they work with. If they won't state something such as "high standards," it doesn't mean they do not exist, but if several workers don't mention that, it could be a good indication that they're not something the company is focusing on.

Being a good detective or investigator can sometimes pay off!

Glassdoor

Glassdoor is a website that allows employees to *review their workplace anonymously*. Isn't it what we tried to achieve a minute earlier? Good for us!

Moreover, Glassdoor provides additional benefits, such as the ability to see not only workers' reviews, but also candidates' personal experiences from the process while describing the interview, the office, and even interview questions and coding tasks. Sites like Glassdoor are a treasure for candidates who want to perform advanced company research and can prepare us for the interview day.

Come to the office early

This is one of the lesser-known tips in company research, yet it is still very effective. When you are invited to the first on-site interview, *early always looks* good. It shows that we are serious and mature, and there's no worry that it can cause negative effects.

But coming early has an additional benefit. It's an excellent method to experience how a day looks in the office. We can sit in the office, make a coffee while waiting, and listen to what employees say.

Do they talk about work? A specific problem? Are they working in different teams (so we can tell the collaboration level)?

If it's morning, *how many workers* do we see in the office? This can be an indication of working hours or work-life balance.

Remember, we won't always hear the complete truth during the interview process regarding different information about the workplace, so seeing things through your own eyes is immeasurably valuable.

To summarize, knowing where we go can make us more ready for the interview process, and it helps us understand if the company we are interviewing for fits our requirements.

As I said earlier, interviews go both ways. We examine the workplace just as much as it examines us. And since it is going to be our next "home," we should invest effort in it as much as we can.

Now that we have done our company research, we need to move forward and apply to those companies. The most popular way to do that is by building our resume.

Building our resume

We now see that performing company research is not a difficult task at all. But there's another side of the equation, and that's us: how do we get an interview with the company we desire?

Being noticeable among dozens or hundreds of other candidates is not easy. Making our resume shine when there are many other great candidates sounds like an impossible mission. It's not a coincidence that some recruiters claim that writing a good CV *is not science but an art*. Sure, there are guidelines on how to do that, but to stand out, we need an artistic touch.

And speaking about art, let's see how looking at our profile as a movie or a book can benefit us.

A resume is like a book or a movie

OK... what?

Imagine you enter a bookstore. You want to pick one or two books, but there are thousands of books in the store. What do you do? You choose a book with an interesting title, turn it over, and go over the *back cover text*. After a few seconds, you have already decided about the book even though you haven't opened it or finished reading the back cover. The reason for that is apparent. You *don't have time* to review so many books, and you decide to invest your time in those with a catchy title and an interesting back cover opening.

The experience I just described is precisely what happens in workplaces that receive many job applications. In big companies, an average resume scanning by a recruiter takes between *six to 10 seconds*. This is a short time to impress someone, isn't it? Well, that's why I said it's like an art more than science.

Now, if we pass that stage, the recruiter decides to read the rest of the resume. Assuming our profile fits the company, we need to *impress the hiring manager*, which is not an easy hurdle at all.

Oh, didn't I tell you? That's the difference from a book. We need several people to read our resume and like it!

Let's see how we nail that challenge together.

Structuring the resume outline

A basic resume outline is based on content importance. We start with our name as the title, contact information, a summary of ourselves, expertise, and then skills, education, and our projects and achievements.

There are indeed different resume outline variants out in the field. For instance, some say adding personal insights, such as hobbies or volunteering activities is also a good idea. Some even add a photo portrait.

But in my perceptive, I think *less is more, regarding resumes*. We should keep it simple, clear, and straight to the point.

Working on design and layout

Well, what about the design and the layout?

There are tons of resume design templates we can download easily from the web. Even though some of them look beautiful, we should remember that the document's purpose is sending a *clear message* about who we are and why we are the best option to invite for an interview.

Since we have only six to ten seconds to catch the recruiter's attention, we should plan our **CV** (*Curriculum Vitae -> "course of life"*) according to that assumption. One of the most famous methods of that is to use something called the **F-Pattern**.

What is the F-Pattern?

Scanning a document quickly sounds straightforward at first. We probably imagine the recruiter starting to read your document and just stopping after a while. The basic assumption, that the recruiter is *reading our document rather than scanning* it, is just wrong.

The **Nielsen Norman Group** (**NNGroup**) had exciting research in 2006. Their researchers gave thousands of documents to more than 200 students and asked them to review them while analyzing the eye-tracking movement quickly.

The findings concluded that users have a constant pattern of "scanning" the documents – they move their eyes in a pattern that looks like the letter F:

1. First, they read the first two rows, from left to right.

2. Then, they move down a little bit, skip some lines, maybe, and read another row, but this time they won't go all the way to the end.

3. Finally, they scan the document from top to bottom and on the left side.

> **Right-to-left languages**
> For right-to-left languages such as Arabic or Hebrew, the F-Pattern is flipped.

Have a look at the following image from NNGroup's website (`https://www.nngroup.com/articles/f-shaped-pattern-reading-web-content-discovered/`):

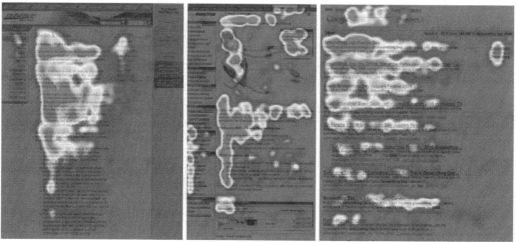

Eyetracking by Nielsen Norman Group nngroup.com NN/g

Figure 1.2 – NNGroup Document Scanning Experiment results

So, why do users do that?

Well, readers have a goal. They want their scanning to be as effective as possible. They aim to grab maximum information from the document with minimal effort and time.

We now understand where the recruiter's eyes go when scanning your resume, but how can we ensure the reader doesn't miss our primary objectives?

Okay, now we are battling for the user's attention, but it doesn't mean we are losing. Here are some tips on how to handle the situation:

- Because of the F-Pattern research, we know that the user invests heavily in our document's top part. We should put our *most meaningful message* to the user in this place. In other words, this is where our "money should be spent."

- The same goes for each section of our document. We always need to *start with the message*. When we describe a project that we were involved with, we should start with our contribution to the project rather than describing the project's history.

- We need to make it easier for the reader to understand what's important and what's not by using typography. For example, **marking primary words in bold** can help us emphasize the document's essential takes (as I did here).

- *Add space* between sections and use big, clear headings. That can help the reader understand the document outline and avoid getting lost in the scanning task.

- Use *short bullets* instead of long, tedious paragraphs. Short bullets take a load of information and display it in a structured list, helping the user to scan and understand what we wanted to say quickly.

Using typography is a great way to help the user understand how to read our resume while taking advantage of the F-Pattern and overcoming its flaws.

Let's break our resume into different pieces. We'll start with your personal information.

What is the personal information part?

Remember, we already said our resume content should be ordered by priority. So, what's more important than us?

Returning to the bookstore analogy, the reader first scans the *book title*. In the CV world, our name is the book's title, and the profession is its subtitle. We can also add certificates and awards to the pile to make the subtitle a bit catchier.

The most important thing about putting our personal information on top is double-checking that all the provided information is accurate. We don't want to be in a position where it is difficult for the reviewer to reach us just because we haven't paid enough attention.

One tricky piece of information is our address.

Personal address

A few words about the personal address, because it's a little bit of a sensitive subject.

Traditionally, resume documents used to contain a personal address. A personal address was a primary part of reaching a candidate and a massive consideration of whether their location suited a company. Even though things have changed, and we live in a different era, many recruiters still expect resumes to include an address.

However, there are a couple of reasons why we don't want to put our full address in the resume document:

- It's *sensitive information*. For privacy and security reasons, it is perfectly understood why some candidates prefer not to have their address details flowing around.

- Some places can find long-distance locations a *problem* and may reject us. There are countries where discriminating by location is illegal, and still, we don't want to put ourselves in a problematic situation.

If we still decide to put an address in our resume, here are some tips:

- We don't have to put our full address. A *city or a region* is good enough for most reviewers.

- If we know that our location can become an issue for many companies, we can state our *willingness to relocate* (if that's accurate, of course).

- Emphasize throughout our resume our ability and experience in **working remotely** (again, be accurate on this). Working remotely for iOS developers is perfectly legit today, especially since COVID-19.

Now, let's continue to our main dish and formulate our personal summary section.

Formulating the personal summary section

The summary section is probably the most crucial part of our resume and plays a significant role in the reviewer's decision to move forward with our application.

Now, even though we call it a "summary," it doesn't summarize our resume, and we'll understand why in a minute.

The first thing we need to do when approaching to write our summary section is to flip sides and think like an employer. What kind of iOS developer are we looking for? What can help our team or our company? What kind of a person can fit into our squad?

Now that we have changed our point of view, we have a good starting point. Now, let's roll up our sleeves and build our summary according to the following tips.

Working according to a structure

Let me start by reminding you of the 6 to 10 seconds it takes for a reviewer to scan our CV and decide.

6 to 10 seconds. This is all we have.

So, we need to write our summary section according to that assumption. Short, simple, and to the point, while keeping it to 3 to 5 sentences and no more than 50 words.

But what exactly do we need to write?

Let's start with how it is built. The basic structure is built upon three things: *who we are, what we offer,* and our *goals.*

Since we are all iOS developers, let me try to describe it as a formatted string:

```
let adjective: String = "Self motivated…"
let role: String = " iOS Developer"
let experience: String = " with 3+ years of experience with
    iOS project.."
```

```
let goals: String = "eager to learn and develop myself"
let summary = adjective + role + experience + goals
```

Perhaps we are not professional in resumes just yet, but Swift we know, don't we?

Find our soft and hard skills

If you're hearing those terms for the first time, it's a good idea to explain what they are and why they are essential.

Soft skills are *not related to a specific role* or industry. Soft skills are non-technical and can help the employee accomplish various tasks. Some examples are time management, communication, and problem-solving.

Conversely, **hard skills** are *technical and role*/position specific, such as working with Swift, Combine, testing, and more. There are cases where hard skills come with certificates and degrees.

We should combine these two skill types in our summary and try to emphasize the skills we are good at.

For instance, if you lack development experience, try to emphasize your hard skills. If you're an experienced iOS developer, you probably gained some tremendous soft skills over the years, and you can highlight them instead.

Adjusting to your workplace using terminology

Now, this is a handy tip: adjust the personal summary to the job posting description *using the exact keywords* and target it to what the workplace needs and wants.

Yes! It means that we may need to create several summary versions for different job postings. And why is it important?

To start, we want to *speak in our reviewer's language*. If they are looking for a "motivated iOS developer," our reviewer will be excited to find exactly what they were looking for.

But it doesn't end here. In the next sections, I'm going to tell you a dark secret most candidates don't know: **Applicant Tracking Systems** (**ATSs**).

What are ATSs?

Back (again!) to the 6-to-10-second scanning process. A recruiter scanning a resume is efficient when the workplace receives dozens of resumes daily. But what do we do when a workplace gets hundreds or even thousands of resume documents daily?

Oh, I know! They hire more reviewers, right?

No.

They use something called ATS, which, among many things, this system does. It can also parse resumes and extract headers, contact information, and keywords.

As a matter of fact, in big companies, most of the resumes aren't even read by humans! The ATS act as *gatekeeper in these places*, filtering out irrelevant candidates. Want to beat the ATS? Include keywords based on the job posting and use clear formatting.

Be aligned with the employer's needs

Every company needs something different from us. One company needs us to deliver an extremely robust SDK, and another company will need us to build a slick UI. SDK and slick UI are two different things. We cannot express how good we are in both areas in 50 words!

We need to choose, and therefore research, and understand what the company's needs are. Following that, we can adjust our summary to answer the company's requirements.

Adjusting to the post-COVID era – be flexible

If there's something that COVID-19 has taught us, it is that nothing is set in stone, and we need to *be as flexible as we can*. Flexibility can be expressed by relocation, role changes, or technology.

If some of these are legit on your side, try to *include that side in your summary* and show how you evolved and adjusted yourself to changes over the years.

Flexibility and willingness to change can give employers confidence, and in some companies, it can be useful to emphasize that side of us.

Focus on specialty

The last tip in the perfect summary is that we all have a specialty – something that we are good at in being a powerful iOS developer.

If we want to stand out from the other developers trying to compete in our role, we need to emphasize the area where we have outstanding capabilities.

Now, the big question is, what if that capability is not relevant to our desirable workplace? The answer is that it *doesn't matter*. Managers are like ninjas and superb developers. If we are striking well in one area, it probably means we can be good in another.

Listing our expertise

Dealing with expertise means that the recruiter or the hiring manager read our summary and decided it was interesting enough to invest more time and effort with the rest of the resume. Kudos to us!

This "Expertise" section contains a list of workplaces and open source projects we worked on. Usually, the list is chronologically ordered, and that's perfectly understood. Our last workplace is the most important one, so it should be on top. But there are three things we need to make sure of when we write that list:

- Focus on our *contribution* to the company and the team, rather than our last or current title. "I created an app from scratch," and "I led the iOS development of the company's primary app" are examples of contributions.

- Cover our contribution with *project names, numbers, and stories*. Some details make our contribution description much more reliable and precise.

- Speaking of reliability, don't miss anything! *Never hide a workplace*, even if you worked there for a few months and got fired. At this point, the recruiter may try to dig into some details about our application, and hiding such an important detail may cost us the job and our reputation.

Expertise is only part of the picture we want to expose. The other major factor is our skills.

Skills

This section aims to show our capabilities and present our knowledge to the reviewer.

First, let's remind ourselves of what we've discussed earlier regarding soft and hard skills. Hard skills are technical skills such as Swift, Combine, and SwiftUI. Soft skills are not particularly related to iOS Development and pertain to our capabilities as employees in general, such as communication and problem-solving skills.

What we need to do now is to list our skills (both hard and soft) cleverly and effectively. Let's see how.

Adjusting our skills to the requirements

Just like the personal summary section, the skills section needs to be adjusted to what you are looking for and the job posting requirements.

For example, if we are looking for remote work, we need to emphasize the soft skills that can help us work remotely. Communication, time management, and independence are all examples of soft skills employers look for in remote roles.

Mixing our skills list

Remember that even after we successfully passed the initial scanning, there's still an attention limit when reviewing our application. We can't put an endless list of skills, and limiting that list to 10 to 15 skills is best.

Don't worry, limitation has a significant upside. It pushes us to *focus* and forces us to *prioritize* our list.

In the 10-to-15 skills list, we must have different types of skills as listed here and create some sort of an interesting skills mix bag:

- *Hard* skills that are relevant to the job requirement are important. Social apps, payment, gaming, and SDK are all examples of relevant hard skills.

- *Soft* skills relevant to the working environment, role, and company size help, too.

- Add a *specialty* skill that makes us stand out compared to the other candidates and shows our capability to shine in specific areas.

Some skills need to be in your personal summary section, and we must ensure our summary is synced with the skills list.

Mixing the skill list will ensure we don't have blind spots and safely cover the hiring manager's requirements.

Miscellaneous

After we present our skills and personality, we move to the part where we need to show some *evidence*.

In this part, we can present our education, certificates, training, blogs, publications, GitHub repositories, and more.

Part of what I just wrote is something we call **Developer Branding**, and we will discuss it in *Chapter 3*.

Avoiding red flags

Our expertise can be extraordinary, and our summary can be well written, but resume reviewers are looking for additional information that we may not like, which are **red flags**.

The first thing we must understand about red flags in our resume is that *no resume is perfect*. Most of us have had issues in the past. We took a very long vacation to organize our lives, got fired, or things just couldn't work out.

So, as a result, we need to ensure our resume is reliable. On the other hand, we need to emphasize our positive side on occasion.

The first red flag we need to address is **job-hopping**. Spending less than a year in one place can raise some eyebrows in a workplace that looks at our resume. It gives the feeling that we are not stable, mature, and that we have trouble with absorption in workplaces. One thing that many candidates do in a job-hopping situation is to eliminate that job from their resume, with the excuse that, "It doesn't have any meaning, anyway."

Now, hiding details from our working expertise is not a good idea. The hole in the resume is there to be seen, and eventually, things like that are always floating and can cause much more damage than we wanted to avoid.

The best thing to do in this situation is to *highlight our accomplishments* in each role rather than our work duration. When we emphasize our experience in each workplace, we show how working across different teams and companies increased our breadth of knowledge and competence.

We should consider taking a disadvantage (job-hopping) and converting it into an advantage (working diversity and broad experience).

Of course, that lesson is relevant for all the other parts of our resume, but when we have a built-in warning alarm, this is doubly true.

Inviting another set of eyes

Once we have finished writing our resume document, it is highly recommended to give it to *someone else to read* and give us their feedback.

But – don't pick just anyone for that job. Your grandmother may be intelligent and honest, but she may not be the profile that we are looking for.

We must pick our "second set of eyes" carefully and ensure our feedback will be as emotionless and professional as possible. Try to pick a recruiter or talent acquisition to review your resume structure and a hiring manager to review your summary and expertise. Even one or two comments can make significant differences.

Preparing for the interview

So, we got a call from a recruiter saying they went over our resume and are interested in moving forward with us! This call means that we did a great job with our resume and succeeded in showing our experience and capabilities just the way we wanted.

But – the hard work is *only ahead of us.*

In *Chapter 2*, we will discuss the interviewing process, the different stages, and their primary goals, but now, I want to discuss the period before the interview.

Taking our time

When the recruiter wants to schedule your first interview, the first thing many candidates do is schedule as soon as possible because of the excitement of getting an interview. Well, that's a bold mistake.

We should take our time and make sure we start this journey 100% ready. A time frame between one and two weeks should be enough to start the first stage.

Technical, personal, and logistics preparations

Being ready for an interview doesn't mean just going over Swift questions. There are three levels we need to ensure we are ready: **Technical**, **Personal**, and **Logistics**.

Technical

Most of the books that talk about iOS interviews deal with technical preparations. In this period, the first thing we need to ensure is that the *foundation of iOS development* is strong and solid. Screwing up on the fundamental questions and tasks will devastate us and risk our job application more than anything.

The second thing we need to do is *get a whiteboard* to practice design and architecture questions. In design questions, we need to get used to drawing a UML or a system chart on a whiteboard. Even though drawing on a whiteboard sounds easy, it requires practice and experience.

Besides the drawing task itself (which is not that easy for many candidates), we need to know how to present a system, decide what we consider a module in our chart, and explain it verbally. We will focus on that in *Part 4: Design and Architecture* of this book, but we need to make time for that in our preparation plan.

The third thing is *building our daily routine*. Whether we have a daily job or are unemployed, without a daily practice routine, it's going to be hard to move forward and close all the knowledge gaps. Are we night or morning people? Knowing who we are can help reserve a slot dedicated to practice in our schedule.

Personal

Our personality is another important side of the process. As part of the interview preparations, we must build our story as developers. What is our story? How did we get into the development world, especially iOS development? Why did we decide to work in the places that we worked in the past? How was it to work in a big or small company? Why do we search now for a new workplace?

The answers to these questions help the interviewer to build our developer profile, so we must not forget that in our preparation planning.

Logistics

This is the easy part, but we must not fall for this one. We first need to *print our resumes*. It is always good to bring them with us. Bringing our resumes shows that we are serious and have got nothing to hide. It also starts the interview by focusing on us, which is precisely what we wanted.

The second thing is to *plan our arrival journey*. Being early can never harm our odds of continuing the process, but late sure can. Never – never be late for an interview.

The third thing may sound weird and unrelated, but it is much more important than you think: *make sure you smell good*. Now, I mention the smell, because many people (interviewers, in our case) tend to associate a smell with the person they talk with. Now, just to be clear, the link between smell and people is not the interviewer's fault; it's just how our brain is built. There's a direct connection between memory, emotion, and our sense of smell. It can be a good idea to put deodorant or perfume in our bag during our on-site interview.

Summary

Throughout this chapter, we've learned what a company profile is and how to build it, how to describe our needs, and how to match with the right company. We also learned how to write a resume for fast recruiter scanning and deep reading.

We've discussed the different skills that we have and tried to find a solution for gaps and issues that might be present in our expertise.

Finally, we discussed being prepared for our first interview with full power.

Company research is a significant part of the interview preparation. It increases our chances of choosing the right place for us and helps us to get through the application process and get our first interview.

But what exactly happens in the first interview and beyond? That's precisely what we will talk about in our next chapter.

2
Going through the Interview Process

Many candidates (or even employers) summarize iOS development as primarily "Swift". But narrowing the iOS developer role to just a programming language is a very simplistic way of looking at it. An iOS developer (in fact, any developer) has a bundle of capabilities, even if we don't feel that way. We must show knowledge not only in Swift but also in computer science. Some iOS development fundamentals are also essential, such as UIKit or Foundation.

Being an iOS developer doesn't sum up to just coding skills. A senior iOS developer must design a robust app with a clean architecture, write unit tests, manage CI/CD processes, deploy beta/alpha versions, manage certificates, and provision profiles.

And what about some soft skills? Communication and time management are essentials in today's dynamic market.

As we can tell from the pointers we just discussed, being an iOS developer means a bundle of capabilities, much, much more than Swift itself. The hiring process goal is to cover all of our abilities, from hard to soft skills.

In this chapter, we will learn about the different stages of a standard iOS developer hiring process. By the end of the chapter, we will be in a position where the process will be familiar for us as if we were actually there!

To that end, we will cover the following:

- Understanding the hiring process

- Getting ready for the screening interview

- All about the iOS technical interview

- Cracking the coding interview

- Passing the architecture interview

As I said, let's begin with understanding how the hiring process works.

Understanding the hiring process

One of the goals of the hiring process is to get a complete picture (as much as possible) of the candidate's skills, both hard and soft.

> **Soft and hard skills**
>
> If you don't remember what soft and hard skills are, **hard skills** are role-specific, such as iOS coding, GitHub knowledge, and more. **Soft skills** are skills that are relevant for many jobs. Communication and leadership are examples of soft skills. Refer to *Chapter 1* for more information.

Think of our candidate picture as a giant puzzle.

When we start the hiring process, each stage puts together another piece of the puzzle, and the process helps our hiring manager see our skill set before they offer.

Each stage examines a different part of our picture as an iOS candidate and, like a knockout tournament, determines whether the newly revealed part of the picture is good enough to proceed to the next stage.

Learning the hiring funnel

I mentioned a knockout tournament just to catch your eye. The reality is that the hiring process looks more like a funnel. Each stage of the funnel goes deeper and reveals more advanced skills.

Here's an example of such a funnel:

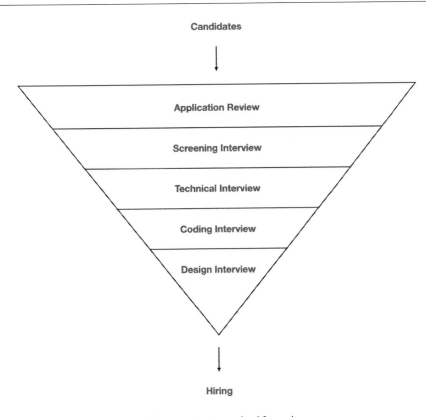

Figure 2.1 – A standard funnel

It is called a "funnel" because it gets narrowed as we move down and more candidates drop out.

But how does that funnel look in the specific workplace that we interview for?

Distinguishing between different companies

The funnel we see in *Figure 2.1* is just an example. Every company has a different hiring process, and there are no rules in this domain.

There are a couple of reasons for that difference:

- **Different roles** require different stages and different topics to check. The different role is not just a developer versus a designer, but also a developer versus a team lead.

- Each company has its **own view** of how such a funnel should look. Some focus on personality, and others focus on coding. Each company has its own DNA (remember that in *Chapter 1*, we compared companies to humans), and therefore looks for a specific type of candidate. This candidate type can be quickly learned from looking at the hiring process. Look at the following two examples (*Figure 2.2*):

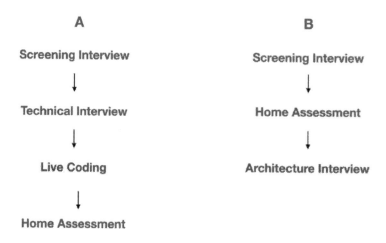

Figure 2.2 – Different funnels for different roles

We can see that role **A** focuses heavily on coding skills while role **B** is more about design and architecture. It might be different roles (developer versus tech lead), but it can also show how the company or the team sees the developer position. In small companies or teams, the developer is much more central and has more responsibility. In this case, role **B** sounds more suitable for a startup company than a corporate one.

The last thing that can affect the funnel is the **product**. A front-facing product may require high UI skills. Focusing on screen design and UIKit/SwiftUI as part of the process sounds like a good idea.

So, here's another (free) tip: we saw in *Chapter 1* that we can learn a lot about the team and the role just by looking at the job posting. Now, we can see that the hiring process can also teach us a lot about the job and the working place expectations.

Now, let's start our funnel journey with a short but essential interview: the screening interview.

Getting ready for the screening interview

In most cases, the first step in the hiring process won't be an in-depth and advanced technical interview.

We succeeded in passing the resume scanning step and getting an interview, but at this stage, we are among many other candidates that also had that luck. Yet, with so many candidates, the workplace must filter as much as possible with minimal effort before it moves to the next stage. That's what the screening interview is all about.

Think of the screening interview as an oversized, coarse filter in the hiring funnel that needs to handle a large number of candidates in a short time. It also means we have about 30 minutes to impress our interviewer to move down the funnel while answering several important questions.

What does the screening interview include?

Most screening interviews revolve around three topics – the company, the candidate's profile, and soft/hard skills.

Let's talk about the company

Usually, the interviewer starts the interview with an **elevator pitch** about the company and its product. I want to clarify what an elevator pitch means because we will need it soon.

Let's imagine ourselves going up in an elevator with another person. We want to present an idea or even ourselves to that person, but we have around 30 seconds before the elevator's destination. That short presentation is called an elevator pitch.

In a screening interview, there are two elevator pitches. The first is the interviewer talking about the company and its product. The second is ours, and we will discuss that soon.

The interviewer's elevator pitch may last more than 30 seconds. What we need to do on our side is to listen carefully to the company and product description. Here are a few reasons:

- Remember we talked about making sure the workplace is suited for us in *Chapter 1*? Now is the time to **verify our assumptions**. In *Chapter 1*, we invested precious time in research. Now is the time to find out the truth. Is this the company we want to work at? Is the development team really at the size we were expecting? Do we hear something that bothers us? We should take advantage of that chance.

- "Is this going to be on the test?" Well, kind of. At the end of the screening interview, the interviewer will ask us if we have questions and will expect us to ask some. We will talk about this point, but we need to ensure we understand the interviewer's pitch so that we can ask **relevant questions**. Asking questions that were answered in the pitch is not a good idea.

- The interviewer's pitch can help us **adjust our answers** to what the workplace is looking for. We need to use the additional and precious information we just got and leverage our offering as iOS developers.

But the interviewer is not the only one that speaks in this conversation or has an elevator pitch – we are also a part of the interview!

Building our elevator pitch

At some point, the interviewer will say, "Please tell me about yourself." That will be our turn to present our elevator pitch.

They say each of us needs to be a little bit of a salesperson, and it's true. Even though our specialization is iOS development, we've got a significant lead, and we need to sell something – our skills and expertise as iOS developers.

Therefore, it is extremely important to **plan our elevator pitch ahead** and come to this moment fully prepared. It is recommended to write down our pitch, read it out loud, practice in front of a mirror, and even read it to a close friend. The interviewer needs to remember us. That's how important it is!

What do we want the interviewer to remember about us?

So how do we build our pitch? First, we need to remember there's no need to unfold our entire resume. The interviewer probably read it already. Even if they didn't, listing our expertise in 40-50 seconds is ineffective.

We need to explain **why we fit the job**, and there are two simple pitch formulas: present, past, and future, and past, present, and future:

- With "present, past, and future," we start by explaining our current role, move to our expertise, and then discuss why we think we are qualified for the job.

- In "past, present, and future", we start with our expertise, move to our current role, and finish by explaining why we are qualified for the job.

Both formulas are great – both have smart logic built in, and both will do the job. But we can tune our pitch better.

It may be a good idea to start our pitch with our current role if it's somehow related to the job posting. However, if our past expertise is more related to the job requirements, we should start with our expertise and only then move to what we are doing now.

Now that we have a formula, we need to remember there's a short time to present our profile. The right approach distills our expertise and current role to achievements and influence. We must market ourselves and not fill our interviewer with dry work history details.

In the "future" part, we need to include our expectations from the hiring process and job searching. Mixing our ambitions and workplace requirements will result in a significant "future" part.

Let's try to spice things up with clickbait now that we have a formula.

Including clickbait

We are all likely familiar with the term "clickbait." If you don't know what it means, clickbait is text or a picture designed to **attract the listener** or the reader to consume more content. It's a common practice in tweets, posts, and articles.

Yes, I know an elevator pitch is not a tweet or a post, but the human brain works the same. A clickbait/teaser creates a "curiosity gap" and exploits it. In our pitch, we need to do the same!

We aim to plant a piece of information that makes us unique and will drive the reviewer to drill down and listen for more. This piece of information will also help us be memorable.

Here are examples of some teasers:

- "I constantly speak at conferences"

- "I have a side project on the app store with many active users"

- "I'm a participant in two big open source projects"

Of course, it goes without saying that the teaser you plant needs to be accurate and reliable. Twisting the truth won't look good when your reviewer starts to dig in.

What not to include in your pitch

The answer to what *not* to include in your pitch may differ between countries and cultures. But I think it is best practice not to include personal beliefs, religion, and anything unrelated to being a great iOS developer. It can even hurt our chances of moving forward with the process.

Saying bad words about our previous workplaces is also not a good idea. It is better to say that even though we might have had issues and conflicts with a specific place in the past, we appreciate the time working there.

Remember that we should never act emotionally in these situations. Being smart is extremely important in job interviews.

Now let's talk about some seriously thoughtful questions such as why we want to change jobs.

Preparing for the "Why do you want to change jobs?" question

If our elevator pitch follows one of the formulas I previously mentioned, it should also cover this question in the "future" section.

However, the interviewer can still question us about our motivation to change our current workplace. Maybe because they weren't listening carefully, or because we had only 30-40 seconds, and it's just not enough.

There are many reasons why a candidate would like to change their job. Here are some of them:

- I don't like my company

- I want higher pay

- I'm looking for opportunities

- I'm doing it personal reasons

- I want flexibility

- I got fired

- I don't like the culture in my company

- I don't get timely training and development

Each one of these reasons is perfectly legit. But there are different ways we can present our reason to the interviewer.

Let's take, for example, the reason *"I want higher pay."*

We can just answer the following:

My current salary is too low, and my workplace won't give me a raise.

Well, that doesn't sound too good, does it? Not only does it sounds whiny, but it also may raise some eyebrows – perhaps there's a reason why we didn't get that raise.

On the other hand, we can send a different message:

I like taking challenges, and getting rewards motivates me to work harder. For me, financial support works as a reward for my hard work.

It is better to tie up salary and motivation than salary and ego. It also gives depth to the statement, "I want higher pay."

When we pick the right reason, we should consider how to formulate it with a positive attitude and tie it to a value the workplace requires.

Preparing for the skills test

As I said, a screening interview is like a giant coarse filter. Besides expertise and personal expectations, there's another criterion the interviewer may check us on: a skills test.

The skills test is much narrower than the advanced process stages. Remember, the interviewer may not be our hiring manager or an iOS developer. In addition, we've got minimal time – after all, it's just a screening interview.

Nevertheless, the skills test is an important part that we should be ready for, and we'll start with discussing our soft skills.

Discovering the soft skills questions

The soft-skills test is tricky! No one will tell us, *"Ok, now we are going to check your soft skills."* Our soft skills are examined throughout the interview in various places. Our elevator pitch is one of those places where our soft skills might be shown, but not the only place.

If we were late for the interview, it might point to **bad time management** or personal maturity, and that's one example. **Communication skills** may arise when talking about what it was like working as part of a team or remotely.

We should see every part or every side of the interview as part of the soft-skills test that we are tested on.

Soft skills are there even in the way we answer hard-skills questions. Remember those? Let's talk about them for a second.

Answering hard skills questions

Unlike soft skills, the hard-skills test is much clearer. Not every screening interview contains hard skills, and it depends on the workplace we are interviewing for.

A hard-skills test may contain basic questions about Swift and UIKit. Their primary purpose is not to check our Swift programming skills level but to ensure we pass the minimum bar to continue the process.

We need to remember that the interviewer may not even be an iOS developer at this stage, and they may have a list of questions and answers.

A typical fundamental question might be:

What is the difference between let and var?

The preceding question may look extremely basic to a standard iOS developer. Still, we must remember that the interviewer doesn't know our **actual** experience and knowledge at this stage. An iOS developer or a recruiter can ask that question because an answer such as *"I don't remember"* is a strong signal the candidate may have worrying gaps in their knowledge of the Swift language.

In screening interviews, there will probably be several multiple-choice questions so that non-developer interviewers can ask and analyze the answer.

Part 2, Swift Language and Coding of this book discusses the Swift language, and meticulously reviewing its chapters will greatly prepare us for most screening interview questions.

For now, let's move to another hidden soft skill in the interview: the ability to ask questions.

Asking, "Do you have any questions for me?"

The interviewer isn't the only one who asks questions. We do too.

That won't be the last time we ask our interviewer questions during the hiring process. In reality, asking the interviewer questions is another task in the screening interview and probably in all the other discussions.

In other words, the answer to "Do you have any questions for me?" is always, always "yes." Answering "no" to that question will significantly reduce our chances of getting an offer at the end of the process, and I must say – rightfully. A candidate with no questions is considered uninterested in the workplace he is interviewing for.

Like any other stage, we should prepare. And in this case – with a pool of questions.

Creating a pool of questions

Sure, we can just prepare a question before the interview. But what if the answer to that question is already covered during the talk? The trick is to prepare a list of questions, and that list will be great not only for the screening interview but for other interviews as well.

Each different question shows another side of our personality. Sounds weird, right? Let's look at some examples and how they work:

- *Can you tell me more about the day-to-day responsibilities of the role?* We show our desire to meet the employer's expectations.

- *How could I impress you in the first three months?* This shows that we think of how to make a positive contribution.

- *Are there opportunities for training and progression within the role/company?* We are serious about our career and are committed to the company's future.

- *Where do you think the company is headed in the next five years?* We show interest in the company and a commitment to a long-term relationship.

- *Can you describe the working culture of the organization?* We show maturity and motivation to fit it.

- *Can you tell me more about the team I would be working in?* We show interest in teamwork and communication.

Do you want to pick the side you want to emphasize? Just select the right question – it's like a restaurant menu! We can see that even a question (not an answer) can send a signal to the interviewer and leverage our chances.

Send a thank-you email

And here's an excellent tip relevant to interviews and meetings and any meaningful communication we may have – sending a thank-you email right after the interview can have significant advantages if it's done right.

Now, why send an email? Doesn't the interviewer already have our email address and other communication methods? Aren't we on his list?

So, we need to remember that the interviewer doesn't look at us only as iOS developers but also as humans. Sending a thank-you email shows that we are a person that appreciates the interviewer's time and has excellent manners.

But a thank-you email also provides two additional advantages: the ability to add more information we didn't have the chance to show during the interview and our signature with important links we want them to see.

Remember that a thank-you email is not just two words but more. But exactly how much more?

Learning what to write

A thank-you email should be short and focused. Writing more than a couple of paragraphs is too much for an interviewer to digest – after all, we are talking about a screening interview.

The email should begin with expressing gratitude to the interviewer for their time and reiterating interest in the position. We then need to remind the interviewer of our qualifications for the role by **highlighting our expertise and skills**.

And now, for our signature, which should contain **links to our LinkedIn profile** and personal blogs we may have.

We need to consider our thank-you email as a personal stamp that should go along with you after you finish your screening interview. As long as it has been done with good taste, it impacts our chances to move with the process.

Next, let's prepare for the main dish: the iOS technical interview.

All about the iOS technical interview

The term "technical interview" is too broad, in my opinion. Does it mean coding with Swift? Questions about UIKit? Design?

When we get an invitation for a technical interview, it mostly means that we are expected to show our general knowledge of iOS development.

No, it doesn't mean that there won't be any questions about design patterns or computer science, but we should come loaded with all our expertise about issues related to iOS in general.

In other words, expect everything in that interview!

What happens in that interview?

Even though anything can happen in an iOS technical interview, still, I think we can narrow it down to several options of how it can look.

Notice that interviewers mix some of those options and include them, so we should be prepared for any scenario.

One of these options is where the interviewer fires questions at us as if we're on a firing range!

The questions range

A "questions range" is probably the most common type of interview because it's the simplest one. This type is simple for the interviewer and the candidate because there's nothing easier than just asking short questions with clear answers.

We should think of this type as a driving theory exam – there is a vast pool of questions, and we need to verify that we know almost all their answers.

But we really need to ensure that we know what is **behind the answer** and not just memorize it. Because this type of test is very general, we are expected to answer questions we may not know very well and have never encountered.

Here are a few examples of such questions:

- *"What is the UIKit View Controller lifecycle?"*
- *"What's the difference between GCD and NSOperationQueue?"*
- *"Can you explain the difference between atomic and non-atomic properties?"*

We will discuss interview questions starting from *Chapter 4*, which is another excellent resource for getting us ready for this part of the process.

Worked-on projects

Our expertise is part of our identity when we start the technical interview. What we know and what we did in our short (or long) working history is something that wraps up our job application. One of our interviewer's goals is to understand **how the reality stands up to our story**.

Showing worked-on projects is a way for the interviewer to bridge that gap between our story and who we are. But bridging that gap is not only the interview's goal – it is ours as well. We want them to see who we really are!

Therefore, coming ready with projects we worked on in the past is an excellent idea for that kind of interview. Bringing our iPhone loaded with apps we worked on in the past can be significant. But even better, we can come with our MacBook filled with Xcode projects already launched.

And that leads me to my next point. One of the preparations we need to make before the interview is to go over what we did in the past so that our explanations will be fluent and convincing.

Picking one or two features that we were part of during their development and trying to explain their design while speaking out loud is excellent preparation that will put us in a great position for the interview.

Remember, we don't need to fake anything. We are great developers, and if we are proud of something we did, we just need to show it. Believe me, excitement is contagious.

Answering Swift and algorithm questions

Swift is probably the primary tool that we have as iOS developers. But when developers say "Swift," many think of something much broader than just a language.

In this case, Swift is much more than "optional unwrapping". Data structures, closures, and memory management are also part of Swift. And sometimes, Swift is just the infrastructure for something even more significant: design patterns and algorithms.

In the iOS technical interview, questions can go from simple unwrapping up to recursive functions and delegation versus reactive programming debate. This huge spectrum makes this type of interview the most challenging part of the hiring process, professionally.

In this book, we will cover many aspects of Swift relevant to interviews and explain why each one is important for our daily work and is part of an interview. Remember, Swift and algorithms are just the first floors. We've got more floors to the buildings, such as UIKit or SwiftUI.

Solving basic questions about UIKit and SwiftUI

Besides Foundation, UIKit and SwiftUI are the only frameworks that will certainly be part of a standard interview. The reason is apparent – UI is a major part of almost any iOS project we will be working on.

I didn't just mention "standard interview" and "almost" for no reason. There are cases where UI doesn't play a major role or even a minor role. For instance, an SDK where we don't have UI features at all, or games where we have UI but we use SceneKit or Unity instead of UIKit or SwiftUI to build them.

But for most apps, learning UIKit or SwiftUI at a high level is mandatory. One drawback with many iOS developers today is that they know one framework very well (for example, SwiftUI) and don't have any experience with the other (UIKit).

If that's the status in our case, we need to gain experience in the other framework and explain that gap during the interview. Even a tiny amount of knowledge shows that we are not disconnected from reality and have a solid capability to fill any gaps in the information we may have.

Remember that many apps make use of both frameworks, so the ability to learn a new framework is crucial.

Mastering development tools

If frameworks are the car our code rides in, Xcode is the tool we use to build and fix that car. And how can we be great iOS engineers without mastering our tools?

Mastering Xcode helps iOS developers debug, write more code efficiently, configure the environment and the project, profile the app, and move faster in their job.

I must admit, asking questions about Xcode is not as common as the other parts I mentioned. Perhaps Xcode is not seen as a core topic or essential. The thing about Xcode questions is that as rare as they are, failing in them is considered a red flag in the interviewer's eyes. We just can't afford to fail on a small topic that can devastate our progress.

Xcode is not just the IDE itself but also all the other tools such as the Instruments app, which is mandatory for every iOS developer, UI debugs, and more.

The technical interview tests the theory behind iOS development. Let's now move to the practical part: the coding interview.

Cracking the coding interview

We know how the world spins around – some people are great in interviews. They are great at preparing for tests, and they are strong interviewees. We know them from school or college, and they always get good grades. But theory doesn't necessarily indicate success when it comes to practical tasks.

That's why sometimes we have another stage in the process: the coding interview.

The coding interview goal is to see how we handle **real-life situations** as closely as possible. In these tests, the results are not always what's critical – the interviewer wants to see how we think, plan, write, and respond to changes and dilemmas.

Even though a coding interview can last 15-20 minutes, it can also be a home assessment that takes one or two days to complete. It sounds like a considerable effort not only from our side but also from the interviewer's side!

That's why most of the time, the coding interview stage will be after the technical interview. The hiring manager wants to make sure they put that extra effort for candidates who are deserving!

There are several ways a workplace can see our coding, which depends on the workplace itself and its culture. The industry is not aligned on what's considered the best way to test a candidate because there's a long debate about that. For example, a home assessment allows candidates to complete a coding test at their own pace in a comfortable environment, while a live coding test provides an opportunity for the company to observe the candidate's problem-solving and communication skills in real time.

First, let's go over the different methods. We'll start with the live coding interview.

Live coding interview

The interviewer will give us a coding challenge in the live coding interview. It can be a class, an algorithm question, or even developing a small project.

The primary goal of live coding is to see our coding in action. The interviewer wants to see us write, plan, and think.

While it may be a stressful experience for some candidates, there are some things we can take advantage of in this situation, such as the following:

- One advantage is the ability to show **how we think and deal with ongoing dilemmas** we may have in our tasks. The interviewer expects us to think out loud. Even if we are stuck, good thinking direction can provide us with winning points in the interview. That's something we just can't get in a non-live coding task.

- The second advantage we may have is the ability to **ask questions during the exam** that can give us a hint of the solution.

As we can see, the best approach to a live coding test is to use it as an opportunity to fully showcase one's knowledge and skills. Another option that takes a different direction is a home assessment.

Working on a home assessment

Live coding has its drawbacks – it's stressful and time-consuming, which makes it also time-sensitive. As a result, it covers fewer topics and areas.

To cover more in the coding test, a standard option is to perform it asynchronously (yeah, just like opening a new background thread in Swift for heavy tasks).

A home assessment usefully covers basic subjects in iOS programming – design patterns, architecture, API calls, and some UI with a data source. We shouldn't expect a complex task – the main goal of home assessment is to see how we handle and approach an entire project, how we separate code and responsibilities to classes and layers, conduct networking and UI, and in general, to see real task results as iOS developers.

Home assessments have clear advantages. They are cheap, as there is no need to spend the interviewer's time. In fact, time is (almost) a non-factor. On the other hand, some workplaces don't like home assessments as they don't test our abilities to solve complex problems in a limited time. Also, home assessments don't show how we think and face dilemmas during our work. To retrieve that information, the interviewer needs to question and go over the code with us, which makes the advantages I mentioned earlier much less significant.

But don't worry! We'll cover both live coding and home assessments in *Chapter 13*.

Up next, we've got the architecture interview for complex architecture problems.

Passing the architecture interview

The architecture interview aims to test complex architectural problems. One of its aspects is to see how we plan, approach a problem, and ask relevant questions. Unlike the coding interview, which handles simple or minor problems, the architecture interview requires us to have a broader point of view of how iOS apps are built. That's one of the reasons why the interviewer will probably be a senior developer, a tech, or a team lead.

The interview covers design patterns, computer science principles, and architecture decisions. This is the interview where we get the chance to shine and show our best as iOS developers. We must lead the discussion, communicate our concerns, and present our thoughts.

We've got *Chapter 11* and *Chapter 12* covering **app architecture** and **design patterns** (we will also discuss the differences between them, don't worry!).

In most hiring processes, the architecture interview is the last stage before we move forward to the HR interview and the offer.

Summary

Throughout this chapter, we've learned about the hiring process and its stages. We have dived deep into the screening interview, as it is the first interview in the process. We also discussed the other interviews – the technical, the coding, and the architectural interview.

The hiring process is much clearer now, isn't it? But before we get into the interviews themselves, in the next chapter, let's talk about the missing piece in our career-building process, which is something we all should have: a fantastic brand!

3
Developer Branding

Up to this point, we have discussed choosing our desired workplace and learned what the hiring process looks like. Now, I want to drill down a little about something not many developers pay attention to: developer branding.

Developer branding refers to the way software developers present themselves and their work to the public. It can include elements such as a personal website, social media presence, and contributions to open source projects.

In this chapter, we're going to cover the following main topics:

- Understanding the importance of developing a brand
- Contributing to the community
- Writing content
- Combining all and more
- Understanding that every in-person interaction is important

By the end of the chapter, we will have the tools to start building our personal developer brand. First, let's understand why it matters to our primary goal: passing the iOS interview.

Understanding the importance of developing a brand

This book talks about iOS interviews, but that doesn't mean it teaches us iOS development. Why? Because I assume that we already know iOS development; the problem is not our skill level but our ability to pass the hiring process.

But passing an iOS interview is more complicated than we think. It combines our iOS development knowledge, which needs to be comprehensive and extensive, and our familiarity with the hiring process. But there's a new factor that can help us get our interview and the offer – and that's our name, or in other words, our *brand*.

Let's dive into the meaning of a "brand".

Learning what a brand is

When we think of a brand, we usually imagine Apple, Google, or Coca Cola and we're right! A brand is a product or service publicly distinguished from others. The product or the company achieves that by building a reputation, specializing in specific areas, and connecting feelings and thoughts to its name.

But – did you know that branding is not only for companies? In fact, it's even not only for businesses. *We, as iOS developers, can build a brand and reputation of our own.*

But what does a "brand" mean? Are we a product?

In the modern labor market of iOS developers, we are considered to be products, and we need to sell and market ourselves just like any product. We also must brand ourselves to create demand, just like in any marketing process.

Usually, when we think of a brand, we imagine specific colors, fonts, or a unique logo. And that's true – these are all visual representations of a brand. But this visual representation goes on top of a deeper layer underneath, and that layer contains much more than that. It includes values, history, contribution, quality, and specializations.

The Apple brand makes us imagine a superior user interface, a premium feel, and the "it just works" slogan. The Coca-Cola brand makes us imagine parties and freedom. If you spend more time thinking about it, you'll find this is true for more brands.

And you know what? That's where the concept of a "brand" meets us. Our goal is to bind specific attributes that set us apart from our name in the market of iOS developers. Once we do that, it can leverage our chances in the interview process.

Increasing our chances of passing the resume scanning

A strong brand can help us get an interview. Do you remember the **profile scanning** process we discussed in *Chapter 1*? That's where our developer's name comes in handy. If we maintain our name and build it, chances are that the recruiter would be familiar with it. Bear in mind the *six to eight* seconds we've got for a first impression, and we can understand the importance of our reputation at this stage.

Imagine going over a list of candidates and suddenly encountering a familiar name. In most cases, it will catch your eye, and you will spend more than the usual eight seconds reading their resume. So yes, the more time spent on our profile, the more chances we'll get an invitation for a **screening interview**. This is how it works. And that also applies, of course, to the interview process itself up until the offer.

Increasing our chances of getting an offer

Our brand influence doesn't stop with getting an interview. It also helps us with the hiring process itself. During the hiring process, our name is part of the recruiting team's internal discussions, and if we have a strong name, these discussions look different. Any way we look at it, it increases our chances of moving to the next stage in the process (or even skip several stages!) and getting an offer at last.

On the other hand, the fact that we have a strong presence doesn't mean we shouldn't stay modest with a low profile. And that has nothing to do with branding or our skill. It is all about our personality and being a pleasant person to work with or be connected to.

Talking about connections leads us to my next point: networking.

Expanding our network

One of the side effects of strengthening our name is the *expansion of our professional network*. You know, some people don't care about networking, either because they are not social in their personality or just want to focus on the job and nothing more. That is legit! But if we want to build a strong brand, our network is part of the bundle.

Networking means going to conferences and meetups. But it also implies participating in social media discussions and constantly creating content. These are all part of branding development, and that's why it goes hand in hand.

Now that we are (hopefully) convinced how important branding is, let's understand how to build it.

So, where do we start?

How to start building your brand

The first and perhaps the primary rule is *focusing on what represents us as developers*. If we feel that being on a stage is not our style, we should find another lane. If writing **blog posts** makes us nervous and itchy, we might consider going in the **open source** direction. If we are not comfortable with what we're doing, the chances we will last in the area are pretty low.

Building our name requires persistence and hard work. Without motivation and enjoyment, it will be difficult to achieve our goal.

Having said that, the second rule is that we *mustn't stay in our comfort zone*. It may sound contradictory to the first rule, but I haven't promised you a straightforward method. After all, life is complex.

In this chapter, I will list some ideas of how we can develop our name, and I encourage you to at least *consider them as an option*. Experiencing them will be the best option.

Let's start with the basics: contributing to the community, and by that, to yourself.

Contributing to the community

I know that "contributing" sounds like a heavy task, but this field is so vast that you can also find your niche here. Contributing means not just participating in a project, but also helping other developers or sharing your achievements in coding.

One good thing about a contribution is the ability to share your solutions in the most practical way, which is *coding*.

We don't need to come up with a new way to contribute, as there are many resources available to help us. In today's age, there are numerous websites that host a large number of developers who share code, ask questions, and exchange ideas. One such website that you may be familiar with is **Stack Overflow**.

Being a star in Stack Overflow

I'm not sure this book is the place to talk about what the **Stack Overflow** website is. But if you are unfamiliar with Stack Overflow, you probably haven't been living on Earth in the past 15 years, so passing an iOS interview is the least of your problems.

But the big question is – what is your presence in Stack Overflow? Stack Overflow has four types of users:

- The first is the *passive reader*, which most developers conform to. In most cases, you are one of them. The passive reader reaches Stack Overflow by a search for a question in Google, but they never ask or answer a question because they are, well, passive.

- The second profile is the *Asker*. The asker likes to ask questions but never answers or comments. As weird as it sounds, asking questions provides us with a rating, but more importantly, it exposes us to the community and opens new communication channels with other developers. The most important about asking a question is to do it right – duplicate questions will be removed or marked as spam. Also, we need to provide all details and code snippets and mark the correct tags.

- To provide answers, we must actively enter Stack Overflow and search for questions or add comments. That is an entirely different use case for the site and leads us to the next user type.

  The *respondent* is the user type that bumps into a question and knows the solution, so they answer it. They don't spend much time on the website but invest minimum effort to contribute. If we want to build our brand, we should be at least a respondent in Stack Overflow.

- The last type is the *heavy contributor*. They enter Stack Overflow daily and search for questions to answer. This is a different type of user – they like to phrase solutions to complex problems, publish code snippets, and conduct discussions about best practices and mythology. It's an excellent way to start our workday while going over questions in Stack Overflow, filtered by tags such as **iOS**, **Swift**, or **UIKit**. It is not an impossible mission to answer questions in Stack Overflow and gain a high reputation; it is just a matter of priorities and effort.

Another lighter way to contribute is to comment on answers and questions. We use comments when we need clarifications, criticize a provided solution, or improve an answer or a question. These options open many new ways to be part of the discussions even though we don't have the perfect answer to the question.

I mentioned all these types because to be a star, we should aim to be the fourth type. If we want to build our brand, contributing to the community using Stack Overflow is a great way to do that.

Once we get more ratings and experience in Stack Overflow, we can start contributing in new ways, such as editing questions or answers, flag questions, and even deleting them.

Contributing to Stack Overflow is a *win-win strategy* – you get to learn so much while getting noticed in the community.

Maintaining a public GitHub repository

We had long discussions about having a great resume in *Chapter 1*. And while having a good resume is essential, we can complete our image as developers with an impressive **GitHub** repository. For example, when we talk about an architect, we expect to see his work. The same goes for a designer or a photographer. Why does it need to be a different case with **iOS** developers?

A GitHub repository is our code portfolio, our way to show what we are capable of. Pushing new updates, ideas, and libraries using social media can significantly influence how we look as iOS developers.

The big problem is – what do we need to put on our **public Git repository**? We can't put our current project from work on it, can we?

Let's break it down.

Sharing solutions using Swift Package or pods

We are iOS developers, and we're good! It means that we've solved dozens, if not hundreds, of complex issues during our careers. Most likely, we are not the first that have encountered them. What if (just an idea, right?) we take one or some of our solutions and *share them with the world*?

Let's try to remember – did we have something unique that we were proud of? Did we build something in a way that can be used in a different project easily? If this is the case, we should create a public repository in our **GitHub** account and share it. The simplest way is using a **Swift Package** or a **pod**.

Creating a side project

Another option for a GitHub repository is creating a side project. Side projects allow us to show our code portfolio, how we build a project from scratch, and maintain it over time. Maintainance is one of the primary challenges with side projects. Here are some tips for maintaining our side project:

- Many developers have ideas for side projects. Starting one is easy: set up a new repository, create a new project, and write some classes. The primary problem, well... is to finish these projects. And that's the first tip with a side project. It is better to start a *modest* project but one that is practical to work on than an ambitious one that we never get to finish.

- Another thing to focus on is its *architecture rather than its functionality*. I'm not saying that our side project doesn't need to function well, but we should remember its goal, and that's showing what we can. If that's the case, it needs to look good. Clean design patterns, good naming conventions, and single-responsibility principles are much more important than fixing one more bug.

- The third tip is our *time management*. I know what it's like to find a slot in our busy schedule to work on a side project. But do the math – 10 minutes a day sums up to five hours a month and 30 hours in half a year. We don't have to quit our job or spend endless nights on a side project. We just need to manage our time better and have a long-term plan with realistic milestones.

- My last tip talks about *priorities in our work*. Trying to nail every minor issue that we bump into and striving for perfection won't bring us to our goal and will just frustrate us. It is better to continually progress and leave leftover to-dos than be stuck on a non-issue. Remember that finishing a side project is much more important than making it perfect, especially from a mental point of view.

Now, a side project is a big deal for some of us. We need ideas, ambition, and time. But we don't have to go that far, as there are other ways to show what we can.

Adding gists and showcase projects

Why build an entire app when we only need to show a design pattern, an algorithm solution, or even a code snippet? If we have a great idea for implementing navigation management, we can just build a project demonstrating our concept. If we want to show how the **binary tree search** (**BTS**) algorithm works in **Swift**, we can build a small app that uses that algorithm. But for that, we don't even need a project to show a piece of code. We can use a GitHub feature called **Gist**.

> **What is a binary tree search?**
>
> A binary tree search is a data structure consisting of nodes arranged in a hierarchical order, where each node has at most two children. It allows for efficient searching, insertion, and deletion of nodes by leveraging the property that the left subtree of a node contains only nodes with keys less than the node's key, and the right subtree contains only nodes with keys greater than the node's key. Although binary tree search isn't in the scope of this chapter, this is a good opportunity to learn about it, implement it in Swift, and create a nice gist to share with the world.

A gist is a GitHub feature that allows us to share code snippets. Do we need to show how to use a **regular expression** to match an email address form? Great! A gist is perfect for that.

Remember that by writing code daily we perform innovative and sophisticated tasks. So, let's take these ideas and create meaningful content. Once we have a lead for a written code snippet or a project, it is essential to add gists correctly. Like everything in life, focusing is the key to success.

How to focus on what matters

Let's start with the obvious – this chapter is not a GitHub tutorial, and this book doesn't explain how to develop an app to solve Swift algorithm problems. The main goal is to help you get an interview and pass it like a king. Having said that, we now understand how important it is to strive for a good-looking GitHub account.

As I said earlier, if our goal is branding, there's a significant weight to how our GitHub looks like. Let's break down what that means.

Making our README file look more interesting

Let's go back again to the resume scanning in the *Building our resume* section of *Chapter 1* – remember that issue? We know that we have six to eight seconds for the recruiter to scan our portfolio and decide whether they keep on reading or move it to the trash. This six-to-eight-second rule also applies to code documentation scanning; not just resumes.

Every GitHub repository has a **README** file, which appears when you enter the repository on the web. Usually, it contains installation and usage instructions, but it always starts with explaining the project.

That explanation allows us to market our project and make it more interesting. Just like our personal summary description, we don't start with what the code does but rather what problem it solves and why that problem is crucial.

Another way to make our project looks more attractive is by adding images or even a GIF animation (depending on the project type). Adding artwork catches the eye and makes the scanning more effective.

Now that we have an excellent README file, let's move to the main course: the code, which must be readable.

Writing readable code

In the end, our code is our portfolio. I said that once and will keep saying that until it is internalized. Even if we take a code snippet from our working projects and put it in a **gist**, we must ensure it looks perfect.

Let's list some tips for a readable code:

- Adding explicit *comments* that explain the reasons for our choices
- Choosing good *naming conventions* for classes and variables
- Using *design patterns* correctly and by the book (unless the book is ours, of course)
- Writing **unit tests** that describe what the code does and its expectations

These are some of the ways to make our code shine!

Remember that the developer who will review our code will not be the recruiter, but the hiring manager or the team tech lead. They know a thing or two about iOS development, so our code needs to look perfect and complete.

Completeness of our project

What about finishing our project before we make it public? That's an important point. Don't leave half-baked projects or even code snippets. It is better to finish a small project than to plan and not finish a big one. We discussed that previously, but when showing it to the world, it gets even more crucial.

A side project is a big deal. It takes time and effort, but it also gives us *points* when we build our brand.

If we want to work on a project but don't want to start our own, there's another way to do that, and maybe that's more suitable for us.

Joining an open source project

There are many reasons why developers like contributing to an **open source** project. One of the top reasons is the *drive to change* a product we often use. Another reason is *empowering our skills*. We are not here to talk about how open source projects help us as developers but how contributing to an open source helps us build *our brand*.

We said earlier that a brand should reflect the developer we are or the style of the developer we want to be.

An open source project requires different skills (both soft and hard) than a personal side project, and contributing to an open source project brings these skills to the front. So, before we **fork** a Git repository and add new code, we must confirm that this work fits our personality.

Previously, I said that the most critical thing about building our brand is to make sure that whatever way we choose is suitable for us and the image we want to create. Enjoyment and fun play a significant role here! And contributing to an open source project can be frustrating at first. We must dive into an existing project, handle intensive communication with other developers, and get used to cruel pull requests rejected with insulting comments. Is this what we imagined when we planned on joining an open source project?

Many developers want to share their knowledge and lessons learned with the world, but open source projects don't always fit their skill set. Fortunately, there is another way of achieving that: writing.

Writing content

Another way of building a brand is content writing. **Blogs**, tutorials, or even books are all great examples of content writing that can leverage our developer brand.

The reason it has a significant influence on our brand is apparent, but content writing can help us pass the interview process in other ways as well, and it is considered a win-win solution. Let's elaborate on that next.

Being experts

Reading a professional article is excellent for learning, but writing a professional article is another level of profundity.

Imagine what is required from us when writing an article – research, coding, edge case covering, the ability the explain why things are done the way they are, and managing alternative discussions.

We understand now that writing an article is not really writing – it's learning! It means being an expert in a specific field and covering it from all angles. The more blog posts we write, the more areas we cover, and that's a fantastic starting point for our hiring process.

But knowledge coverage is not everything. It also provides us the capability to explain that knowledge, which leads us to my next point.

Improving wording and expression capabilities

Another skill we get when writing content is the wording and self-expression ability. Content writing organizes our thoughts coherently, allowing us to list cons and pros, discuss alternatives and explain (for example) why we need to force wrap an **IBOutlet** and not make it optional.

The **self-expression capability** is crucial in interviews. Starting from the next chapter, we will learn how to answer questions, but mostly, we will learn that there are many questions without clear answers. In these cases, our ability to discuss or even debate these questions is essential.

Writing content creates discussions not only in interviews but also as a reaction to the blog post itself. So, here's another benefit we have! Connections!

Increasing our network

Remember when I said content writing is a "win-win" effort? Now, we see that it's a gift that never stops giving.

After we publish our post, we will start getting responses from iOS developers worldwide. Each answer is a lead for a discussion thread, and that thread creates a new connection.

Also, each blog post brings new followers, which in turn adds more questions and creates new connections, so that process is even exponential!

An extensive network and a high number of followers can help us get our first interview during the interview process. I remember interviewing for a job where the interviewer was one of my followers, and he even used one of my blog posts to solve his problem. That illuminates the interview in a different light, doesn't it?

The example I just gave also brings up another benefit: exposing our knowledge to the world.

Making the world aware of our knowledge

The mission of passing an interview is part of a competitive world where we need to "play the game".

It's not enough that we know how smart we are. We need others to see that as well. That may sound superficial, I know. But yes – that's part of building a brand and marketing ourselves and our capabilities.

The fourth benefit of sharing our knowledge is *exposing to the world what we know*, how we think, and our abilities to perform research in new and exciting fields. When we think of it, managing a blog or having our own book opens a window to our knowledge, our mindset, and our way of thinking. This might sound creepy initially, but it can significantly benefit applying for a job posting when we do it right.

Let's think about it for a second – our first and perhaps most challenging goal is passing the resume scanning stage, which we can only do if the reviewer thinks we are suitable for the role. For some reviewers, the fact that we have our iOS development knowledge laid bare acts as a certificate of what we are capable of. It's a huge benefit, especially if the reviewer is also the hiring manager.

So, we can see we have several advantages of content writing, and it's practically a win-win situation. But how does it fit with other ways we discussed earlier? We will see that in the next section.

Combining all and more

You know, writing content is excellent and valuable to our brand development effort. But the real power comes when we use the content as an infrastructure for our brand and combine it with the other methods we mentioned, such as being active in GitHub and Stack Overflow.

For example, if we write an article about a specific topic, we can *build upon it*. A GitHub repository explains our central idea, and by doing so, we earn another way to share our skills. We can then use our repository or article as a reference when answering a question in Stack Overflow and gain even more exposure.

But what can really make a big difference is upgrading that package to the extreme. Two great options that can make us stand out are *speaking at conferences* and *authoring a book*. I didn't mention them before because, unlike the other options, being a public speaker or writing a book requires special skills, time, and resources.

Dreaming about standing on a stage or seeing our book on Amazon is thrilling and exciting. These two options can leverage our brand to new highs and open new doors in the industry.

Before we summarize the chapter, I want to take us back to the ground and talk about the basics of the basics: in-person interactions.

Understanding that every in-person interaction is important

In *Chapter 2*, we discussed how important it is to leave a good impression in interviews. But the discussion was in the context of getting hired. We should remember that impressing people in person is not just essential for interviews, but also for creating our brand.

Open source contributions, Stack Overflow questions, blog followers, and more are all examples of places where we are *required to handle a certain number of interactions* with other developers.

Looking forward, these interactions also help us to shape our image in the industry. Sometimes, that single interaction is the only chance we've got to show who we are to other developers.

What is the impression that we leave behind? Like every industrial product, our name goes in front of us and is built upon thousands of talks, help sessions, and correspondences.

Summary

We just covered an exciting and unique topic! Developer branding is way beyond just Swift and UIKit practicing – it can also help us in our development career. But what's more interesting is that its scope is very flexible. We can start with just a code snippet in Gist and move up until we're speaking in public and writing books. We can choose where we want to be according to our resources and skills.

We've learned what a brand is, why contributing is part of it, how to maintain a GitHub repository, be a star in Stack Overflow, and produce our professional content.

By now, we should have the essential tools to start our branding development plan toward becoming a rising star in the iOS development community!

But one thing is missing: our ability to successfully pass the technical interview… (after all, this is why we are all here, right?). Fortunately, in our next chapter, we will discuss something we all enjoyed learning – Swift language and coding. The fun is just beginning.

Part 2:
Swift Language and Coding

Moving on to the second part of the book, we begin to look at the crucial Swift topics that interviewers commonly ask about and consider valuable. In this part, we will find a dozen interview questions covering areas such as data structures, optionals, memory management, generics, and testing. By the end of this part, we will have the knowledge to tackle most Swift-related interview questions.

In this part, we have the following chapters:

- *Chapter 4, Data Structures and Algorithms*
- *Chapter 5, The Swift Programming Language*
- *Chapter 6, Managing Your Code*

4

Data Structures and Algorithms

We spent time and effort on our resume, performing company research and building our developer brand. But what for? To start an interview process at a company we want to work for, and *get hired*!

So, now that the first step has been achieved, we will turn to our next challenge, passing the iOS technical interview.

The first topic to pass the iOS technical interview will cover data structures such as classes, structs, dictionaries, and arrays. While we could begin with the fundamental principles of the Swift language, that could be considered a more technical subject. In contrast, *data structures involve more abstract concepts*. Therefore, we will leave the Swift language for *Chapter 5*.

This chapter will cover the basic data structures often asked about in iOS technical interviews. To that end, we will cover the following topics in this chapter:

- Learning the importance of data structures
- Answering classes and struct questions
- Answering questions about Swift array
- Covering the Codable protocol
- Preparing for dictionary- and set-related interview questions

Before we begin, let's take a moment to understand the significance of data structures and why I have chosen to start our technical discussion on this topic.

Learning the importance of data structures

Data structures are the building blocks of our iOS development. In fact, data structures are the building blocks of many programming languages, and having a deep understanding in that area is the key to success in development and, therefore, passing an iOS interview.

What are considered to be data structures? Well, classes, structs, arrays, dictionaries, and sets are all examples of data structures.

But what precisely makes data structures so important? Here are a couple of reasons why data structures are an integral part of an iOS interview. Let's list them before we go over some interview questions.

Increasing efficiency

We always have shortages and constraints when we discuss resources. Even though iOS devices have become much more powerful in the last few years, iOS development is no exception to the need for efficiency.

Each data structure has its own strength in terms of time and space complexity; therefore, it will have a different usage in our code. Sometimes, the difference in performance can be so significant that it can cause our app to run much slower on even the most powerful iPhone.

> ### What is "space and time complexity?"
>
> Time complexity refers to the amount of time required to execute an algorithm or solve a problem as a function of the input size. It is usually measured in terms of the number of basic operations performed by the algorithm.
>
> Space complexity, on the other hand, refers to the amount of memory required to execute an algorithm or solve a problem as a function of the input size. It is usually measured in terms of the amount of memory used by the algorithm to store data and intermediate results.

Showing a drastic knowledge gap in an interview will raise a big red flag, and having basic knowledge is a minimum requirement for an iOS developer, even juniors.

Nevertheless, let's try to change the book atmosphere – not everything is red flags, and we can even earn points in an interview. Modularity is one example.

Making our code modular

Call me a "super-geek," but I think a great use of data structures is making our code look like a piece of art. Modularity is perhaps the best example of an artistic code.

Data structures provide a way to organize and encapsulate our code, making it easier to read and maintain.

Developers who follow my online content already know that I'm a big fan of the **single responsibility principle**, which is part of SOLID set of principles. This principle states that each module, function, class, or even variable should have its one and only one responsibility.

> **About SOLID principles**
>
> SOLID is an acronym for a set of principles in object-oriented programming that help to design more maintainable, scalable, and reusable code. The SOLID principles were introduced by Robert C. Martin in his paper *Design Principles and Design Patterns* in the early 2000s.
>
> The five SOLID principles are as follows:
>
> - **Single Responsibility Principle (SRP)**: A class should have only one reason to change
>
> - **Open-Closed Principle (OCP)**: Software entities should be open for extension but closed for modification
>
> - **Liskov Substitution Principle (LSP)**: Subtypes should be substitutable for their base types
>
> - **Interface Segregation Principle (ISP)**: Clients should not be forced to depend on interfaces they do not use
>
> - **Dependency Inversion Principle (DIP)**: High-level modules should not depend on low-level modules; both should depend on abstractions

Let's look at the following code:

```
class Employee {
  var name: String
  var salary: Double

  // responsibility 1: store employee data
  init(name: String, salary: Double{
    self.name = name
    self.salary = salary
  }

  // responsibility 2: calculate payroll
  func calculatePayroll() -> Double {
  }
}
```

We've got an `Employee` class with two responsibilities – the first is to *store* the employee's personal data, and the second is to *calculate* the payroll.

I'll start with the basics – this is not a piece of code you want your interviewer to see, as it mixes two responsibilities in one class. It is much better to take the `calculatePayroll()` function and move it to a separate class named `Payroll` (for example).

The reason why code separation is essential is that we understand that having control of what's happening in our code is crucial. If a class or a struct has more responsibilities, it can create a side effect that may lead to other issues.

We always need to explain (to the interviewer and ourselves) the goal of the class or the function we just wrote, what its role is in the design pattern we chose, and do the same thing for methods and variables.

Modular code is not only for logic separation – it also plays a significant role in my next point, which is reusability.

Reusing our code

Do I need to explain the importance of code reuse?

But just in case, when writing code that can be used in different places, code reuse can prevent bugs and inconsistent behavior.

Code reuse in data structures refers to the reuse of both logic and data. This can include using classes and structs to reuse logic and data structures, such as arrays and dictionaries, to store and access data in a reusable manner.

And that's where code reusability relates to the previous point of modularity – if a data structure has one responsibility, it is easier to reuse, as there are no side effects that can prevent us from using that code in other places.

Another example of code reuse in data structures is *class inheritance*. When we create a subclass, we can use all the superclass code.

In general, interviewers love to see reusable code, as it makes our code more effective and less error-prone. A data structure can also make our code less error-prone in another way, which is an API and interfaces.

Using data structures for an API

Another excellent usage for the data structure is for an **API** and interfaces. We should think of a data structure as a way to represent an entity or some other complex data collection. Creating API interfaces between the different components in our code is much easier if you think of it that way.

Let's have a look at what it means in code by writing a `sendPersonToServer()` function:

```
func sendPersonToServer(name: String, age: Int, email:
    String, phone: String, address: String) {

}
```

The `sendPersonToServer()` function's goal is to send a person's details to the server, but we can easily see the main problem here. First, we need to provide a long list of parameters, which is very inconvenient. But, much more importantly, it looks like all the parameters together *can be encapsulated* into a data structure that we can call – `Person`.

Let's see how the function interface looks once we extract it to a `Person` struct:

```
struct Person {
    let name: String
    let age: Int
    let email: String
    let phone: String
    let address: String
}

func sendPersonToServer(person: Person) {

}
```

It's much more elegant, isn't it?

It looks like the interface for `sendPersonToServer()` function is much clearer now but also more consistent. Whenever we add a new variable to `Person`, we won't have to update our functions header anymore because it is now capsulated within the struct definition.

That's why interviewers often appreciate seeing solutions that involve the reuse of functions and API interfaces when discussing potential strategies.

We discussed the importance of data structures – we mentioned efficiency, modularity, reusable code, and interfaces. My main goal was to provide you with a knowledge infrastructure to help you build your answers during the interview.

Now, let's review some interview questions about data structure, starting with *classes* and *structs*!

Answering classes and struct questions

Under the umbrella of data structures, classes, and struct questions are probably the most basic forms we use in our projects. The reason is that not only do classes and structs contain data, but they also provide the main logic of the app and the objects they represent.

When Apple announced Swift, they constantly pushed using structs over classes in many cases. The trend became even more extreme when **SwiftUI** was announced, which was based solely on structs over classes. So, it goes without saying why classes and struct questions play a significant role in iOS interviews.

Let's move to the first and the most popular question – classes versus structs.

"What's the difference between a class and a struct?"

Why is this question important?

A class and a struct have many features in common – they are both used to define complex data types, **methods**, and **properties**.

"Functions" or "methods?"

Having a job interview in iOS development means that we need to be professional. As part of being professional, terminology is crucial, so it is important to distinguish between a function and a method. A function is a code block that performs a specific task and can be called from anywhere in the program. In contrast, a "method" is a function that is associated with a class or a struct.

However, classes and structs also have some significant differences that influence our choice when approaching a problem we want to solve.

What is the answer?

There are three main differences between classes and structs:

- The first difference is that *classes are reference types*, while structs are *value types*. This means that when we pass an object that is based on a class to a function or another instance, we are actually working and modifying the original instance because the object we passed is just a reference. That's not the case with structs – whenever we pass a struct to a function, we work with a copy of that struct, not the original one.

  Have a look at the following code:

  ```
  struct A {
      var name: String
  }

  var a = A(name: "Avi")
  let b = a

  a.name = "John"

  print(b)
          print(a)
  ```

  The result of the code will be `Avi`, and then `John`. However, if we declare A as a class, the results would be `John` and `John` because it's a reference to the original variable.

- Another difference is the fact that *we can inherit classes*, and by that, we mean we can derive a class from another class, including properties and methods. Structs cannot be derived from another struct (or class, for that matter).

- The last difference is **mutability**. Because a struct is a value type, we cannot change its properties if we mark it as let. That's not the case with a class – if a class is marked as let, we can still mutate its properties.

The following code will raise an error:

```
struct A {
    var name: String
}

let a = A(name: "Avi")
a.name = "John"
```

However, if we change A to a class, that will work:

```
class A {
    var name: String

    init(name: String) {
        self.name = name
    }
}

let a = A(name: "Avi")
a.name = "John"
```

> **Important note**
> Before we continue, let's clear up something – there's no such thing as "better" in topics such as data structures. There's always a trade-off; we should emphasize that fact in our interviews.

Let's now move on to the next question.

"Which is better, a class or a struct?"

Why is this question important?

To thoroughly impress the interviewer, it is essential to not only be able to distinguish between a struct and a class, but also to demonstrate an understanding of when it is appropriate to use each data structure in different situations.

As we discussed earlier in this chapter, structs and classes have different features, so their use cases are also different. This is a more practical question than just knowing the differences.

What is the answer?

Both are great data structures for different purposes. It's a good idea to start with a struct and see whether it meets our needs. If we need additional capabilities, we can change it to a class.

We should use a class if we need to do the following:

- Use it as a *reference* type
- *Inherit* from another class (such as subclassing **UIViewController**, for example)

We should use a struct if need to do the following:

- Pass it between *threads*
- Optimize *performance*

It is important to state that there's no such thing as "better" without context. It is all based on the use cases and the requirements of our code.

"Why are structs faster than classes?"

Why is this question important?

This question may not be meaningful on its own, but interviewers like to ask it because they want to check how deeply the candidate understands how structs and classes are stored in a device's memory. Knowing the answer to that question or even explaining the difference in other cases can give us points on our interview scoreboard.

What is the answer?

Structs are faster than classes because of the way *they are stored in memory*. Structs are value types; therefore, they are stored in the **stack**, which also stores local variables and function parameters.

On the other hand, classes are reference types, and they are stored indirectly in the **heap**. The heap is used to store dynamically allocated objects.

The stack is faster than the heap because it is organized more predictably, and I/O operations are performed faster.

It is important to say that the performance difference is not significant. We should first choose the proper data structure according to our needs. Only if we encounter performance issues should we consider optimizing it.

Classes and structs are extremely important topics in iOS development. We meet these data structures daily, and knowing them well is crucial to writing compelling and great code.

But in coding, data structures are often created upon other data structures. That's the case with arrays.

Let's make sure we have a complete understanding of how arrays work in Swift.

Answering questions about Swift array

Unlike many other data structures, arrays are considered tricky. On the one hand, arrays are great to store a collection of data and are valuable in many widespread use cases, such as managing lists of objects and entities. On the other hand, we need to know their strengths and weakness to use them effectively.

Interviewers like to ask questions about arrays that check our more profound knowledge about how they work internally.

Questions such as, *"How do you declare an array?"* are not that common because it is given that an iOS developer knows how to create an array.

So, what are exciting interview questions about arrays?

Usually, questions about arrays focus on pros and cons, memory management, and data manipulation.

Let's start with the advantages.

"Please list the Swift array advantages"

Why is this question important?

Swift arrays have several advantages that make them useful. If a developer is unaware of these advantages, an array might not be the correct data structure to use. It's essential to remember that for every advantage, there may also be a disadvantage.

What is the answer?

There are several advantages to arrays:

- **Easy element access by index**: Elements can be retrieved or modified quickly by providing the index number of the desired element

- **Type-safety**: An array can hold only an element from a pre-defined type

- **Built-in operations**: Arrays have many actions, such as adding, removing, filtering, sorting, and more

Remember, questions such as these are the foundation for many more to follow, such as *"What are the use cases for arrays?"* or *"List the disadvantages of arrays."* Diving into the material can help prepare you for any unexpected surprises.

"How to remove duplicates from an array?"

Why is this question important?

Unlike the Set data structure, a Swift array can contain duplicate items. The question tests our ability to manipulate an array of data and discuss the solution with the interviewer. There are several ways to solve that, and showing some of them will give the interviewer the feeling that we can manipulate the data from different directions.

What is the answer?

Let's see the possible solutions.

Solution #1

The simplest way to remove duplicate elements is to convert the array to Set and then back to the array. Set is a data structure that cannot contain duplicates, and converting the array to Set removes these duplicates. Let's see that in action:

```
let arrayWithDuplicates = [1, 2, 3, 3, 4, 5, 5]
let arrayWithNoDuplicates = Array(Set(arrayWithDuplicates))
```

This simple and elegant code snippet will work great! But for some interviewers, doing that may seem like "cheating."

Remember that converting to a Set may *disrupt the order* of the items, so if the order is important, this may not be the best solution.

So, it is better to make clear that we have additional solutions to the problem.

Solution #2

Another solution would be to build a new array and add items only if they do not exist:

```
var newArray: [Int] = []
for number in array {
    if ! newArray.contains(number) {
        newArray.append(number)
    }
}
```

While this solution will work, it is considered a **brute-force** solution.

> **What is a "brute force" solution?**
>
> A brute-force solution is an algorithm that relies on sheer computational power to solve a problem rather than using a cleverer approach. This can often be a simple and straightforward approach, but it can also be very time-consuming and may not be the most efficient solution for more significant problems.

One way to make the loop more efficient is to use Set to check whether the item already exists, instead of using `array.contains()`:

```
var newArray: [Int] = []
var newAddedItems = Set<Int>()
for number in array {
    if ! newAddedItems.contains(number) {
        newArray.append(number)
        newAddedItems.insert(number)
    }
}
```

Unlike the array's contains method, the contains method of Set has an average time complexity of O(1), which would improve our answer.

Solution #3

A more elegant way is to use the array's **filter** method:

```
let numbers = [1, 2, 3, 3, 4, 5, 5]
let uniqueNumbers = numbers.filter { number in
    numbers.firstIndex(of: number) == numbers.lastIndex
```

```
        (of: number)
    }
```

Generally, we should always prefer the filter method over looping elements. The filter method is easier to read and more efficient because of native optimizations of the Swift language (we don't need to get into details during the interview, even though I admit it is fascinating).

"How do you implement a queue using an array?"

Why is this question important?

This is a simple question if we know what a **queue** means in computer science and the basic array manipulation methods.

These are the reasons why this question is relatively popular. It demonstrates our understanding of the basic concepts of a queue and the general trade-offs when using an array for that task.

What is the answer?

To create a queue using an array, we should start by creating a Queue struct with basic methods, such as isEmpty, count, enqueue, and dequeue.

The Queue struct contains an underline array, and we can use the append and removeFirst array methods to execute the queue's basic functionality. Let's see an example of that:

```swift
struct Queue<Element> {
    private var array: [Element] = []

    var isEmpty: Bool {
        return array.isEmpty
    }

    var count: Int {
        return array.count
    }

    mutating func enqueue(_ element: Element) {
        array.append(element)
    }

    mutating func dequeue() -> Element? {
        return array.isEmpty ? nil : array.removeFirst()
    }
}
```

Don't be scared. There's no need to memorize that solution!

The best thing to do is improve our understanding of queues and remember the `append()` and `removeFirst()` array methods.

It is better to practice once or twice to ensure we nail this question the first time.

"How do you create a new array by mapping the elements of an existing array in Swift?"

Why is this question important?

Aside from searching arrays, an iOS developer also needs to know how to manipulate and transform data from one data structure to another. This capability is not only for arrays but also dictionaries and sets.

Transforming or mapping data is a common practice in development, especially in the world of **combine** and **reactive programming**.

What is the answer?

We can use the `map` method to map an array to a new one. The map method takes a closure as an argument and, for each element, returns a new value. That way, the map method produces a new array with new values.

Let's see a basic map method that takes an array of integers and returns a new array by doubling its values:

```
let array = [1, 2, 3, 4, 5]
let doubledArray = array.map { element in return element * 2
}
```

After the loop has ended, the array contains the [2, 4, 6, 8, 10] values.

An even more elegant way to use a map is with a Swift feature called **implicit closure parameter syntax**. Using that feature, we can create even shorter and more readable code:

```
let doubledArray = array.map { $0 * 2 }
```

`$0` represents the first argument in the closure, and there's no need for the `return` keyword, making the statement look even shorter!

We can see that arrays are fundamental in Swift and iOS development, playing a major in data storage, states, API interfaces, and many more cases where we need to handle collections. Manipulating arrays elegantly and efficiently is something that interviewers like to test!

Now, we are done with simple data structures and will move on to serialize them with Codable.

Covering the Codable protocol

The **Codable** protocol is an important Swift feature that allows us to *convert serialized data such as a string to a data structure* we can work with.

The first thing to know about the Codable protocol is that it combines two other protocols – "Encodable" and "Decodable." These two protocols help us to convert data both ways.

Data objects (such as structs) need to conform to the Codable protocol so that we can convert them back and forth.

Here's a simple code snippet:

```
struct Person: Codable {
    var name: String
    var age: Int
    var address: String
}

let person = Person(name: "John", age: 30, address: "123 Main St.")
let encoder = JSONEncoder()
let data = try encoder.encode(person)

let decoder = JSONDecoder()
let person = try decoder.decode(Person.self, from: data)
```

As we can see in the preceding code block, `Person` conforms to Codable, and therefore, we can convert it to data in both directions.

The second thing we need to know about Codable is that all struct properties must conform to it.

In the preceding code snippet, we can see that `Person` has three properties from the `String` and `Int` types. `String` and `Int` already conform to Codable, so we don't need to do anything else. However, if we want to add additional custom properties, we need to make sure they conform to Codable as well.

The following example adds the `Child` property to `Person`:

```
struct Person: Codable {
    var name: String
    var age: Int
    var address: String
    var children: [Child]
}

struct Child: Codable {
    var name: String
    var age: Int
}
```

The fact that the `Child` struct conforms to Codable makes the `Person` struct also conform to Codable.

Let's go over some questions about the Codable protocol!

"How do you handle optional properties when using the Codable protocol?"

Why is this question important?

Optional properties are essential when working with Codable because it is helpful in cases where we need to work with APIs. Sometimes (or should I say, often), the returned data may not include all the properties we define in our struct.

Being familiar with how Codable works in common API use cases demonstrates your understanding.

What is the answer?

To handle optional properties, we simply need to declare them as optional using the ? parameter.

Let's take the `Person` struct from the previous example:

```
struct Person: Codable {
    var name: String
    var age: Int?
    var address: String?
}
```

We can see that both the `address` and `age` properties are optional. If we don't receive these values in an API response, they will remain nil.

On the other hand, if a value is not marked as optional and no default value is set, an exception will be thrown if the corresponding key is not present in the JSON response.

"How do you use CodingKeys enumeration to map the keys in a JSON object to the properties of a custom data type?"

Why is this question important?

CodingKeys enumeration allows us to customize the keys used in the **encoding/decoding** process.

A good answer about CodingKey shows us that we fully understand how Codable protocols work and can handle more complex parsing when needed.

What is the answer?

The way Codable maps keys to properties is by using their names. If we take the `Person` struct example, the `name` property will be mapped to the `name` key in the JSON structure because they have an identical key name.

However, we can customize that easily using CodingKey enumeration by defining a custom mapping.

We need to create `enum` under the struct that conforms to CodingKey and define a new mapping value.

Look at the following example:

```
struct Person: Codable {
    var name: String
    var age: Int
    var address: String

    enum CodingKeys: String, CodingKey {
        case name = "full_name"
        case age
        case address
    }
}
```

According to our code snippet, the `Person` struct has a `name` property, but that property is now mapped to a `full_name` key that will appear in the JSON.

Here's the JSON with the `full_name` key:

```
{
    "full_name": "Avi Tsadok",
    "age": 42,
    "address": "Hamargalit Street
}
```

Using CodingKeys helps us go through different naming between our structs and the data we need to parse. However, CodingKeys doesn't help when converting one data type to another. In that case, we have a decoder. Let's see an interview question explicitly related to that.

"How can you convert a formatted date string to a date object in Codable?"

Why is this question important?

When working with APIs, there's no way of representing a date value other than with `String` or `Double`.

If we want a struct that contains a date value, we need a way to convert the `Double` or `String` value to a date object.

We need to understand that these kinds of use cases are not rare.

There are more examples where we need to convert a value we have in a JSON object to another type we have in our struct. Here are some of these examples:

- Converting a JSON value to enum.
- Creating nested objects
- Handling default values in the case of optional properties

Ultimately, parsing API responses is a common and important responsibility for iOS developers, and proficiency in this area is essential.

What is the answer?

We use several features to convert a string-based date to a date object. The first is CodingKey to map the keys and properties, as we learned in our previous question. Second, initialize the struct using `init(from decoder: Decoder)` struct, and finally, use `DateFormatter` to convert the string to a date object.

Let's see an example. This is the `Person` properties list:

```
struct Person: Codable {
    var name: String
    var age: Int
    var address: Address
    var birthday: Date

    enum CodingKeys: String, CodingKey {
        case name
        case age
        case address
        case birthday
    }

    enum Address: String, Codable {
        case home
        case work
    }
```

And this is the `init(from decoder: Decoder)` function:

```
init(from decoder: Decoder) throws {
    let container = try decoder.container(keyedBy:CodingKeys.self)
    name = try container.decode(String.self,forKey: .name)
    age = try container.decode(Int.self, forKey: .age)
    address = try container.decode(Address.self,forKey: .address)
    // Decode birthday using a custom date formatter
    let dateFormatter = DateFormatter()dateFormatter.dateFormat =
    "yyyy-MM-dd"
    if let birthdayString = try? container.decode(String.self, forKey:
    .birthday) {
        birthday = dateFormatter.date(from:birthdayString) ?? Date()
        } else {
        birthday = Date
```

This is a lengthy piece of code worth mentioning!

During an interview, it's important to provide a detailed explanation of how to implement the features that were mentioned earlier in this section.

`init(from:)` is called when we want to create a struct based on serialized data.

With this method, we can enter the keys container of the received data and map them to the struct properties. This provides us complete flexibility when parsing more complex data structures.

One important note about Codable before we move one is that, technically, we don't "have" to use Codable in our projects. There are other solutions to parse and serialize objects and structs. But in modern Swift development, Codable is a major player in API management and data storage; therefore, it is a must topic for interviews, and we need to ensure we are fully prepared.

The Codable protocol is a great match for structs, yet it's not the only option to manage complex data structures. Dictionaries are a flexible method of organizing data of diverse types and structures, and they are often utilized in interviews.

Preparing for dictionary- and set-related interview questions

Dictionaries and sets are both highly effective data structures that enable fast storage, retrieval, and data manipulation. In particular, dictionaries offer the ability to store data using a key-value format, and they also serve as the foundation to encode and decode complex data structures.

As an iOS developer, there are some use cases where we can use dictionaries in our projects:

- **Quick lookup**: Dictionaries are excellent to save and retrieve data quickly, since they use key-value to store data. This makes dictionaries ideal to save user accounts, lists of settings, cache data, and so on.

- **Counting and frequency tracking**: When the dictionary key represents the item's type, and the value is the number of instances of that type, we can use it to track the frequency of words, items, and so on.

- **Encoding and decoding complex data structures**: Dictionaries are so flexible that we can store almost any data structure. Moreover, dictionaries are in the form of JSON, so they are suitable to encode and decode API requests and responses.

- **Configuration data**: The key-value nature of dictionaries makes them ideal to store configuration data.

Try to think of these use cases as a basis for interview questions about dictionaries. Knowing the primary dictionary's advantages and usage can easily help us pass dictionary-related questions.

Sets are similar to dictionaries in the sense that they are both effective ways to store and retrieve data quickly. However, sets do not use the key-value structure as dictionaries do. Instead, they are lists of unique values that can be accessed with a time complexity of `O(1)`, which makes them very efficient data structures in so many use cases.

In fact, it is more appropriate to compare sets to arrays. If we do not need our list of items to be sorted or include duplicates, sets are a superior choice to arrays in most cases.

Just like dictionaries, let's look at some set use cases:

- **Removing duplicates from an array**: Do you remember the example of using sets to remove duplicates from an array? This is a classic application of sets.

- **Fast membership testing**: Sets help determine whether a particular value has already been used. The `contains` function in sets is much more efficient than an array and can be helpful in many situations.

- **Relationships between entities**: Sets are an ideal data structure to create relationships between two entities, such as `User` and `Product`, because they do not require sorting or duplicates. This is why sets are the default choice for "to-many" relationships in core data.

Now, we look at some interview questions related to sets and dictionaries.

"Can you use a dictionary to store configuration data?"

Why is this question important?

As previously mentioned, dictionaries are a valuable tool to store key-value pairs of data, and configuration data is a common use case for this data structure. This question involves creating a "configuration manager" class that utilizes a dictionary as its primary data structure and designing an interface to store and retrieve values from the dictionary. The task combines multiple coding skills, including creating a class and implementing a dictionary data structure.

> **And here's a great tip!**
>
> Generally speaking, as an iOS developer, this is a pattern we meet in our day-to-day work and, therefore, in interviews.
>
> Let's go over the pattern again:
>
> - Decide the data structure suitable for the task
>
> - Encapsulate the data structure within a class
>
> - Design and create a simple interface to work with that data structure
>
> Following these guidelines is the key to many answers!

What is the answer?

Here is a great code example to store configuration data in a dictionary:

```
class Configuration {
    static let shared = Configuration()
    private var values: [String: Any] = [:]

    func setValue(_ value: Any, forKey key: String) {
        values[key] = value
    }

    func value(forKey key: String) -> Any? {
        return values[key]
    }
}

// Setting configuration values
Configuration.shared.setValue("Dark", forKey: "theme")
Configuration.shared.setValue(true, forKey: "enable_notifications")
```

Looking at the code, we can see the three principles I mentioned – a data structure (dictionary), a wrapping class (`Configuration`), and an interface (`setValue()` and `value()`). That would be a perfect answer.

"How do you use the filter method to select a subset of key-value pairs from a dictionary based on a condition?"

Why is this question important?

This question tests our ability to manipulate dictionary data. To do that, we need to accomplish two tasks – *iterate* the dictionary values and create a *new dictionary* for some of the values according to a condition.

This operation is helpful in many different types of programs, as it allows you to focus only on the key-value pairs relevant to a particular task. For instance, you might use it to select only the key-value pairs for students who received an "A" grade on a test, or only the key-value pairs for words used frequently in a text.

What is the answer?

There are several ways to tackle this question – the `for` loop, filtering, and iterating the dictionary keys.

Solution number one – the for loop

The for-loop solution iterates the dictionary keys and values and performs a simple `if-then` check to fill up a new filtered dictionary, as shown here:

```
var wordFrequencies: [String: Int] = ["apple": 4,
    "banana": 3, "cherry": 2, "date": 1]
var highFrequencyWords: [String: Int] = [:]
for (word, frequency) in wordFrequencies {
    if frequency >= 3 {
        highFrequencyWords[word] = frequency
    }
}
print(highFrequencyWords)  // prints ["apple": 4, "banana": 3]
```

Remember the syntax to iterate a dictionary using the `for` loop:

```
for (key, value) in dictionary {
  // code to be executed for each key-value pair
}
```

That will be useful in other questions as well.

Solution number two – using the filter() method

The `filter` method solution is considered much *more elegant* than the `for` loop because it is more readable and optimized. Moreover, it combines the two operations (iterating and filtering) into one method.

Let's see how to perform the same task with a filter method:

```
let wordFrequencies: [String: Int] = ["apple": 4,
    "banana": 3, "cherry": 2, "date": 1]
let highFrequencyWords = wordFrequencies.filter { $0.value >= 3 }
print(highFrequencyWords)  // prints ["apple": 4, "banana": 3]
```

Look at how much less code we used here. This is how the professionals do it!

Solution number three – looping the keys

It is not necessary for the condition in the filter to be based on the dictionary's values; it could also be found in the keys. In this case, we would need to iterate through the keys and apply the filter to them.

The following code filters the same dictionary, but this time, it creates a dictionary subset of fruits whose name starts with a:

```
var wordFrequencies: [String: Int] = ["apple": 4,
    "banana": 3, "cherry": 2, "date": 1]
var highFrequencyWords: [String: Int] = [:]
for (word, frequency) in wordFrequencies {
    if frequency >= 3 {
        highFrequencyWords[word] = frequency
    }
}
print(aWords)  // prints ["apple": 4]
```

This solution allows us to perform more powerful dictionary filtering for more potential use cases and questions.

"What is the time complexity of common set operations, such as inserting an element or checking for membership?"

Why is this question important?

The **time complexity** for operations is a popular topic in data structures questions, mainly when we discuss sets.

If you are unfamiliar with this term, it's time to catch up! One of the decisions we make as iOS developers is choosing the proper data structure for the right task.

One of the key advantages of using a set over an array is its operation efficiency, such as inserting an element and checking for membership. Therefore, we will choose a set when handling caching, avoiding duplicate items, and so on.

What is the answer?

The time complexity of common set operations is as follows:

- Inserting an item into a set has an average time complexity of $O(1)$ and a worst-case time complexity of $O(n)$
- The same goes for checking for membership – the average time complexity of $O(1)$ and the worst-case time complexity of $O(n)$

Sets can have an average time complexity of O(n) in common operations because there are cases where a set can be clustered, and the time complexity depends on the size of the set.

Either way, a set is much more efficient than an array in inserting and checking.

"Is it possible to store any type of data in a set collection in Swift?"

Why is this question important?

This question evaluates our comprehension of Swift's set data structure and the process of hashing data types.

Working with primitive data types such as Int or Double is straightforward. But that's not the case with other types, especially those we define ourselves, such as structs or classes.

As a result, understanding how to use the **Hashable** protocol with a set data structure is crucial for iOS developers.

What is the answer?

It is possible to store any type of data in a set collection *as long as it conforms to the Hashable protocol*. The Hashable protocol allows custom types to generate a unique value that needs to be stored in set and dictionary data structures.

Let's see an example of how to store a struct named Person in a set:

```
struct Person: Hashable {
    var age: Int
    func hash(into hasher: inout Hasher) {
        hasher.combine(age)
    }
}

let newSet: Set<Person> = [Person(age: 21),
    Person(age: 35), Person(age: 49)]
```

It's crucial to understand the Hashable protocol when working with sets and dictionaries in Swift, as it determines how values and keys are stored in these collections.

Summary

In this chapter, we discussed the importance of data structures and why they are so important in interviews. We covered structs and classes, arrays, the Codable protocol, sets, and dictionaries.

This was a crucial chapter, and we now know so much more about data structures!

 However, that was just a warmup because, in the next chapter, we will go over another critical topic in iOS interviews – nothing less than the Swift language itself.

5

The Swift Programming Language

As we discussed in *Chapter 4*, understanding data structures is a crucial and complex skill for any developer, regardless of the platform or language they work with. Data structures are the foundation of computer science programming and algorithms, and mastering them is essential for success as a developer. Now that we have a solid understanding of data structures, it's time to move on to another important aspect of iOS development: Swift.

Swift is a highly popular topic in iOS interviews, and it's not only a programming language for iOS developers but also the core foundation of Apple's new frameworks and technologies.

Therefore, understanding Swift's primary features such as structs, property wrappers, generics, and more is vital to succeeding in iOS development and passing an interview. The close relationship between Swift and Apple's latest technologies makes a deep understanding of the language crucial for any iOS developer.

In this chapter, we will learn about optionals, access levels, and closures. We will also review computed and lazy properties, extensions, generics, error handling, protocols, and memory management questions.

To that end, we will cover the following topics:

- How do we master all Swift features?
- Basic Swift features
- Advanced Swift language features

It's essential to ensure that we have a good grasp of the primary language features to excel in the iOS interview process. But how can we ensure that we are fully covered in knowledge and understanding? We will see in this chapter.

How do we master all Swift features?

First, reading this chapter will get us through most of the important Swift features interviewers ask about in the iOS technical interviews.

But that's not enough.

To become a true professional, we must start acting like one.

For example, reading the *official Swift documentation* is an excellent start to ensure we are covered with the latest Swift enhancements. We will ensure we cover the basics by going over access levels, error handling, and extensions. But don't think of Swift as just a programming language. Some features were developed with deep thinking and interesting methodology.

Ideally, we shouldn't answer Swift interview questions just by memorizing the technical documentation – the interviewer would like to hear our thoughts, best practices, and recommendations.

Let's explain that idea with extensions.

A typical answer to the question *"Can you please tell me about Swift extensions?"* would be, *"Swift extensions allow us to add functionality to an existing class or struct."*

While this answer is not a mistake, it is still very technical. Try to think deeper:

- Why do we need extensions?

- How do extensions help us to write better code?

- What are the use cases that make extensions so powerful?

A better answer would be as follows:

Swift extensions are a powerful tool that allows developers to add new functionality to existing classes, structures, enumerations, and protocols. They enable code organization by grouping related functionality together, making it easier to read and maintain. They also increase the code reusability, readability, and testability.

Of course, we must ensure we fully understand extensions to phrase this type of answer.

Our next step would be to take what we've just learned about extensions and implement it on other topics, such as optionals, protocols, generics, and other Swift features. That's precisely what we're going to do in this chapter.

Do we need to know all Swift features? The answer is yes. Do we need to know all the features exceptionally well? It's highly recommended, but we can pass some of the interviews without expertise on some of the features.

That's why I grouped the Swift features into two levels: basic and advanced.

Let's start with some basic language features such as optionals, access levels, and closures.

Basic Swift features

Having a solid understanding of Swift's basic concepts is essential, as a lack of knowledge in these areas can cause significant issues for iOS developers, not to mention job interviews.

Answering optionals questions

Optionals are a fundamental concept in Swift and help us to write safe and robust code. These can handle the possibility of a variable having no value (nil). We define optional by adding ? after the variable type.

Here's an example:

```
var name: String?
```

In the preceding line of code, `name` can contain a value or nil.

A simple way to unwrap an optional and extract its value is the `if let` statement:

```
var name: String? = "Avi"

if let unwrappedValue = name {
    print("The unwrapped value is: \(unwrappedValue)")
} else {
    print("The optional was nil")
}
```

As we can see from our code snippet, the `if let` statement safely "extracts" the value from the `unwrappedValue` variable and provides an `else` statement in case it is nil.

Notice that since Swift 5.7, it is possible to unwrap more elegantly, keeping the optional name as it is:

```
var name: String? = "Avi"

if let name {
    print("The unwrapped value is: \(name)")
} else {
    print("The optional was nil")
}
```

The `if let` shorthand makes it simpler to unwrap as it doesn't require us to create another variable/constant with the same name as the optional.

Now, let's move to some interview questions.

"Can you give an example of a situation where you would use an optional in your code?"

Why is this question important?

This question tests our practical understanding of Swift optionals. Because optionals are a widespread feature that involves API interface design, functions declarations, and control flows, the interviewer needs to see if we understand correctly how to use it.

What is the answer?

We can use optionals in our code in a few everyday situations. Here are some of them:

- An optional parameter in function declarations:

```
func checkPerson(name: String, age: Int, address: Address?) ->
Bool
```

- Handling situations where a function may return null:

```
func getParentViewController() -> UIViewController?
```

- Handling missing data in JSON response using optionals in a struct:

```
struct Person {
    var name: String
    var age: Int
    var address: String?
}
```

We should use optionals in every place where we understand that we *may not receive a value* and receive nil instead.

"List all the options you know to unwrap an optional"

Why is this question important?

There are several ways to unwrap an optional. It doesn't mean that all of them are alternatives to each other – each method solves a different use case. Knowing most of the ways and their use cases shows our ability to unwrap optionals in our code elegantly and effectively.

What is the answer?

Let's go over some of the ways to unwrap an optional:

- Use `if let` syntax to perform a code block with an unwrapped value:

```
if let value = optionalValue {
    // Do something with the unwrapped value
}
```

- Use Optional Chaining to avoid multiple `if let` statements:

```
if let country = person.address?.country {
    print("The person lives in \(country).")
} else {
    print("The person's address is unknown.")
}
```

- Use `guard let` to have a stop condition and exit the scope if the value is nil:

```
guard let value = optionalValue else {
    return
}
// Do something with the unwrapped value
```

- Use the `!` operator. Force unwrap if we are certain the optional contains a value:

```
let value = optionalValue!
// Do something with the unwrapped value
```

- Use nil coalescing (`??`) to provide a default value:

```
let value = optionalValue ?? defaultValue
```

There is no preferred way to unwrap a value. It all depends on the control flow and the situation.

"Using force unwrapping will crash our app in case of nil. So why would we use it?"

Why is this question important?

That's a tricky question often asked in interviews. Take the following line of code:

```
let value = optionalValue!
```

If `optionalValue` is nil, we'll get an exception. So, why are we using that method?

This interview question is not really about optionals – it's about our ability to *manage exceptions* in our code and crash the app when needed.

What is the answer?

The most straightforward answer would be, "When we are certain the value is not nil." Here is an example:

```
var maybeString: String?
maybeString = "Hello"

if let unwrappedString = maybeString {
    // If the optional has a value, print it
    print(unwrappedString) // Output: Hello
    print(maybeString!) // force unwrapping
}
```

But that answer is not a complete one. Why would we even approach the maybeString variable, even if we just unwrapped it?

As mentioned earlier, this question tests our ability to manage exceptions using optionals. There are cases where an optional must contain a value. Otherwise, the program cannot continue.

One popular example would be declaring an IBOutlet as forced unwrap:

```
class ViewController: UIViewController {
    // Declare an IBOutlet
    @IBOutlet var label: UILabel!

    override func viewDidLoad() {
        super.viewDidLoad()
        // Force unwrap the label outlet
        label.text = "Hello World!"
    }
}
```

We'll get an exception if the label is nil. In general, we don't want our app to crash, but in this case, a crash indicates that *our program setup is broken* – we either disconnected that outlet or even removed it from the storyboard.

Another good example is force-cast UITableViewCell in a cellForRow method. Even though it's a casting operation, it is related to optionals because the result of casting is an optional value, and we force it to succeed.

Our program is not relevant if this casting fails, therefore we will use force-cast for that:

```
override func tableView(_ tableView: UITableView, cellForRowAt
indexPath: IndexPath) -> UITableViewCell {
    let cell = tableView.dequeueReusableCell
        (withIdentifier: "customCell", for: indexPath) as!
            CustomTableViewCell
    // configure the cell using the properties and methods
```

```
        of the custom class
    return cell
}
```

In summary, force unwrapping is not a common technique, but it can be helpful in certain situations where normal unwrapping is not applicable.

Solving access-level questions

At first, access-level questions seem like a small topic. Technically speaking, it is a small topic. Learning and remembering the different access levels is pretty straightforward.

The question is always, do we use access levels properly?

While a single keyword represents access levels, they influence code encapsulation, visibility, project and organization, and readability.

Access levels also influence how our interfaces between the simple app components look.

We should come to our interview knowing what the different levels represent and what they mean to our project structure.

"What are the different access levels in Swift, and what are their use cases?"

Why is this question important?

This question is considered a screening question, and its goal is to ensure we understand the basic access levels in Swift before we move on to more advanced questions on this topic.

> **A screening question**
>
> A screening question is a question that the interviewer asks to make sure we pass the minimum qualifications for the position and that we have the basic knowledge for the role. Experienced developers may find these questions weird – but we should remember that the interviewer doesn't have a previous acquaintance with us. We should be careful with these questions and ensure they won't be a trap in our interview. A screening question is also called a "fundamental" or "core" question.

What is the answer?

There are five different access levels:

1. *open* – Entities marked as open can be accessed and subclassed by any other module, including other frameworks. This level is used when we want to allow our class or method to be subclassed or overridden.

2. *public* – With public, we allow the entity to be accessible from any other module or framework *without subclassing* it. Sometimes, because of backward compatibility or security, we don't want other users to subclass our class, and using public is a great way to ensure that.

3. *internal* – We should use the internal access level when we want our entity to be accessible *within the same module* but not from the outside. Marking an entity as internal is not mandatory – that's the default access level in case we didn't define it explicitly. But in libraries, it is a best practice to mark classes explicitly as internal.

4. *fileprivate* – Entities marked as fileprivate are accessible *within the same file*. This is used when we have a class named A, and we want to add another class relevant only to class A. The `fileprivate` entity will ensure that constraint if we write both classes in the same file.

5. *private* – private methods and variables are accessible only for the *same class or struct* (enclosing declaration). With private, we can hide code implementation outside the entity.

"How do access levels affect code organization and readability?"

Why is this question important?

Just like the previous question, as iOS developers, we shouldn't look at access levels as technical features. Access levels tremendously influence how our code is organized and viewed. As a matter of fact, in some way, access levels have a part in our code documentation, as it describes what methods are part of the interface and what methods are part of the implementation.

What is the answer?

Access level affects code organization by separating it to interface and implementation. For example, let's take the following Game class:

```swift
class Game {
    private var gameOver: Bool = false

    public func restart() {
        gameOver = false
        // Other restart logic here
    }
}
```

We can see that Game has a gameOver property which is declared `private`, and a `restart()` method, which is `public`. We understand that gameOver is hidden and cannot be modified directly from outside the class. The only way to change it is by using the `restart()` method, and that leads us to my main point – readability.

By looking at the Game class, we can immediately see that there's only one way to stop the game: by calling restart(). They can safely ignore any other private methods or variables as it is used only for implementation. If gameOver was not private, it was possible to modify it from the outside without calling the necessary steps that are being done in the restart() method.

In short – the access level explains how to use the class or struct and separate them nicely to interface and implementation.

Handling questions about Closures

Closures replaced what used to be Blocks in Objective-C and are widely used in Swift development. But the reason I put it under *basic Swift features* is because closures became a fundamental part of many advanced Swift features. It is used as completion handles, advanced collection type functions, SwiftUI, and Combine. Not knowing closures well can affect our ability as iOS developers to move fast and implement advanced features.

"How do you use closures to handle callbacks in iOS?"

Why is this question important?

I chose to start with this question because callbacks and asynchronous operations are typical examples of how to use closures in many Swift applications. Unlike delegates, closures can make asynchronous tasks look simple and always in context.

What is the answer?

Closures are passed to a function as a parameter and can be executed later. Suppose the asynchronous operation is based on a delegate or any other mechanism where the response is out of the function scope. In that case, we can handle that dependency by saving the closure to an instance variable and calling the closure whenever we finish the task.

Here's a code example to explain that:

```swift
class SomeClass: SomeDelegate {
    var completion: ((Bool) -> Void)?

    Func startAsyncOperation(completion: @escaping ((Bool) -> Void)) {
        self.completion = completion
        // Start async operation
        NetworkManager.shared.performAsyncOperation (delegate: self)
    }

    func operationDidFinish(success: Bool) {
        self.completion?(success)
    }
```

```
}

protocol SomeDelegate: AnyObject {
    func operationDidFinish(success: Bool)
}
```

And now, let's see how to use the closure without using any delegate:

```
let someObject = SomeClass()
someObject.startAsyncOperation { success in
    if success {
        print("Async operation succeeded")
    } else {
        print("Async operation failed")
    }
}
```

In the preceding code blocks, I demonstrated how to encapsulate the delegate inside SomeClass, and expose only a closure to be run when the async operation ends. This pattern provides a clearer interface to the developer when calling startAsyncOperation.

"Can you explain how closure capture semantics in Swift can lead to retain cycles and how to avoid them?"

Why is this question important?

This classic interview question is a common pitfall junior developers fall into when working with closures.

In iOS development, topics are related to each other, even though we deal with closures and not memory management.

Closures are powerful, but when we don't use them correctly, they can produce memory leaks and affect our app performance.

This question tests our understanding of how closures work. It checks our knowledge of what happens in our app memory when we create and call closure and how scopes are handled.

What is the answer?

Closures capture variables and constants from the surrounding scopes with a **strong reference**. One of these constants might be the objects that hold the closure itself, which can cause a **retain cycle**.

Look at the following code:

```
class SomeClass {
    let someProperty = "property value"
    var closure: (() -> Void)?

    func setupClosure() {
        closure = {
            print(self.someProperty)
        }
    }
}

let someObject = SomeClass()
someObject.setupClosure()
```

We can see that SomeClass has a strong reference to closure, and closure prints someProperty, which requires closure to have a strong reference to SomeClass (aka self).

The simplest way to avoid a retain cycle is to declare self as a weak reference and, by that, untie the retain cycle:

```
class SomeClass {
    let someProperty = "property value"
    var closure: (() -> Void)?

    func setupClosure() {
        closure = { [weak self] in
            guard let self else { return }
            print(self.someProperty)
        }
    }
}
```

We can also use unowned instead of weak, but this is a dangerous approach – the closure may still be alive while self gets deallocated, and that may lead to an exception. However, there are cases where using unowned instead of weak is safe, and that can be derived from the relationship between our classes. A good example would be the Country class and the CapitalCity class. A country has a reference to its capital city, and the capital city can have an unowned reference to its country. We understand that the lifetime of a capital city is aligned with its country's lifetime, and therefore, it cannot exist without its country. Therefore, using an unowned reference in this scenario would be more practical, and if an exception occurs, it indicates an error in the code implementation.

Here's a code example that demonstrates using `unowned` between a `Country` class and a `CapitalCity` class:

```swift
class Country {
    let name: String
    var capital: CapitalCity?

    init(name: String) {
        self.name = name
    }

    deinit {
        print("\(name) is no longer a country.")
    }
}

class CapitalCity {
    let name: String
    unowned let country: Country

    init(name: String, country: Country) {
        self.name = name
        self.country = country
    }

    deinit {
        print("\(name) is no longer a capital city.")
    }
}
```

Having an `unowned` reference between `CapitalCity` and `Country` ensures that we avoid the retain cycle while still maintaining references between our classes.

Now that we have been through the basic Swift features, we are moving to more advanced Swift features to ensure we are covered over there.

Advanced Swift language features

Generally, interviewers like to start up softly with Swift features, checking different language aspects and trying to locate any red flags we might have about Swift.

In this section, we will go through more advanced features of Swift, beginning with computed and lazy variables.

Solving computed and lazy variables questions

Computed and lazy variables are both advanced features of Swift variables, providing efficient ways to improve performance and code readability.

First, let's be aligned about what computed and lazy variables are:

- **Computed variable** – a variable that calculates its value *based on other properties*, doesn't store its value in memory, and calculates it every time it's accessed

  In the following `Rectangle` class, `area` is a computed variable that is based on `width` and `height` values:

  ```
  class Rectangle {
      var width: Double
      var height: Double
      var area: Double {
          return width * height
      }
  }
  ```

- **Lazy variable** – a variable whose initial value is *calculated once* when it's first accessed

  The following code example explains what a lazy variable is:

  ```
  class ExpensiveObject {
      // Some expensive initialization
  }

  class MyClass {
      lazy var expensiveObject = ExpensiveObject()
  }
  ```

  The `expensiveObject` variable is only initialized when we first access it. We can see the `lazy` keyword prefixed the variable declaration, making it lazy.

Many iOS developers make little use of computed and lazy variables, and most of the time, the reasons are a lack of understanding and premature optimization.

Now, let's dive into our first question.

"When would you use a computed property instead of a stored property, and vice versa?"

Why is this question important?

That's a thoughtful question, and it helps to test our understanding of how to apply the theory in practice. Both computed and stored properties have their advantages and disadvantages in terms of performance and accuracy, so the question goes beyond just technical considerations.

What is the answer?

Computed properties are used when the value needs to be calculated every time the property is being accessed. A computed property usually uses other properties to calculate its value. Some examples are date formatted, the area of a rectangle, or a full name value that is based on other properties such as first and last name.

Stored properties, on the other hand, are stored and changed from the outside of the class based on user input or other events — for example, username, configuration value, and more.

Computed properties have a more dynamic nature. They are being calculated constantly and are, therefore, more accurate. The downside is that they are less efficient in many cases, especially when the value tends to change.

There is a tension between computed and stored properties. Stored properties are excellent for performance, but we need to maintain their data accuracy. Computed properties are the opposite – they are always accurate but are calculated all the time.

"How can you use lazy variables to improve the performance of an app that loads large amounts of data?"

Why is this question important?

Lazy variables are significant for performance and memory consumption. This question tests our ability to optimize our app and UI loading using lazy variables.

What is the answer?

Lazy variables can improve our app's performance by delaying the data's initialization until it is needed. Loading an object is always considered a heavy task, as the runtime environment needs to initialize the object and its properties. So, variables that need to initialize and load a large amount of data can affect the loading time (and the memory consumption) of the object being loaded. If there's a possibility to postpone the data loading for later, it can improve the object loading time.

Here's an example of a lazy loading code:

```
class MyData {
    lazy var largeData: [String] = {
```

```
        // load large data from a file or remote API
        return loadLargeData()
    }()

    private func loadLargeData() -> [String] {
        // perform the expensive operation to load the
           large data
        // here we just return an array of string but it
           could be some large data
        return ["large","data","loaded"]
    }
}

let data = MyData()

// the largeData is not loaded until this point
print(data.largeData)
```

We can see from the preceding code that the `largeData` variable can take time to be initialized, so we declared it as `lazy`. When we allocate `data`, `largeData` is still not allocated, not until we call it using the `print` command.

Solving extensions questions

Some of the features we discussed are related to code organization. For example, access levels are not just for technical restrictions; they are also part of organizing our code and declaring what's part of the interface and what's encapsulated.

Another important feature in that area is **extensions**.

Extensions in Swift have several important roles:

- Extensions allow us to *add new functionality to existing classes*, structs, and enums without modifying their source code
- Extensions can help us to *group related functionality* and improve our code readability and organization
- Extensions are used to *add protocol conformance* to types, aligning their interface with other types conforming to the same protocol

We can see how many extensions are essential to Swift language, as they are widely used in our daily iOS development.

Even though extensions are powerful, they are effortless to use and understand. That's why we must be highly prepared for this topic, as any mistake can raise a red flag for our interviewer.

Now let's move to our first question.

"Can you add new properties to a struct or class using an extension?"

Why is this question important?

This question seems like a simple yes/no question, but the reality is that it hides two more layers of understanding the interviewer wishes to hear.

First, they want to hear the practical layer – what is and is not *possible* in extensions (aka the full answer).

But second, and this is a bonus, they want to hear *why extensions work the way they work*. That will show how deeply we understand Swift memory usage.

Don't worry, we'll cover both layers in our answer.

What is the answer?

The short answer is "no," we cannot add stored properties in extensions. But it is worth mentioning that it is possible to add computed properties. The reason is that we can add new functionality to a type but not its memory layout, which can imply to us what can/can't be added to a type using extensions.

There are several workarounds for that – wrapping the original type or using a global variable to store the property value, but the idea stays the same.

Now for the "bonus" part of the answer: a type's memory layout is *determined in compile-time* and embedded in the binary. This means that we cannot add new stored properties on the fly using extensions, as they will make changes to the memory layout set earlier. Adding that fact to the answer would give us additional points in the interview!

"Can you use an extension to add a method to a protocol? If so, how?"

Why is this question important?

This is a tricky question. Protocols are not types. Extending the protocol is like adding new functionality to the conforming types. Confused? That's why this question is tricky… Let's see the answer to clear things up.

What is the answer?

Yes, it is possible to extend a protocol. Extending a protocol adds new functionality to all types that conform to that protocol, allowing us to add a default implementation to protocol methods.

Let's see a code example of extending a protocol:

```
protocol MyProtocol {
    // existing protocol requirements
```

```
    }

extension MyProtocol {
    func newMethod() {
        // implementation
    }
}
```

We can see that the `MyProtocol` extension adds a new method: `newMethod()`. The new method can be used in all types that conform to `MyProtocol`. Let's continue the code example to explain that:

```
struct MyStruct: MyProtocol {
    // existing struct properties and methods
}

let myStruct = MyStruct()
myStruct.newMethod()
```

I hope it's clearer now, as `myStruct` can call `newMethod()` even though it wasn't defined in the original protocol declaration.

Solving generics questions

Generics are Swift features that allow iOS developers to write reusable code that can work with any type of data.

For iOS developers, generics are particularly important because they can be used to write reusable and type-safe code. This means developers can write code used in multiple places within an app without worrying about typecasting or other type-related issues. Additionally, generics can help to prevent runtime errors and improve performance by allowing the compiler to optimize the code at compile time. Overall, generics are powerful tools that can help iOS developers write more robust and efficient code.

Now, let's see an example of a reverse method for an array that can work with any type:

```
func reverseArray<T>(arr: [T]) -> [T] {
    var reversedArr: [T] = []
    for i in stride(from: arr.count - 1, through: 0, by: -1) {
        reversedArr.append(arr[i])
    }
    return reversedArr
}

let numbers = [1, 2, 3, 4, 5]
let reversedNumbers = reverseArray(arr: numbers)
```

```
// reversedNumbers is [5, 4, 3, 2, 1]
let words = ["apple", "banana", "cherry"]
let reversedWords = reverseArray(arr: words)
// reversedWords is ["cherry", "banana", "apple"]
```

The most important thing to understand about that code snippet is this line:

```
func reverseArray<T>(arr: [T]) -> [T]
```

The `reverseArray()` method receives an array from a specific type and returns an array at the same time. Perhaps that's the core concept of generics – not just creating reusable code but also maintaining type safety and avoiding type-casting issues.

"Can you give an example of a problem that can be solved using generics?"

Why is this question important?

Like previous questions, this question challenges us by taking a theoretical topic and asking for a real-life example of how to use it.

Compared to other Swift features, it is harder to understand generics' benefits without going over real-world problems and solutions.

What is the answer?

A caching class is an excellent example of a problem that can be solved using generics. If we want to cache data, we need to create a separate class for each type we want to cache or create a different method in some abstract class.

In this case, generics let us reuse the same code for different types:

```
class Cache<T> {
    private var cache = [String: T]()

    func set(value: T, for key: String) {
        cache[key] = value
    }

    func get(for key: String) -> T? {
        return cache[key]
    }
}
```

This is how we use the `Cache` class with `Int`:

```
let cache = Cache<[Int]>()
cache.set(value: [1, 2, 3, 4, 5], for: "numbers")
```

```
let cachedNumbers = cache.get(for: "numbers")
// cachedNumbers is [1, 2, 3, 4, 5]
```

A cache is a good example because it doesn't require us to cast the returned type. We can initialize a new cache instance that works with a different kind of data each time.

"How do you use associated types in a generic protocol?"

Why is this question important?

Associated types are features that iOS developers rarely use, but I still want to dedicate one question to them. The reason is that it can give you a better picture of generics' usage and examples in Swift. It is difficult for many iOS developers to find practical use cases for generics, so providing an example from a different perspective may help your interview readiness.

What is the answer?

Associated types are actually *generics for protocols*. They work the same way as classes and structs work with generics.

To use the associated type, we need to define it in a protocol using the keyword `associatedtype`:

```
protocol DataSource {
    associatedtype Data
    func fetchData() -> Data
}
```

The `DataSource` protocol contains a `Data` `associatedtype`, but it is not specified what kind of type it will be used. We do that in the protocol implementation.

For example, this is an implementation of `DataSource` with `Int` as `Data`:

```
struct LocalDataSource: DataSource {
    typealias Data = [Int]
    func fetchData() -> [Int] {
    }
}
```

Of course, other structs or classes can implement the protocol using a different type by defining it in the `Data` type alias, which makes this protocol flexible and reusable.

Solving error-handling questions

Error handling is an essential topic in every language and platform. It lets us respond to unexpected events or conditions (which makes them "expected" when we think of it).

Error handling and Swift are interesting when we discuss job interviews – first, this area *improved tremendously* when we moved from Objective-C to Swift. Still, it also improved dramatically between the different Swift versions. Consider that by the time you read this book, probably more changes will have been made in error handling, so it is worth having a look.

Moreover, the *increasing popularity of Combine and SwiftUI* made error handling even more popular. We can confidently say that error handling is a fundamental part of Combine data streams, and if that's an area we feel insecure about, now is the time to catch up!

"How do you use the try? and try! operators for error handling in Swift?"

Why is this question important?

try? and try! are operators that handle errors more concisely.

It is important to explain the difference between the two operators and implement them in our code flow.

What is the answer?

Instead of using the do-catch flow, we can use the try? operator to bypass it, similar to how we unwrap an optional:

```
let result = try? someThrowingFunction()
if result != nil {
    // Use the result
} else {
    // Handle the error
}
```

In this code example, we wrap the call for someThrowingFunction() with the try? operator. The result is an optional value – if the function throws an exception, the returned value will be nil.

However, try! is exactly like force unwrapping. If the function throws an exception, our program will be terminated:

```
let result = try! someThrowingFunction()
```

Notice that we should use try! with caution and in cases where there's no point in continuing our program if the function throws an exception.

"Can you explain and give an example of how you would write a function in Swift that throws an error?"

Why is this question important?

Many developers know how to perform a basic do-catch block, mainly because it is required in many cases.

The natural step forward is to perform the throwing action ourselves. Knowing how to write a function that throws an exception shows a good understanding of Swift's error-handling mechanism.

What is the answer?

There are three things we need to do to have a throwing function:

- The first thing is to *add the* `throws` *keyword* to its declaration:

```
func readFile(at path: String) throws -> String { … }
```

- The second thing is having some kind of an *error to throw back* in case of a problem:

```
enum FileError: Error {
    case fileNotFound
}
```

- The third will be the implementation and *throwing the error in case of an exception* (complete code ahead):

```
enum FileError: Error {
    case fileNotFound
}

func readFile(at path: String) throws -> String {
    guard let data = FileManager.default.contents
        (atPath: path) else {
        throw FileError.fileNotFound
    }
    return String(data: data, encoding: .utf8) ?? ""
}
```

Remembering these three fundamental components of throwing functions will help us nail this function efficiently.

If you still feel insecure about error handling, try to return to one of your projects and add error handling in places where you think it's relevant. There's nothing like practical experience to deal with topics with which you don't feel strongly about.

Solving protocol questions

One of the most important principles in computer science is the **Separation of Concerns**. To achieve that, one of the things we want to do is reduce coupling between different parts of our code – decoupling objects and classes.

Protocols play a significant part in this task, making our code more flexible and reusable. In modern iOS development, protocols are a fundamental part of the development, and we can find them heavily used in almost every API and SDK.

"Can you explain the use of protocol-oriented programming in iOS development?"

Why is this question important?

Even though that's an open-ended question, it is common in interviews. Maybe because it is an open question, interviewers like to ask it so they can understand how candidates think.

Protocols are like spices in cooking – technically, they are easy to use. The problem starts with how much and when.

We should be ready for this question, and it is also a chance to spread our methodologic point of view of protocol's role in our code writing.

What is the answer?

The first thing to understand about **Protocol-Oriented Programming** (POP) is that it's a programming paradigm. This means that POP is a set of guidelines and rules for organizing and structuring our code.

The main idea of POP is that objects communicate with each other using protocols. This makes our code much more flexible and reusable, as different types can implement different behaviors and still work with other objects by conforming to the same interface.

POP works with **Object-Oriented Programming** (OOP) and doesn't replace it.

"How do you decide when to use a protocol in your iOS app?"

Why is this question important?

This question takes a theory topic (protocol) and moves it to the practical world of considerations and tradeoffs. The interviewer doesn't want to hear a dichotomous answer but rather a more profound solution involving our point of view on Swift's development.

What is the answer?

I'll start with the bottom line: we shouldn't always use protocols. We should use them only when it is effective and they don't make our project more cumbersome than it is already. We should do that with caution and according to the following factors:

- *Interface reusability* – if we want to reuse a specific interface between different types.
- *Abstraction* – A protocol provides another level of abstraction to our code by defining a set of methods and properties used by different objects.
- *Dependency injection* – We can use protocols to inject dependencies into a class and, by that, make it more flexible and testable.

To summarize, protocols are a great solution whenever we need more flexibility and decreased coupling in our code.

On the other hand, protocols can add a layer of complexity to our code, adding a virtual layer between classes. And that's an expected trade-off in programming – *complexity versus coupling*.

Solving memory management questions

Memory management for iOS developers has been a critical issue from the beginning days of iOS development.

I must say that things have become better over the years – Apple added **Automatic Reference Counting** (**ARC**), debug tools became better, and the hardware has evolved dramatically.

Having said that, efficiency is still essential when discussing resource management.

Be prepared for some questions on that topic in your next iOS technical interview.

"What is the difference between a strong and a weak reference in iOS?"

Why is this question important?

Strong and **weak** references are the core components of the memory ownership concept we have in Swift.

Ownership is the key to ARC, which is the basis of the memory management mechanism in iOS, and if we don't understand how that mechanism works, we are on the path of creating **memory leaks** and **retaining cycles**.

What is the answer?

The answer is fairly simple: a strong reference (which is the default reference unless defined otherwise) is a way to indicate an object is being held in memory by one or more elements. In contrast, a weak reference allows the object to be deallocated when it is no longer needed.

A strong reference *increases* the reference counting by one, while a weak reference *doesn't change* the reference counting at all.

A good example of weak reference usage is **a delegate pattern**.

Let's see an example:

```
class ViewController: UIViewController {
    var delegate: ViewControllerDelegate?
}

protocol ViewControllerDelegate: class {
    func didTapButton()
}
```

```
class AnotherViewController: UIViewController,
    ViewControllerDelegate {
    weak var viewController: ViewController?

    override func viewDidLoad() {
        super.viewDidLoad()
        viewController = ViewController()
        viewController!.delegate = self
    }


    func didTapButton() {
        // Perform some action
    }
}
```

In this code example, we can see that the ViewController has a strong reference to its delegate object, while the delegate object has a weak reference to its ViewController. The reason for this arrangement is to avoid a retain cycle and, as a result, increase our app memory usage.

"How do you handle low memory warnings in iOS?"

Why is this question important?

This question is designed to assess our understanding of managing resources. There are situations where it is acceptable to receive low memory warnings, but the question is how we should handle it when it occurs. Having control over the resources in our app allows us to manage and respond to these situations appropriately.

What is the answer?

One thing we need to do when we get a low memory warning is to release any unnecessary resources and reduce the app's memory footprint.

Here are some examples of how to reduce our app's memory footprint:

- Release cache data
- Use autorelease pools
- Use weak references
- Release unused resources such as off-screen views
- Use NSCache

That's the time to dig in our memory from past projects and try to remember resources we could have released when we get low memory warnings.

Summary

In this chapter, we discussed the many topics in Swift development, both basic and advanced. We covered optionals, access levels, closures, computed and lazy variables, extensions, generics, error handling, protocols, and memory management.

These are a lot of topics! But on the other hand, we are experienced Swift developers, and these all need to be familiar.

As I said earlier, we are good iOS developers and know the job well. We just need to organize our knowledge to be prepared for our interview.

Our next chapter deals with something different than just Swift – we will talk about code management.

6
Managing Your Code

In *Chapter 5*, we covered the essential aspects of the Swift language. In this chapter, we will cover more topics related to iOS development, such as UIKit and various frameworks.

Preparing for iOS interviews is mostly around Swift, UIKit, and coding. It is obvious why – these are the bread and butter of iOS development. But being an iOS developer is much more than that.

In my experience, developers who know how to plan their tasks, solve/test complex bugs, and document their work are true professionals, regardless of their code quality. I think that this is what separates a good developer from a true pro-iOS developer.

In a good and effective hiring process, these skills are tested as part of the manager interview or the home assessment stage, and we should be ready for them. Unlike most other topics, the *principles* for good quality work are vital to remember here.

This chapter will cover the following four main topics in managing our project:

- We will ensure that we have the capability to *plan* our projects and features and gain knowledge on how to develop a technical document.

- We will cover *testing*, not only unit testing but also integration and performance tests. We will also learn what it means to write testable code.

- We will go over *debug* techniques for different types of issues.

- We will answer some questions about *documentation* – how to comment correctly and handle documentation as part of a bigger team.

Let's start with the essential part of this chapter, in my opinion: planning.

Planning

Planning and design are both critical aspects of being a developer, certainly a senior one. Many think of "planning" as a way to estimate delivery dates, but the delivery date is really only a tiny part of the story.

The real story behind planning is going down to the details. In my perspective, planning is equal to learning. When we plan, we perform research about our task, trying to understand the following:

- Can we *understand the product requirements* and translate them into tasks?

- What are our *dependencies* with other teams/developers?

- What things do we need to perform *additional research*? Do we need a **Proof of Concept (POC)**?

- What tasks will be complicated, and what tasks will be simple?

- Are we handling *edge cases*? Can we define them?

When we plan, we consider different aspects and challenges we may encounter. Therefore, "planning" is much more than estimation; it is really a learning session.

Being a professional means learning our task before we start it. From my experience, not all interviews emphasize that point. In many hiring processes, planning is not even a part of the interview.

I advise bringing it up even if we are not explicitly asked for it. We are interested in leading the conversation with our interviewer to the places where we want to show our strengths.

"How do you create a project timeline and plan for the iOS app's development process?"

Why is this question important?

Similar to many questions we'll find in this book, this one also doesn't have a clear right or wrong answer. But the interviewer doesn't care about the answer's details. Their main goal is to assess our experience, organization skills, and our development process point of view.

In *Chapter 2*, we talked about "soft skills." Planning and time management are indeed essential soft skills our interviewer wants to see. An iOS developer who understands how to plan, challenges and dependencies, manage time, and prioritize tasks is a great addition to the team.

What is the answer?

Regardless of the details we are required to provide, there are three points we need to ensure to highlight in our answer:

- **Demonstrate our experience**: Providing examples, approaches, and lessons learned is a great way to show we understand and have handled challenges in the past.

- **Show we understand the development process**: Task management, estimation, resources, and priority are all good examples of tools that can help us to provide a good plan.

- **Show we can collaborate**: Working on a development project involves heavy collaboration. We need to highlight the fact that we are not working alone. Collaboration means task ownership, collaborative tech design, reviews, dependencies, and working with designers, QA teams, product managers, and backend developers.

Why are these steps crucial to highlight? Because, in most cases, we are joining an existing team and project. Understanding what a good and healthy process looks like is essential.

Now let's dive into a standard framework for a project planning process:

1. Understand the *project's requirements*, purpose, and audience.

2. *Break the project down* into small, manageable tasks: design, coding, and testing.

3. Provide a development *estimation for each task* and a result: a timeline.

4. Assign *resources* between the different team members.

5. *Monitor* progress to ensure we are on time.

6. *Testing* and deployment.

We need to look at this question as a chance to bring our point of view and experience to the table while taking a standard process and breaking it down into the three key points I mentioned.

"How do you estimate development time for a task?"

Why is this question important?

Time estimation is one of the most challenging tasks for developers, and how we approach task estimation shows our experience.

Development time estimation is both a soft and hard skill.

On the one hand, it requires a broad technical knowledge of the development challenges and risks, breaking them into smaller tasks and managing them.

On the other hand, we need good communication skills to work with other teammates, excellent time management skills, and the ability to analyze dependencies that can affect our schedule.

After all, we chose to develop professional iOS applications, and that's a complex job to do…

What is the answer?

The answer is similar to the previous answer about the project timeline. The difference is that in task estimation, it is simpler to get into the small details and understand the risks.

Let's go over the list of the stages we need to go through:

1. Understand the *requirements*.

2. *Break* them down into small sub-tasks.

3. *Assess the complexity* of each sub-task, and consider any potential risks and challenges. If needed, research such risks or even create a POC to understand.

4. *Consider dependencies* to make sure we are not blocked from moving forward with our development process.

5. Add more time for *reviewing and refining* the results.

I think that point number three is perhaps the most important. When a development task doesn't meet its estimation goals, it is primarily because of risks we didn't consider. It is hard to go wrong when setting up a standard **user interface** (**UI**) screen, but the unknown issues are what make our task overdue.

"How do you create a technical design document for an iOS task?"

Why is this question important?

This is a question that continues from the previous two. We started with project planning and task time estimation, and now we are trying to understand how to design a single development task.

Technical document creation encapsulates our expertise in approaching a technical task. Even if we don't usually write technical documents, the process of designing a feature from a technical point of view is crucial for developers.

Put aside the suggested answer – try to go over technical documents you've used in the past and retrieve what the process that led to this output was. Bringing your own experience to the table is the best answer because it will be easier to explain.

What is the answer?

A technical document contains the following topics: introduction, requirements, architecture, flows, data model, testing, and deployment.

These are the following steps to create it:

1. **Plan and research**: Collect information about the project, including requirements and constraints.

2. **Outline the document**: Write the sections and sub-sections to ensure we are not missing any important topic.

3. **Describe the requirements**: Specify requirements in detail.

4. **Discuss the system architecture**: Describe the system architecture in detail. Write down the different layers involved in the feature.

5. **Define the data model**: Describe the entities and the different API calls.

6. **Specify the user interface**: Include screens, UI components, and navigation flows.

7. **Outline the testing strategy**: Include types of testing, tools, and goals.

8. **Discuss the deployment process**: Include beta rollout, A/B testing, and app versions.

It's important to say that most, if not all, of the steps I detailed are not explicitly related to Swift – this is one of the good things about this question. Planning is a language and platform-agnostic task, and you can find plenty of people that can help you understand how to approach a technical document design even if you haven't done one before.

Testing

Testing is a crucial part of being an iOS developer. It ensures our codebase's quality and reliability and improves levels of confidence in our projects.

Questions about testing in interviews are much more than just technical. Writing a unit test is an easy task and can be learned quickly. But experience in testing shows a different side of us as iOS developers. It offers our approach to managing a reliable and healthy code base.

Answer the following questions:

1. Do we write tests after a bug fix?

2. How simple is it to test our code?

3. What is the test role in the deployment process?

Being a professional doesn't mean just writing good code but also maintaining it well.

Unlike most topics in this book, it is difficult to gain knowledge of testing without having some experience. I advise you to take one of your projects and write some tests. You need to feel it with your fingers before you approach the interview.

"What is the meaning of unit and integration testing in the context of iOS development?"

Why is this question important?

The testing world is full of different terms and approaches. Defining unit tests and integration tests is essential because they represent different use cases and coverage.

This question aims to see whether we have enough experience understanding the different use cases.

What is the answer?

A **unit test** checks the behavior of an individual component, while an **integration test** checks how different components work together.

It's crucial to consider the app's context when investing more time in unit or integration testing.

For example – unit tests mainly check logic functions such as the following one:

```
import XCTest

class MyClassTests: XCTestCase {

    func testExample() {
        let myClass = MyClass()
        let result = myClass.doSomething()
        XCTAssertEqual(result, 42)
    }
}
```

We can see that the preceding code block tests a specific logic function. It doesn't care about other app components such as the network, core data, or the app state, but rather isolates the scope to the function itself.

On the other hand, an integration test checks a use case that involves multiple layers and functions, such as a network request:

```
import XCTest

class MyAppTests: XCTestCase {

    func testExample() {
        let apiClient = APIClient()
        let user = User(username: "testuser", password: "secret")
        apiClient.login(user) { (error) in XCTAssertNil(error)
            let data = apiClient.fetchData() XCTAssertNotNil(data)
        }
    }
}
```

The preceding code shows how we can test how two layers of our project work together. The network layer can work well, as can the local function of `apiClient`. But when working together, we may encounter a problem, and that's an integration test.

Most iOS apps need integration tests over unit tests because most functions handle user interaction and different app layers versus logic code. This is an essential insight into the balance between integration and unit tests.

"How do you perform performance testing in iOS applications?"

Why is this question important?

Performance testing is less common in iOS development than unit or integration testing and is considered a more advanced topic. This question aims to gauge your depth of knowledge and experience in testing. It is a good idea to set up one performance test to understand how it works, but there is no need to have significant experience with it.

What is the answer?

Setting up a performance test is much simpler than it sounds. The first thing we need to do is to choose the function or code block we want to measure.

Second, we need to write a test function that performs that code block, usually multiple times. Why do we need to run it multiple times? Because it is simpler for us to measure a test run with big numbers. If one test run takes around 3–4 milliseconds, it will be hard to measure the change over time. But if we run it 100 times, it will be much easier to measure any small tweaks we can make in the function's code. Let's see what a performance test looks like:

```
import XCTest

class MyClassPerformanceTests: XCTestCase {

    func testPerformanceExample() {
        let myClass = MyClass()
        measure {
            for _ in 0..<1000 {
                let _ = myClass.doSomethingExpensive()
            }
        }
    }
}
```

The XCTest framework uses the average running time as a baseline, and every time the test is run, XCTest compares the results to that baseline.

One disadvantage of performance tests is that their results depend on the device they run on. It is best practice to ensure performance tests run *on the same device*, preferably an actual device and not a simulator.

"Can you explain what it means to write a testable code?"

Why is this question important?

Sure, we are now talking about tests, but **testable code** is much more than preparing our codebase for tests – it is about writing code that we can easily maintain and decouple.

In this question, interviewers like to see that we understand what makes code testable, ensuring our code can be maintained easily.

What is the answer?

Writing testable code means writing code designed to make it easy to write unit, integration, and performance tests for it.

In practice, testable code means the following:

- **Keep the principle of separation of concerns**: When each part of our code base has a single, clear responsibility, it is easier to test a use case without requiring several layers or classes.

- **Ensure loose coupling**: High coupling makes it hard to test one component independently.

- **Design our objects for easy mocking**: A clean, well-defined interface can help our objects to be easily mocked. One great example is the usage of **Protocol Oriented Programming (POP)**.

- **Use more pure functions**: Pure functions are functions that don't have a shared state or side effects. They are isolated in a way that makes them very easy to test.

Here's an example of testable versus non-testable code. I'll start with the testable version:

```
class Calculator {
  func add(a: Int, b: Int) -> Int {
    return a + b
  }
}
```

And now the non-testable code version:

```
class Calculator {
  func calculateResult() -> Int {
    let a = UserDefaults.standard.integer(forKey: "a")
    let b = UserDefaults.standard.integer(forKey: "b")
    return a + b
  }
}
```

In the first example, we can see that the add() method takes two parameters and use them solely to return a result.

However, in the second example, we see a function dependent on two `UserDefaults` keys that may return different results each time we run it. In testable code, we should get the same results each time we run the test, so that's not an excellent example of testable code.

That's a great example of testable versus non-testable code snippets.

Tests are a crucial part of interviews, much more than they used to be several years ago. The reason is that tests are not a topic of their own – they represent a whole approach to development, code design, and maintenance. Tests are a clear win in terms of our striving for perfection.

Debugging

A famous quote says:

> *"Programming is not about being the best at writing code, it's about being the best at debugging code."*

This quote sounds weird, right? But, when we think about it, we spend many coding hours debugging our (or others') code.

Our debugging skills can sometimes determine whether a phase lasts a few days or weeks.

One of the mistakes developers make when practicing for job interviews is focusing only on code writing and forgetting about debugging. But debugging is one of the most important tools we have as developers, and we can expect at least one or two debug questions in our interview.

"Can you explain how to debug memory leaks in iOS applications?"

Why is this question important?

First, let's be aligned on what a memory leak is. A memory leak doesn't mean an app with high memory usage – that's a widespread misconception.

A memory leak means an app was allocated memory for something and then stopped using it, but the memory space wasn't released.

The result might be high memory usage, but increased memory usage does not indicate a memory leak.

Memory leaks are hard to debug but point to inefficient resource consumption and can lead to app termination. That's why memory leak debugging is an important topic in iOS development.

What is the answer?

Having said that, memory leaks are hard to debug. Fortunately, there are many ways to solve this:

- **Instruments**: Instruments is a powerful tool that comes with Xcode that can help us profile different aspects of our app, including memory allocations and leaks. It's an advanced tool that can profile a specific object, log its retains/release operations, and even direct us to a particular location in our code base.

- **Memory graph debugging**: It's a relatively new feature, and not many are aware of it yet. Using memory graph debugging, it is possible to stop the run at any point and look at the live objects list and the relationships between them. It can also highlight what it identifies as a memory leak and points to the reason.

- **NSZombie**: NSZombie is a tool that lets us detect and track elements before they are deallocated.

- The `deinit` function: In certain cases, we can put a print statement or a breakpoint in the object's `deinit()` function. The `deinit()` function gets called just before the object is deallocated. That's a nice and simple way to see whether an object leaks without launching external and heavy tools.

- **Memory gauge**: We can use Xcode's memory gauge regularly to see whether memory is being deallocated and doesn't grow constantly. It's a great sign we should investigate the issue further using the other tools on the list.

As we can see, there are plenty of methods and tools to debug memory leaks in iOS. Some are there to *monitor our memory* consumption, and some are very advanced and *help detect* precisely where and when the leak occurs. The combination of the tools provides us with the perfect toolset to track and fix memory leaks.

"Can you explain how to debug UI-related issues in iOS applications?"

Why is this question important?

Up until now, most of the questions dealt with Swift only, without the context of the relevant layer of the framework. But moving forward with our book, we'll find there is much more than Swift in iOS development. The UI is another main topic for iOS developers, and as part of it, debugging it is considered to be a very challenging task. If you have worked with UIKit, you have probably investigated issues with the UI throughout your career. The following answer organizes things for you.

What is the answer?

"UI-related" is an extensive definition of a problem. Some issues are related to the UI life cycle, some to user interaction, and others to layout and animation.

So, the answer can be divided into three parts:

- **Inspect the layout**: We have four primary ways to debug our UI layout:

  - **Debug View Hierarchy**: Debug View Hierarchy is a built-in tool in Xcode that lets us debug our layout in runtime with a nice 3D view showing up the different layers of the screen, allowing us to inspect each layer for its properties, including color and layout. That's a great way to understand how the UI is organized, how the Auto Layout equations mechanism works, and what the hierarchy is.

  - **Open Accessibility Inspector**: This tool is part of the Xcode development suite and can help us debug our views from an accessibility point of view. **Accessibility Inspector** is a less widely recognized tool that assists us in examining our application's handling of accessibility issues.

  - **Color our views**: This is a primitive yet helpful way to debug our UI. We can just set our views' background or border colors in the code and then rerun the app to examine the results. Other tools are more advanced, but coloring our views can sometimes be a very fast and efficient way to debug, for example, in animations and sophisticated layouts.

  - **Simulator debug tools**: The iOS Simulator has built-in debug tools for our UI, including color views and slow animations. These are great for a quick look at our layout during runtime.

- **Life cycle debug**: Life cycle debug means debugging our screen's various stages – when it is created, appears, pushed, and more. The way to do that is mainly around breakpoints and print statements. We can set breakpoints in life cycle methods such as `viewDidLoad` and `viewDidAppear`. Another great tip is to use **logs** to track UI flows. Following those logs can help us debug during development and also debug QA issues. We can also inspect life cycle events using the **Instruments Time Profiler** to track calls during screen launch.

- **User interaction debugging**: We can also use the Accessibility Inspector, print to console, add breakpoints, and use **View Debugger** to understand the different hierarchies and properties.

There are many ways to debug a UI! And there's a reason – UI debugging requires experience and many "hit and miss" tries, so we will need every possible tool.

"How do you debug performance issues in iOS applications?"

Why is this question important?

In today's mobile development world, performance is not as big a topic as it used to be. We are now handling powerful devices, and most chances are that our product requirements are not even close to challenging the least powerful machine out there.

Bad coding and design can lead to annoying lags and long waited for operations. These are the cases where performance debugging can help us nail problems quickly.

This question tests a crucial skill set for an iOS developer, as users expect apps to be fast and responsive. It also checks the understanding of the iOS platform and the different debugging tools available.

What is the answer?

There are several ideal steps to take when debugging performance issues:

1. **Reproduce the performance issues**: Rerun the app and ensure we can quickly reproduce the problem. It's not an obvious task at all – because we don't know the issue's root cause yet, we can't tell for sure that the problem will be reproduced.

2. **Profile the app**: Use the Instruments time profile and/or **Core Animation Instrument** to inspect the app and collect information about the problem.

3. **Analyze the information**: Try to make an assumption about the cause of the issue.

4. **Perform a fix or a change**: Implement some sort of solution. It doesn't have to be the final solution; it can be some temporary code modification to isolate the issue.

5. **Test and verify**: Rerun the app to see whether there's a change. Restart the process if needed.

Notice that these steps are only an outline for a recommended debug procedure, and it is great for an interview answer. However, we should note that performance issues are more complex and may require additional or different steps.

Documentation

Documentation questions are typically not included in technical job interviews, but they may be part of interviews whose purpose is to gain insight into us as developers.

However, documentation is an essential part of being an iOS developer, and that part gets a special place when we are part of a team.

Here are some reasons why documentation is crucial:

- **Better collaboration**: Documentation makes it easier for multiple developers to work on the same code base, where they need to explain smaller parts of the code.

- **Improve code understanding**: Do you know what it's like to write code and one week later look back and not understand why you did what you did? It is a common thing among developers. Documentation doesn't eliminate that but can improve it dramatically.

- **Onboarding new members**: That's a critical point. Explaining something to an old-timer developer is straightforward, but doing the same for a new team member is much more complex. That's another reason why documentation plays a significant role here.

- **Improving code reviews**: A "code review" is an event where someone who didn't write the code tries to read and understand it. It goes without saying why documenting it is a crucial thing to do.

Looking at the list, we can understand why documentation is a powerful tool, especially in teams, and why it is not a part of the technical interview but rather part of the "personality" review. But documentation is an integral part of being a professional developer, so it is better to be prepared with examples and point-of-view statements.

"Can you explain how you document your iOS code?"

Why is this question important?

We already went through why documentation is essential as an iOS developer. Now, the interviewer wants to see our techniques and approach to comments and documents.

What is the answer?

The basis of iOS code documentation is done using comments throughout the code base.

There are several types of comments we can use to document our project:

- **A "Why" comment**: This doesn't need us to explain *what* we did, but rather *why* we did it (that's a typical mistake developers make). These comments should be in places where there is a reason for our decision, but it is not reflected in the code. This comment can help other developers, but also we can benefit from that. Here's an example of such a comment:

```
let password = "secret_password_1234"

// Use the hashValue property to get a unique
   identifier for the password string
let passwordHash = password.hashValue
```

We're adding a comment that explains why we used `hashValue` and not the fact that we used it.

- **Code organization**: One good use of comments is to organize code; a common practice is using a "pragma mark." A pragma mark helps us separate our code into sections to be more readable and easier to navigate. Let's see how to organize our code with pragma marks:

```
// MARK: - Properties

var name: String
var age: Int

// MARK: - Initialization

init(name: String, age: Int) {
    self.name = name
    self.age = age
}
```

```
// MARK: - Methods

func sayHello() {
    print("Hello, my name is \(name) and I am \(age) years old.")
}
```

Xcode knows how to read these types of comments and provides an easy way to jump between the different sections.

- **Method documentation**: We can document methods, properties, and classes using code-generation comments. These comments can be generated automatically by Xcode or other third-party tools and be a part of our project documentation. This can be done easily using the /** **/ marks:

```
/**
 * Generates a random password of a specified length.
 *
 * @param {number} length - The length of the password
   to generate.
 * @return {string} The generated password.
 */
function generatePassword(length) {
  // Implementation details
}
```

The results of adding @params and @return information to our function declaration comment provide Xcode (or other relevant tools) the ability to automatically generate documentation similar to what we can find on Xcode Developer Documentation.

In the end, it is important to understand the different types of comments to structure a good answer. A short answer such as "Explain what I do" is not a "pro" answer and doesn't reflect our expertise.

It is also worth saying that good naming conventions for methods, classes, and variables can make our code much more readable and self-explanatory and, by that, reduce the need for documentation.

"Can you explain how to document design patterns and best practices in iOS development?"

Why is this question important?

Technical design documents are not something junior or even mid-level developers do, but instead, senior developers and tech leads.

So, this question's relevance depends on our interviewing role.

Also, our expertise in technical design documents is probably based on our current and previous workplaces. Small start-ups are not always strict about technical documents, and that's something we can mention when receiving this question.

What is the answer?

A technical design document is not there just to create one. It is there to answer the following questions:

- What is the *purpose* of the feature?
- What were the *alternative* solutions?
- Why did we *choose* the selected solution?
- What is the *preferred solution* in detail?

Now that we have these questions in mind, we understand that a technical document reflects the thinking process behind our solution and not just describes it.

To document a feature, we need to follow these steps:

1. **Choose a format**: Choose a suitable format for the document that will be consistent across different features.
2. **Include an introduction**: Explain the feature's goal and what it includes.
3. **Discuss alternatives**: Explain the different ways to solve that feature and their tradeoffs.
4. **Describe the selected option**: Describe the choice among the alternatives.
5. **Describe the selected option in detail**: Provide code examples, diagrams, and flow charts to explain what we did.

It is important to note that technical document formats and processes differ from place to place, but the idea stays the same. As long as we provide a detailed answer with confidence and understanding, it will be good enough to pass that question.

"How do you handle the documentation of code that multiple team members are developing?"

Why is this question important?

Writing documentation for ourselves is straightforward. Most likely, we can communicate with ourselves easily…

The real challenge starts when our code documentation needs to serve our teammates.

This question tests how we see code documentation as part of a team when we need to read and write such documentation and maintain it over time.

What is the answer?

There isn't a magic answer for that, as it depends on culture, project, and team size.

But some best practices are helpful to follow:

- **Establish a documentation standard**: The team must agree on some comments and document format guidelines. For example – what methods to comment? What types of comments to emphasize? How to explain design decisions? Guidelines are a great start to managing documentation in a team.

- **Use a collaboration tool to manage documentation**: Plenty of collaboration tools can help us work on the same document with our teammates, including comments and discussions. We should take advantage of these tools to ensure the whole team participates in the documentation.

- **Encourage collaboration**: This is not just using a collaboration tool. If we want everyone on the team to take part, we should encourage the team to review each other's documentation and comment on their code as part of the code review. Remember – reviews are also part of the collaboration.

- **Provide training**: Onboard new team members on how to comment and write documents. Training doesn't have to be overhead – it can be short or as part of a weekly meeting. Cross-team alignment is essential to make sure our documentation is effective for everyone.

Following these guidelines is a great start to ensure the whole team is responsible for documentation *together* with high standards and motivation.

Summary

In this chapter, we discussed topics that are not directly related to coding, but as iOS developers, they are crucial. Remember that most mobile teams are small – sometimes, a team includes only one developer, so being a mature and professional developer is crucial.

This chapter is unique – instead of talking about coding, it examined quality and communication. These skills are harder to test and even harder to show in an interview. But in good workplaces with an effective process, these topics will pop up in one way or another.

In the next chapter, we will discuss perhaps the most crucial framework of iOS development: UIKit. No iOS interview can conclude without questions being asked about that framework.

Part 3: The Frameworks

In this part, we take a significant step forward and begin to cover the different frameworks we use to build great apps. We will address interview questions related to UIkit, SwiftUI, Combine, and persistent memory. Additionally, we will discuss CocoaPods and Swift Package Manager. By the end of this part, we will be familiar with the primary popular frameworks.

In this part, we have the following chapters:

- *Chapter 7, Building Great User Experiences with UIKit*
- *Chapter 8, SwiftUI and Declarative Programming*
- *Chapter 9, Understanding Persistent Memory*
- *Chapter 10, Libraries Management*

7
Building Great User Experiences with UIKit

In *Chapter 6*, we took a break from coding and discussed topics that evolve our code, such as testing, debugging, and more. Now, it's time to go back to what we love to do, and what is more loveable in iOS development than building a great UI experience?

For most iOS developers, UIKit is considered to be the most critical framework right after Foundation, and in iOS interviews, it's a mandatory topic.

Even though UIKit is a huge framework, this chapter will cover the essential topics required for iOS developers:

- We will go over the **Auto Layout** system
- We will discuss the different `UIView` features
- We will ensure a deep understanding of `UITableViews`
- We will talk about `UIViewController` and its role in our app
- We will dive into the navigation world
- We will learn the basic concepts of animations

As I said – UIKit is an enormous topic, and there are many more, but we are focusing on the mandatory interview issues.

We will start with what is driving our layout, and that's the Auto Layout system.

Answering questions about Auto Layout

UIKit is a vast topic, and over the years, it has become even more significant, gaining more and more capabilities.

The engine that drives how things are placed on the screen is what Apple calls Auto Layout, which is why I chose to start the UIKit chapter with that topic in mind.

Auto Layout is Apple technology that defines the *relationships between the different elements* on the screen and tremendously influences our ability to move fast with UI development. We can say that mastering Auto Layout sets us up with the ability to provide a great UI in a decent amount of time.

But there is more than just time efficiency – Auto Layout can help us *adapt our app to different screen sizes* or even platforms (**iPad** versus **iPhone**). It can also help us automatically set the UI direction according to the current localization.

We'll go over some of the most common Auto Layout questions now. Isn't it an excellent start for a UIKit chapter?

"Can you explain what content hugging and compression resistance are in Auto Layout and how they are used to control the layout of UI elements?"

Why is this question important?

Compression resistance and **content hugging** are two essential concepts in Auto Layout that define views' behavior when their size and layout change. At this stage, the interviewer assumes we already know the basics of Auto Layout and wants to see how we handle more complex situations where two different views are "fighting" over limited space to satisfy all their constraints.

What is the answer?

Compression resistance and content hugging are two of UIView's properties that define the layout behavior when there isn't enough space to satisfy all the constraints.

Let's go over what these terms mean for constraints:

- **Content hugging**: When content hugging is set to high priority, the view wants to become *as small as possible* with a specific axe
- **Compression resistance**: When the compression resistance property is set to high, the view wants to become *as big as possible* with a specific axe

One great example to demonstrate a possible conflict between two views is a UIView (let's say `UITableViewCell`) with two subviews – a leading label and a button (see *Figure 7.1*):

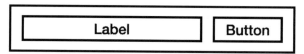

Figure 7.1 – A view with a label and a button

Looking at *Figure 7.1*, we can see a possible use case – both the label and button can have a short text, and as a result, their intrinsic content size is small. If these two views try to set their width according to their content, one will have to "give up" and fill the remaining space. To ensure that the button will try to become as small as possible and the label will fill the remaining space, we need to set their content hugging and compression resistance accordingly. Let's see how to do that in code:

```
class MyTableViewCell: UITableViewCell {
    @IBOutlet weak var label: UILabel!
    @IBOutlet weak var button: UIButton!

    override func awakeFromNib() {
        super.awakeFromNib()

        label.setCompressionResistancePriority (.defaultHigh, for:
.horizontal)
        button.setContentHuggingPriority (.defaultHigh, for:
.horizontal)
    }
}
```

Calling `setcompressionResistencePriority` for `label` means that when the cell is resized horizontally, the auto-layout system will try to maintain the intrinsic content size of the label and *prevent it from being compressed*.

However, calling `setContentHuggingPrioirty` for button means that when the cell is resized horizontally, and there is extra space available, the auto-layout system will *try to expand* `button` to fill the available space and prevent it from being stretched too much.

We can set these priorities in the code and Interface Builder quite easily.

There are many other examples where this settlement is needed, such as a page title's width that conflicts with its alignment or complex screens with dynamic font size.

"Can you explain how to use size classes in Interface Builder to adapt layouts for different screen sizes and orientations?"

Why is this question important?

This question is important because it tests our understanding by taking Auto Layout and trying to adapt our layout to *different sizes and orientations*.

Notice I didn't mention iPad or iPhone – these terms are irrelevant when discussing Auto Layout. We must consider our layout fully responsive according to different size levels, aka, size classes.

What is the answer?

Size classes are a feature that allows us to create one UI for various screen sizes. A screen size can be an iPhone or an iPad, but it can also be an iPad app being presented on a split screen and therefore needs to change its layout to an iPhone app.

The classes we have today are **Compact** and **Regular**. Compact usually means an iPhone or an iPad app in a split screen, and Regular means an iPad app. As mentioned, we shouldn't think of these classes as iPhone versus iPad. Size classes allow us to think responsively regardless of our app's device.

To use size classes in Interface Builder, we first need to open the storyboard we want to work on. Then, in the bottom right corner of the **Interface Builder** window, we'll see the Size Classes tool. By default, it shows the w Any h Any class, which means the layout will be the same for all devices and orientations. We can select another size class from the control to create a different layout for a specific screen size or orientation. For example, we can choose the w Compact h Regular class to create a layout for iPhones in portrait orientation.

One good use case is a login screen, where on a small screen, we want the username and password text fields to be laid out vertically, and on a bigger screen, we may want them to be laid out horizontally. The layout of the text fields according to size can be managed using size classes.

More examples of different values in different size classes are fonts, Auto Layout, and constant size.

"What is the purpose of the safe area in Auto Layout, and how do you ensure that your views are properly positioned within the safe area?"

Why is this question important?

The **safe area** is an important topic when working with layouts across different devices. Every iOS developer must know how to handle the safe area, which contains the status bar, sensors, and round corners of modern iPhones. This question tests our experience working with different devices and creating a layout agnostic to the device type we work on.

What is the answer?

The safe area is a feature in Auto Layout that provides a **layout guide** that helps us position elements above and below areas on the screen reserved for sensors, round corners, and generally areas the user isn't supposed to touch.

However, we can position non-interactive views in the safe area zone, such as videos or backgrounds. Still, we must consider that iOS elements, sensors, and screen round corners may partially cover these views.

To ensure we position a view outside the safe area, we can use a property named `safeAreaLayoutGuide`. Here's an example of positioning a label below the top safe area using `safeAreaLayoutGuide`:

```
NSLayoutConstraint.activate([
    myLabel.leadingAnchor.constraint(equalTo:
        view.safeAreaLayoutGuide.leadingAnchor),
    myLabel.trailingAnchor.constraint(equalTo:
        view.safeAreaLayoutGuide.trailingAnchor),
    myLabel.topAnchor.constraint(equalTo:
        view.safeAreaLayoutGuide.topAnchor, constant: 30),
    myLabel.heightAnchor.constraint(equalToConstant: 20)
```

We can see that `view`, the UIViewController main view, has a property named `safeAreaLayoutGuide`, and that guide represents the end of the safe area zone. This guide is equivalent to the screen edges in older devices, but in modern devices, it means the interactive part of the display.

It is best practice to check your layout with different devices to ensure it is usable in all displays.

Auto Layout is a fundamental topic in UIKit and iOS development. There's no way to get into UI development without working closely with Auto Layout, and the UI is an important topic in iOS. If you started your iOS development career with SwiftUI, ensure you are familiar with Auto Layout, at least for the basic terms.

Solving UIView questions

UIView is the basic building block for user interaction in iOS UIKit. At its roots, it represents a rectangle on the screen that can display graphics and handle user interactions and animations.

Before we go over any interview questions, it is crucial to understand the roles of UIView in UIKit, and its relationship with CALayer.

Let's go over the main features of UIView:

- **Manage subviews**: UIView can contain additional UIViews called **subviews**, which can include their own subviews. This capability allows us to build complex UIs and reusable components. UIView is also responsible for handling the layout of its subviews using the Auto Layout system we discussed in the previous chapter.

- **Respond to user interaction**: Another important role UIView has is to respond to user interaction, which is not a minor topic. Preparing for the interview involves learning about the **responder chain**, which handles user interactions with UIView's hierarchy.

- **Draw graphics**: UIView can draw graphics: lines, shapes, images, and texts. UIView does that using another framework called **Core Graphics**, which is responsible for drawing basic graphics using the **CPU**.

So, what about CALayer? Well, we already know the UIView can draw using Core Graphics, but that's not an efficient way. Therefore, it has a CALayer. The CALayer is responsible for drawing the content inside UIView, which uses **Core Animation** and the device's **GPU**. Each UIView has a primary CALayer that can have sublayers of its own.

The CALayer is responsible for the content drawing, and UIView is accountable for the layout and user interaction.

"Can you explain how the responder chain works in iOS?"

Why is this question important?

The responder chain is a key concept in iOS UI development. The idea discusses the management of user interaction in multi-layer screens.

The question is vital because user interaction is a critical topic in UI development, and the responder chain is not a simple concept to understand at first glance.

What is the answer?

The term "responder chain" refers to a mechanism in which the user touches the screen, and each UIView passes the touch forward to its corresponding subviews until one of the views responds.

Let us explore this in *Figure 7.2*:

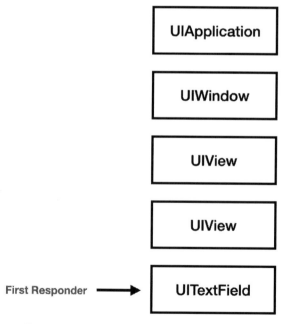

Figure 7.2 – Example of a responder chain in iOS

As shown in *Figure 7.2*, the touch starts with `UIApplication` and goes down until it reaches the first view that responds to the touch, in this case, `UITextField`. The respond chain "asks" each of the views if it is the first responder by calling the `becomeFirstResponder()` function. That's why calling directly to `become FirstResponder()` on a text field brings up the keyboard and makes the text field the currently active input field.

In short, a responder chain is our ability to control which view catches the user interaction while views are placed on top of each other. There are more cases where this comes in handy, such as transparent views or scrolls.

"How can you respond to device orientation changes in UIView?"

Why is this question important?

In many apps, responding to device orientation is crucial because it provides the user with an optional layout for the app just by rotating the device.

But that's not the real reason why it's essential to understand that question correctly. We should know how to structure our UI to support different screen proportions and adjust the layout and the controls according to the new orientation.

The question tests our flexibility and readiness for a radical layout change.

What is the answer?

Handling device orientation changes requires tackling that problem from different angles. Let's list some of the things we can do:

- **Verify our Auto Layout constraints**: Auto Layout is a great technique to ensure our layout will stay usable after changing the screen bounds. We can define constraint relationships and limit view size or margins to ensure our layout is updated correctly with changing orientation.

- **Animate changes**: If possible, we should animate changes to our views to provide our users with a seamless and smooth change experience.

- **Override the willTransition(to:with) method**: The `willTransition(to:with)` method gets called just before the view transitions to a new size or a trait collection. That's where we can modify the view appearance in addition to what Auto Layout already changed. For example, we can show or hide subviews, change texts, or modify constraint values.

- **Update layout**: Position or rearrange views, and in general, make changes to our layout to fit the new orientation. That, of course, is according to our design and product requirements.

Not all app makers support landscape and portrait states in their products, as this is more a design decision than an engineering one. But building our views with orientation change in mind is a good practice.

"Why does UIView not have a 'viewDidAppear' method as UIViewController does?"

Why is this question important?

We haven't discussed view controllers just yet, but that's a question many candidates struggle to answer. This question aims to see whether we understand the relationship UIViews have with their view controller. Many junior developers ask themselves that question because understanding the UIView role isn't intuitive. More experienced developers should answer that question more easily.

What is the answer?

UIView doesn't have a `viewDidAppear` method like **UIViewController** because the primary role of UIView is to be a visual component and not handle life cycle events.

When we look back to the **MVC** design pattern Apple tried to implement with UIKit, it is simpler to understand the different roles we have on our screen. UIViewController manages the relationship between the model and the view. Therefore, the view controller is also responsible for the different life cycle events, such as `viewDidLoad`, `viewWillAppear`, and `viewDidAppear`. If we need to perform tasks in the life cycle events such as performing network requests, loading data, or setting a state, we should do it in the view controller and update the view accordingly. Doing any of these is not part of the UIView's role.

MVC will be discussed in detail in *Chapter 11*.

"Can you explain the difference between setNeedsLayout, layoutSubviews, and layoutIfNeeded in UIView? When would you use each of these methods, and how do they impact the layout process?"

Why is this question important?

These three UIView methods (`setNeedsLayout`, `layoutSubviews`, and `layoutIfNeeded`) tell the story of UIView rendering cycle optimization. This is not a go/no-go question but more like a bonus question. I have interviewed hundreds of iOS developers in my career, and most of them can't fully answer this question as they don't understand how the layout system works precisely.

Answering this question correctly will benefit us in an interview situation.

What is the answer?

First, let's understand how the layout system works – UIView refreshes the layout of its subviews once every screen refresh rate (in 60Hz, it's once every 16.67 milliseconds), only if it needs to. What does that mean? For example, if the view changes its frame, it must refresh the layout of its subviews. The reason it happens every 16.67 milliseconds is because of efficiency. If we change the UIView's frame multiple times within these 16.67 milliseconds, it will refresh the layout of its subviews only once.

Now, what does it mean "refresh the layout of its subviews"? It means that the system runs the `layoutSubiews()` method, which we can override and perform additional changes if we like.

We understand now that changing the UIView frame marks the view as "dirty," so in the next run loop, it will run `layoutSubviews()`. But we don't have to change its frame or one of the related constraints to mark the view as dirty. We can just call `setNeedsLayout()` to ensure that the view will update its subviews in the next run loop.

Sometimes, we need the view to run `layoutSubviews` immediately without waiting for the next run loop. One good example is animations and constraint changes. In this case, we can call `layoutIfNeeded()`, which will call `layoutSubviews()` only if UIView is marked as dirty.

It is now clear why we never call `layoutSubviews()` directly – the system does that for us much more efficiently, and it is better to stick with the natural process.

As I said at the beginning of this section – UIView is our UI building block and one of the fundamental parts of MVC and **MVVM**. Understanding how it works beyond adding and removing subviews is essential to us as iOS developers and can help us influence our app performance and experience. Additionally, some of the discussed questions in this section will be asked in an interview.

Now let's move on to another important side of the MVC pattern: UIViewController.

"What is the difference between the frame and bounds properties?"

Why is this question important?

Even though `bounds` and `frame` are quite similar, the difference between them is crucial to understand how the layout system works. The difference is important, especially when dealing with animations, positioning, and transitions.

What is the answer?

In short, the `frame` property represents the position and size of a UIView relative to its superview's coordinate system, while the `bounds` property represents the position and size of a UIView relative to its own coordinate system.

Here's an example of the bounds and frame properties for the same view, positioned in *x*:50 and *y*:100:

- Frame:
  - Origin: (*x*: 50, *y*: 100)
  - Size: (width: 200, height: 150)

- Bounds:

  - Origin: (*x*: 0, *y*: 0)

  - Size: (width: 200, height: 150)

We can see that the origin is different, but the size is the same. That's because the origin in the frame is relative to its superview.

However, it's important to note that there are cases where the frame and bounds sizes can differ. Unlike the `bounds` property, which represents the view's size in its own coordinate system, the frame size is calculated and can change during animations. Therefore, it is possible to observe different size values between the `frame` and `bounds` properties. While the bounds size property remains constant, the frame size property can reflect the current size values during animations or transformations.

Understanding everything about UIViewController

UIViewController is a core class in iOS development and behaves as a building block for most iOS apps that use UIKit.

UIViewController has multiple roles in iOS development:

- **It is the C in the MVC pattern**: If the UIView is the V (View) and our model is the M, the UIViewController is the one that coordinates between the presentation layer and the business layer. That role affects many of the features UIViewController has, such as life cycle events and memory management functions.

- **Handling life cycle events**: We explained this role of UIViewController in the previous section. UIViewController has another function: to manage the various life cycle events on the screen. By creating subclasses of UIViewController, we can take advantage of its different methods to handle all stages of a screen's life cycle.

- **Leading player in the navigation system**: We can present UIViewController above another UIViewController or push and pop it into and from a navigation stack. As such, UIViewController plays a significant role in iOS app navigation by representing a "screen" in our project (note – a UIViewController isn't equivalent to a "screen," but a screen always has a root view controller).

- **Loading and unloading views**: Usually, we don't present views on the screen without a UIViewController that handles them. We can indeed add a UIView to the app window, but that's an edge case. Adding a view to the window brings with it issues such as life cycle management, model and data linking, and many more, and they are considered not ideal.

I'm not sure that, as iOS candidates, we will encounter an interview without a question about UIViewController.

"Can you list all the life cycle events or methods of a UIViewController, in the order in which they occur?"

Why is this question important?

That is probably one of the most common questions interviewers ask. It isn't a difficult question and is also easy to learn and complete.

This question is usually considered a critical factor in the interview process, as not doing well can lead to concerns for most interviewers.

Let's understand why – our understanding of UIViewController life cycle events influences the decisions of where to load and release data, how to build our UI, perform animation, and provide a good user experience to the user.

It is also important to be familiar with the UIViewController life cycle to handle user interaction and view updates.

We need to ensure we don't have any gaps in our answer to this question.

What is the answer?

Let's list the life cycle events, ordered by their call timing:

- `loadView()`: This is called before the view hierarchy is created. UIKit doesn't create the view before `loadView()` is called, so we'll get nil when accessing the UIViewController `view` property.

- `viewDidLoad()`: This is called after the view is loaded. That's where we can perform additional setups to the view, such as adding subviews and observers. Unlike many other life cycle methods, `viewDidLoad` is called only once.

- `viewWillLayoutSubviews()`: This is called just before the view lays out its subviews. We can make additional changes to constraints at this time.

- `viewDidLayoutSubviews()`: This is called after the view lays out its subviews. We can do tasks that require a final layout. For example, position views, scroll view content size, and animations.

- `viewWillAppear()`: This is called before the view is presented on the screen. UIKit calls that method one or more times. That's the place to load data if needed.

- `viewDidAppear()`: This is called after the view is already presented on the screen. UIKit calls that method one or more times. Generally, that's an excellent place to show start animations.

- `viewWillDisappear()`: This is called just before the view is removed from the parent view controller or is hidden by a modal view controller. We can do some cleanup tasks here, such as stop timers and animations, perform savings, or stop media playback.

- `viewDidDisapper()`: This is called after the view is removed from the parent view controller. We usually perform tasks that do not influence the user experience – for example, logging, states, cleaning temporary files, and resetting data.

It is imperative to mention that some of the methods in the list *can be called multiple times* in different use cases. For example, `viewWillLayoutSubviews` can be called when the main view changes its size, such as an orientation change. The `viewWillDisappear` method might be called when a model is presented above the view controller. We should provide examples of each one of the life cycle events to show our understanding.

"Can you explain the concept of UIViewController containment? How would you implement it in your app?"

Why is this question important?

Compared to the previous question, this question is more advanced and requires knowledge of design patterns and architecture.

UIViewController containment creates modular and reusable UI interfaces and increases our project flexibility.

What is the answer?

With UIViewController containment, we can add a view controller to another view controller and make it a child view controller. This differs from adding a subview because UIViewController represents an independent MVC unit and has its own responsibility.

Take a look at *Figure 7.3*:

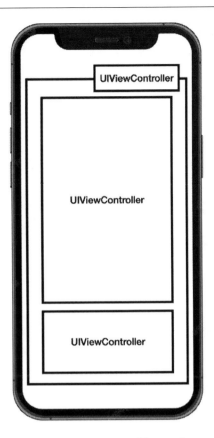

Figure 7.3 – Divide our screen into different view controllers

Figure 7.3 shows that a screen represented by a UIViewContoller is divided into two additional view controllers.

There are two main ways of adding a view controller child:

- **Drag a new view controller in the storyboard**: We can use Xcode **Storyboard** to drag a new view controller to an existing view controller. That creates a container view that is linked to another view controller. Because a single **XIB file** represents a single view controller or a view, we can do that only in storyboards and not in standard XIB files.

- **Adding a child controller using code**: We can easily add a new child view controller in code using the addChild(UIViewController:) method. Let's see an example of that:

```
// Add child view controller
parentViewController.addChild(childViewController)
parentViewController.view.addSubview (childViewController.view)
childViewController.view.frame = parentViewController.view.bounds
childViewController.didMove(toParent: parentViewController)
```

There are four steps we need to do:

I.   Call the `addChild` method to ensure the new UIViewController is added as a child in the view controller hierarchy.

II.   Add the new view controller main view *as a subview* to the parent view controller. The views hierarchy needs to correspond to the view controller hierarchy.

III. Set the child view controller *view frame or constraints*. It can be whatever we need.

IV.   *Notify the system* that the child view controller has been moved to the parent.

One of the advantages of adding the new view controller "according to the guidelines" is that we can sync the life cycle events we discussed in the previous question. A `viewWillAppear` method being called on the parent view controller is also called on its child view controller, as long as they are added correctly. The life cycle events sync is critical when reusing the view controller as a child view controller on different screens.

> **We are already using UIViewController containment in our apps!**
>
> You may feel that UIViewController containment is strange to you if you haven't tried that before. But – most likely, you already used some kind of child view controller implementation in your apps. Let's see two good examples:
>
> **UINavigationController:** Navigating in UIKit is done with a parent view controller (UINavigationController) and a child view controller, the top view controller. Imagine yourself implementing your own navigation controller – how would you do that? How will you implement the push and pop view controllers' actions? This is a great thinking exercise that can prepare you for the question.
>
> **UISplitViewController:** Apple provides a split view controller for apps that run on iPads. In UISplitViewController, we have two additional child view controllers – master and detail view controllers. Both divide the screen into two different areas, each of which is a separate view controller. Now that you know how to add a child view controller, that's easy.

"How do you pass data between view controllers in iOS?"

Why is this question important?

Passing data between view controllers is an important task in iOS development. The dynamic nature of apps presenting the same UI with different information requires us to update a view controller with new information constantly. The question tests our knowledge of the various design patterns of passing data between objects in general and between view controllers explicitly.

What is the answer?

There are many ways of passing data between view controllers! The problem is that all those ways make it extremely easy to answer the question. And therefore, we need to explain the use case and reason for each one of the ways we present to the interviewer. Let's see some examples:

- **Using a delegate**: If we have a child-parent relationship, we use a delegate to notify of events and data between the child and the parent view controller. A delegate is a simple pattern based on a protocol used when we want to implement a simple update with a well-defined interface. However, the delegate pattern is considered a bit outdated as we have more advanced patterns today.

- **Using dependency injection**: One way to pass data to a new view controller when presenting or pushing it into the stack is to use dependency injection. This can be achieved using the `init` function or setting one of its properties. One example can be a screen that displays contact information. In the `init` function, we can pass the contact entity that needs to be displayed. It's important to note that this approach creates a one-way data stream and can be used whenever a new view controller needs to be displayed.

- **Using a closure**: If we pass the information in one direction only, closure is a great way to do that. We can define a closure on the destination view controller and set it on the source view controller. Whenever we want to pass information from the source to its parent, the source just needs to run the closure with the relevant parameters. That's a simple way to pass data with minimal coupling.

- **Using Combine**: Combine is an advanced and reactive version of closure. It lets us stream data updates, including error handling, async operations, and data manipulation from one object to another.

- **Post notification**: If the two view controllers have no reference to each other, a notification may be a good solution. Even though we can attach data to the notification, posting a notification is considered to be an anti-pattern by many developers. A notification doesn't have a straightforward interface; all living objects can observe it and respond. These two reasons alone make it less recommended than the other methods.

You are already aware of all the methods I just presented, but listing them can help you answer that question and help you with design-pattern tasks and home assessments. That is one of my goals in this book – to organize your thoughts.

Making sure we are ready with UITableView

UITableView, followed by UICollectionView, is one of the oldest UI components in UIKit. In fact, UITableView was there from the start, and UICollectionView was added four years later.

Why is UITableView considered to be a fundamental component? The reason is apparent.

Both UITableView and UICollectionView are specialized in displaying a significant *amount of data* efficiently and straightforwardly.

UITableView does more than that – it provides an interface for displaying items in a way suitable for *small screens*, including features like multi-selection, editing, headers, and footers. It became the primary way of displaying menus and data in many apps.

Apple ensured a component style, UITableView, was carried over to SwiftUI from day one to keep this capability with us.

"How does the queuing mechanism work in a UITableView, and what are some best practices for optimizing its performance?"

Why is this question important?

Like several other questions we discussed earlier (for example – UIViewController life cycle), that's another go-no-go question you probably want to make sure you are ready for. This question tests our understanding of the primary mechanism of UITableView that enables its efficiency and performance.

The UITableView queuing mechanism is the foundation for many on-top features and issues we may encounter, such as async operations during scroll, optimizations, and state management.

That mechanism is also the basis for additional controls such as UICollectionView and MKMapView.

What is the answer?

The UITableView mechanism ensures efficiency and high performance when scrolling with a large amount of data.

The main problem with displaying a large number of items is *memory*. Allocating so many views, most off-screen, creates a memory overload, eventually leading to app termination.

What we want to do is to allocate only the views we see on the screen and release off-screen views while we are scrolling the list.

But allocating new views each time raises a performance issue. If the user scrolls fast, allocating and creating new views takes a few milliseconds, which causes lags even when running on powerful devices.

This lag is where the queuing solution comes into practice. Instead of deallocating the view when it goes off-screen, UITableView puts it in a deque pool and pulls it from where it needs to display a new view in the list.

The queuing mechanism makes the UITableView scrolling fast and smooth. But dequeuing cells also creates new problems, some of which are detailed here:

- **Working on an existing cell**: Before we display the cell, we must remember it might already have existing information. We need to clear the cell after it moves out of the pool by calling the `prepareForReuse` method or overriding its properties before we display it.

- **Verify responses from async operations**: A common issue in UITableViews is loading images async from a backend service. We start the request when the cell is being displayed, but when we get the response, the cell is already dequeued and connected to another entity. In this case, we need to ensure that the data we get in the response matches the current entity the cell is supposed to represent.

- **Working with multiple pools**: There are cases where we have numerous types of cells, probably based on different classes and UI. In this case, we need to create multiple deque pools, which we also need to handle and ensure.

To summarize, UITableView provides an excellent mechanism to display big chunks of information but also brings us new issues we must handle.

"What is pagination in UITableView, and how would you implement it to efficiently load and display large amounts of data while maintaining good performance and user experience?"

Why is this question important?

When we think of a UITableView, we imagine a contacts list or pizza recipes. But there are cases when it either takes time to load the data or the list is so big that it creates a memory overload. For example – social media posts, images, and data from the backend. From our point of view – an infinite number of items.

The interviewer wants to see how we handle a more complex situation than just displaying a closed list of items.

What is the answer?

Pagination in a UITableView is a technique that involves loading and displaying data in small batches based on the table view scroll position.

We use pagination when we have a large amount of data, and loading everything simultaneously is inefficient. For example, if we have data from our backend or large images and videos stored in our persistent store.

With pagination, we load the data we want to display on the screen (and a little bit more), and when the user keeps scrolling, we load "another page" of data. This technique of loading data on demand is much faster for initial loading, doesn't create memory overload, and is much more efficient overall.

However, pagination creates some other challenges we need to tackle, which are detailed here:

- **Decide the page loading trigger**: To perform the additional loading operation, we need to decide the loading trigger. For example, load more data when the user reaches the last visible row or a scrolling offset. Also, we need to ensure we are not sending multiple requests simultaneously since the trigger might be happening multiple times during that scroll.

- **Showing a loading indicator**: It is important to provide the user an indication there's more data to view and is currently being loaded. It is common practice to show the indication in the last row at the bottom of the list.

- **Load data in the background**: To provide smooth scrolling without blocking the UI and creating lagging, we should load the data in a background thread using async functions, GCD, or `NSOperation`.

- **Handle the "no more data" use case**: That may sound like a weird issue, but developers sometimes forget to handle it. When the user scrolls to the last item on the list, the trigger for loading more is activated. If the request returns empty, the trigger might be activated again because our list meets the trigger condition. In this case, the list will enter an infinite loop of trying to fetch data without a result. The solution might be to use some temporary flag to avoid ongoing fetching.

Pagination is a technique that has pros and cons and should be considered carefully. It involves both the backend and client and can provide high performance and good user experience but requires us to deal with more complex fetching patterns.

"What are the different approaches for adjusting cell size in a UITableView, and how do you determine the optimal size for cells based on the content they will display?"

Why is this question important?

Cell size in UITableView was always an issue for iOS developers, mainly when the need for accessibility and dynamic font size evolved over the years.

This question tests our knowledge of UITableView delegate, our ability to use Auto Layout with cells, and the tradeoffs we need to make between performance and simplicity.

What is the answer?

There are two ways to adjust a cell size:

- **Set a custom height for each row**: Implement the `tableView(_:heightForRowAt:)` delegate method that returns a different height for each row. In this way, we need to calculate the size of each row ourselves. It can be a constant size or according to the cell content. Calculating the cell size ourselves can be inaccurate if not done right, but it can be faster and more efficient in terms of performance when dealing with large datasets. Here's an example of such an implementation:

```
func tableView(_ tableView: UITableView, heightForRowAt
indexPath: IndexPath) -> CGFloat {
    let cellData = dataSource[indexPath.row]
    let height = cellData.text.height
        (withConstrainedWidth:
```

```
            tableView.frame.width - 32, font:
            UIFont.systemFont(ofSize: 14))
    return height + 16
}
```

In this code example, we pull the cell data according to its row index and calculate the size based on the UITableView size. We can see how error-prone this code snippet is, as it needs to be very accurate. But – since we are not using the Auto Layout system, it is much faster.

- **Using self-size cells**: The other option is to use self-size cells. In self-size cells, the cell's height is set automatically by its content, using Auto Layout constraints. Some things to notice here are as follows:

  - We must ensure a *continuous sequence of constraints* from top to bottom for the cell to get a valid intrinsic content size.

  - We need to ensure that the UITableView `rowHeight` property is set to `automaticDimension`.

  - We said that self-size cells are less efficient in terms of performance. To "help" UITableView measure its size, we can use the `estimatedRowHeight` property or implement the corresponding `tableView(_:estimatedHeightForRow:)` delegate method to provide a row height estimation until the cell is shown on the screen.

The self-size cells should be good enough for most cases, and it needs to be our go-to approach unless we encounter performance issues that will require us to set custom heights for cells.

UITableView is a central topic in iOS development and interviews. The coding or the home assessment will probably include UITableView as a primary component. Make sure there are no mistakes with this control!

Performing navigation well

Navigation is a critical component in UIKit and iOS development. Navigation allows us to move the user from one UIViewController to another intuitively and simply.

There are two ways of navigating the user to another screen:

- **Present a modal view controller**: If we need to present a screen with a task to complete or to make a decision, a view controller can present another view controller on top of it.

- **Push another view controller**: If we want to navigate the user down the app hierarchy to the next stage, we can push a new view controller to the stack. This technique requires a UINavigationController to handle the push and pop operations and provide a navigation bar to ease the transitions.

Interviewers do not generally ask questions about the push and present, as these actions are fairly simple to understand and implement. Most questions and challenges are related to transitions, navigation bars, life cycle methods, and design patterns.

"What is the purpose of the navigationItem property in a view controller, and how can you use it to customize the behavior and appearance of a navigation bar in iOS development?"

Why is this question important?

The navigationItem property is just that, a property. Why on earth is there a question about a specific property?

Well, that's because navigationItem holds an entire concept behind it. This question tests our ability to understand how the navigation controller works and the design concept of empowering view controllers to impact the navigation bar's appearance, despite it being a component of the navigation controller.

Generally, the way navigationItem and view controllers work is an interesting design pattern that can be used in other cases and is worth learning.

What is the answer?

Every UIViewController has a property named navigationItem. That property contains several properties and methods used to customize the navigation bar's behavior with data associated with the view controller itself.

For example, navigationItem contains the title property, which is used to set the *current title* value displayed in the navigation bar.

Other important items of information that can be set in navigationItem are the *left and right buttons*. Let's see an example of how the view controller modifies the navigation bar using the navigationItem property:

```
class MyViewController: UIViewController {
    override func viewDidLoad(_ animated: Bool) {
        super. viewDidLoad (animated)
        navigationItem.title = "My Title"

        let button = UIBarButtonItem(title: "Button", style: .plain,
            target: self, action:#selector(buttonTapped))
            navigationItem.rightBarButtonItem = button
    }
    @objc func buttonTapped() {}
}
```

In our code example, the navigationItem property contains a title and a right bar button with the "Button" title. When the user navigates from that screen, the navigation controller will get a new navigationItem property from the next controller and update its navigation bar properties.

It's a technique that empowers the navigation controller to update its navigation bar based on the context of the visible view controller. Thinking further, we can use this technique in other cases as well.

"What are some of the preset options for presenting a UIViewController in iOS, and why is it important to understand these options?"

Why is this question important?

Presenting a view controller with another view controller is a familiar and straightforward task iOS developers do all the time.

However, there are several ways of presenting a view controller. Each one of the options is suitable for a different use case and can influence the presenter's view controller life cycle events.

Our job is to explain the different options to the product team and select the one that fits our use case.

What is the answer?

There are several preset options available to us. Each one influences the look and feel of the presented view controller.

Let's name some of them:

- `Fullscreen`: The presented view controller takes up the entire screen.
- `PageSheet`: The presented view controller doesn't fill the whole screen, and the screen can be pulled down using a simple swipe gesture.
- `overCurrentContext`: The view controller is presented and hides the current view controller context.

Obviously, the different types of presentations need to be suitable for the user experience we want to provide to our users. But we also must consider the influence of these types on the different life cycle events being fired.

For example – if we use **Page Sheet** and not **Over Current Context**, `viewWillDisappear` and `viewDidDisappear` of the presenting view controller *are not being called*. In Page Sheet, we assume the underlying view controller is still visible. Therefore, some life cycle events related to appearance are also not being called.

In this case, we must change how we present the modal view controllers or communicate any changes or updates using a delegate pattern or Combine.

The rule is simple – we need to adjust the preset option to the user experience we want to provide to our users. Do we hide the underlying screen? That's a good starting question.

"How would you design a navigation system for an iOS app using the coordinator pattern, where view controllers don't decide where to go next, and a coordinator object is responsible for managing the navigation flow?"

Why is this question important?

That's an advanced question about navigation in iOS apps, and it's not related directly to how to technically implement UINavigationController or present a view controller modally.

This question deals with the separation of concerns principle and design patterns we can use in our project to provide more flexibility and modularity.

That's one of the questions that doesn't come with a school-ready answer, and you can think about your answer during your interview and discuss it with your interviewer. More important is to develop a set of principles and ideas for how to nail this challenge.

What is the answer?

A **coordinator pattern** is a popular design pattern that separates the navigation logic from the UI.

So, let's discuss how to approach this question and decide on the basic principles we want to keep:

- The view controller (or its view model, for that matter) *doesn't decide where to navigate* but only sends touch events
- We keep the navigation *logic in another class* called `Coordinator`
- We can create one `Coordinator` for each view controller or a `Coordinator` for a single flow
- The `Coordinator` has a reference to the navigation controller and *can push or pop view controllers* as needed
- The `Coordinator` needs to *observe events* that happen in the currently displayed view controller

Based on these assumptions, we can imagine the following pattern (*Figure 7.4*):

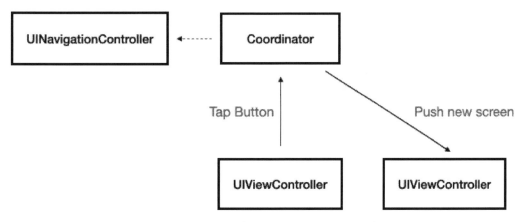

Figure 7.4 – A coordinator pattern (suggestion)

Notice this is just a suggestion, as this pattern is not set in stone.

Here are some modifications we can suggest according to different project's needs:

- If the project becomes more prominent, we can have *several coordinators* and sometimes even a hierarchy of coordinators.

- We can decide that the coordinator *observes state change* in the view model.

- We also don't have to use observers for navigating but provide the view controller a *reference to the coordinator*. The view controller can send the coordinator what happened, and the coordinator can decide what to do next.

We can play with the pattern if we keep the basic design principles and explain what we do well.

Empowering user experience with animations

Unlike what many think, animations in iOS are not for "fun"- they play a significant role in providing our app with a sleek and smooth experience. As a result, they are part of our developer's tools set.

Animation in iOS relies on a framework called **Core Animation**, which is one of UIKit's dependencies. So, even though this chapter discusses UIKit, we can find Core Animation in many classes and methods in UIKit.

Going over the core concepts of animation in UIKit

So, what do we need to know about animations when practicing for an interview?

We need to know several classes, terms, methods, and techniques. Let's go over them before we move on to an advanced interview question.

Performing UIView animations

UIView animations are probably the simplest animations we have in UIKit. In a UIView animation, we provide a closure with our final state, and UIKit runs the animation automatically. Let's see a code example that takes a view and fades it out by changing its `alpha` value:

```
UIView.animate(withDuration: 0.3) {
    myView.alpha = 0.0
}
```

We see a simple code that receives a duration and a closure and animates the changes inside the closure, in this case, changing the `myView` alpha property to `0.0`. Notice that Core Animation doesn't animate all UIView properties. Here is the list of UIView animatable properties: `frame`, `bounds`, `center`, `transform`, `alpha`, `backgroundColor`, and `tintcolor`.

Animating Auto Layout constraints changes

We need to understand how to animate constraints changes because it is not as straightforward as the other properties we modify. Constraints are part of the Auto Layout, and UIKit performs Auto Layout changes every run loop (every 16.67 milliseconds). This means we need to "force" Auto Layout to perform the changes inside the animation closure by calling the `layoutIfNeeded` method. Here's an example of a constraints change of a view:

```
UIView.animate(withDuration: 0.5) {
    myView.topAnchor.constraint(equalTo: superview.
        topAnchor, constant: 100).isActive = true
    superview?.layoutIfNeeded()
}
```

We can see that it's not enough to create or modify the constraint within the animation closure. We also need to "force" the changes to happen on time; therefore, we call the `layoutIfNeeded` method.

Playing with timing and easing

We can adjust the animations to create what we want the user to perceive using timing and easing. Timing means different duration and delays, so we can have a longer or shorter animation. **Easing** means the animation's rate over time. For example, an **ease out** animation starts fast and finishes slower to provide a gentler animation at the end. When adjusting our animation to the experience we want to create, these terms are essential to understand. We also have `springWithDamping` and `initialSpringVelocity` that can help us achieve even more customized animation easing. Let's see an example of that:

```
UIView.animate(withDuration: 1.0,
              delay: 0.0,
              usingSpringWithDamping: 0.5,
              initialSpringVelocity: 10.0,
```

```
        options: .curveEaseInOut,
        animations: {
         myView.transform = CGAffineTransform
             (scaleX: 1.5, y: 1.5)
        },
        completion: nil)
```

We scale the myView size by modifying its transform property and doing that animatedly. We can also see that we pass these two important parameters:

- usingSpringWithDamping: This controls how much the spring effect is damped, with higher values resulting in less oscillation and a quick settling time
- initialSpringVelocity: This controls the initial velocity of the animation, with higher values resulting in a faster start and a more substantial effect

It's important to play with these values to achieve the desired result.

Building keyframe animations

For more complex animations, we can use keyframe animation. Keyframe animation allows us to create animations in stages or sequences. We can define the different stages and provide a relative duration and start time for each one of them. Here's an example of a keyframe animation:

```
UIView.animateKeyframes(withDuration: 3.0, delay: 0.0,
    options: [], animations: {
    UIView.addKeyframe(withRelativeStartTime: 0.0,
        relativeDuration: 0.5, animations: {
        view.transform = CGAffineTransform (rotationAngle: .pi / 2)
    })
    UIView.addKeyframe(withRelativeStartTime: 0.5,
        relativeDuration: 0.5, animations: {
        view.transform = CGAffineTransform.identity
    })
}, completion: nil)
```

How do we read this code block? It's easy. The total animation duration is 3 seconds and is split into two sequences.

The first sequence starts at the beginning (relative time 0) and takes half the total time (relative duration 0.5, meaning 1.5 seconds).

The second sequence starts in the middle of the total animation time (relative time 0.5, meaning 1.5 seconds) and takes half of the animation time (relative duration 0.5, implying 1.5 seconds).

The sequences don't have to sync with each other, and it's up to us to sync them if we need.

Performing transitions between screens

UIKit allows us to perform transitions between screens, or to be precise, between UIViewControllers. We can pick one of the built-in transitions or even create our own transition.

This is how we present a UIViewController with a dissolve animation:

```
let viewController = MyViewController()
viewController.modalTransitionStyle = .crossDissolve
present(viewController, animated: true, completion: nil)
```

UIKit provides a short list of built-in animations that, in many cases, are not sufficient. Therefore, we have the option to create a custom animation and even an interactive animation.

Now, in the context of an interview – just like many other topics, it is important to understand how the custom transition works. We are not required to remember every API's detail, but we need to know what we are capable of, what possibilities it opens up, and how to build it so it can be reused across our project.

Manipulating CALayers

We touched on CALayer earlier when we discussed UIView but haven't discussed its importance for us as iOS developers.

We already know that iOS graphics is built with layers – UIViews (backed up with CALayers) and underneath we have Core Animation, which is built upon **Metal**.

CALayers provides hardware-accelerated rendering components, which lets us manipulate graphics and perform sophisticated animations and image processing. We can also blend layers and add visual effects. Overall, CALayers help us to go down the graphics architecture and get closer to the hardware and the GPU to achieve more power and efficiency.

Understanding the core concepts of animation techniques can help us achieve a better user experience. As iOS developers, we are expected to be familiar with the essential tools and classes to provide the desired animations our product team requires.

Now let's review an interesting interview question related to animation in UIKit.

"How can you create custom transitions between UIViewControllers in an iOS app?"

Why is this question important?

We discussed custom transitions a little earlier when we went over the animation core concepts, and this question tests our experience with the custom transition API. The Custom UIViewController transition API requires us to handle reusability, a deep understanding of how animations work, how view controllers work with each other, how to perform advanced techniques such as snapshotting, and how to implement a relatively complex UIKit API.

Custom animation is considered an advanced topic, and we should at least understand the basics of it.

What is the answer?

To create a custom transition between UIViewControllers, we must implement the `UIViewControllerAnimatedTransitioning` protocol (any object can conform to that protocol).

This protocol has two functions: `animateTransition(using:)` and `transitionDuration(using:)`.

In `animateTransition(using:)`, we handle the view hierarchy, constraints changes, and animations.

In `transitioDuration(using:)`, we return the duration in `TimeInterval`.

`UIViewControllerAnimatedTransitioning` defines a transition, present or dismiss. To determine precisely what happens in each scenario, we must implement `UIViewController-TransitionDelegate` to specify which object handles each use case.

Once we do that, to use our custom transition, we need to set the UIViewController `modalPresentationStyle` property to custom and the `transitionDelegate` property to the object that conforms to `UIViewControllerAnimatedTransitioning`.

Since we have two different protocols to implement and things get a little complex here, let's look at *Figure 7.5* to understand how everything is related to each other:

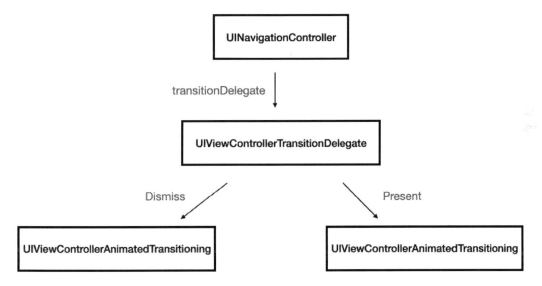

Figure 7.5 – Custom UIViewController transition delegate

We can see that the leading role of `UIViewControllerTransitionDelegate` is to decide which object will handle the animation when presenting or dismissing the presented view controller. It's worth saying that all three components can be the same object, and this is where the reusability concept comes in. If we want to be able to reuse our transitions across the project, we need to do two things:

1. Separate the *different components* of different objects.
2. When animating, reduce coupling between the presented/presenting view controller and the transitioning object *using protocols* and not explicitly the original view controller class. For example, suppose we are animating a view from one controller to another. In that case, we shouldn't use a direct reference to the view but rather a protocol with a `getView()` method so that we can reuse that with another view controller.

As we can see, transitioning between view controllers is a task that involves different techniques expected from a senior iOS developer. However, the concept needs to be done at least once to understand it fully.

Summary

In this chapter, we discussed many crucial topics related to UIKit, such as UIView, UIViewController, UITableView, navigation, and animations. UIKit has a massive presence in iOS developers' day-to-day work and significantly influences the user experience.

But – UIKit is also considered the "old" UI framework. The iOS development world is transitioning to a new, more modern era of declarative programming.

Our next chapter will handle just that – SwiftUI and declarative programming.

8
SwiftUI and Declarative Programming

The previous chapter was highly intensive. We discussed the most critical framework in iOS development besides **Foundation**.

This chapter is more than just discussing a framework – we will discuss an idea, a **programming paradigm**.

We can't approach a job interview today in iOS without a basic knowledge of declarative programming, a topic that was no more than "nice to have" a few years ago.

If you have gaps in your knowledge or limited experience, read this chapter thoroughly to fill that knowledge gap before you start your interview.

This chapter covers these exciting topics in declarative programming:

- Exploring a new era in the development
- Understanding declarative programming
- Learning states and observable objects
- Navigating SwiftUI views
- Expertise with the SwiftUI life cycle
- Expertise with Combine

Let's start with a brief background about declarative programming.

Entering a new era of development

SwiftUI and Combine are not only interesting frameworks but also symbolize a new direction that Apple is leading us toward. This direction is not disconnected from the current industry standards, as we can observe from the presence of **React**, **Flutter**, and RxJava in the everyday work of many developers.

The reason why I chose to dedicate a whole chapter to two frameworks that are still not widely used is that these two frameworks mark how iOS projects will look in the following decade.

If you haven't gained any experience with SwiftUI and Combine until now, the minimum you should do is understand the basic terms and concepts, which are part of the current chapter goal.

First, let's go over the most critical concept – declarative programming.

Understanding declarative programming

Declarative programming is a whole new programming paradigm that provides us with more readable and robust code. Declarative programming is not a new concept at all – in fact, we can find the roots of declarative programming 30–40 years ago. But only in the last decade has declarative programming gained popularity.

Let's try to get into more detail about declarative programming by answering some questions we may encounter during an interview.

"What's the difference between declarative programming and the "classic" programming paradigm, also known as imperative programming?"

Why is this question important?

If the workplace we interview for uses Combine or SwiftUI in its projects, we will probably have to answer some variant of this question. The reason is that the difference in how we approach code is so big that we cannot avoid restructuring our thoughts to answer that.

What is the answer?

In declarative programming, we *focus on the outcome and results of our code*. We observe changes and define precisely what the results would be on other objects and how data will be manipulated.

In imperative programming, we *focus on the steps that lead to our results*.

At first glance, the difference doesn't look clear. What does "focus on the results and not the steps" mean?

Let's try to explain that in code examples.

We have a screen with a button (`UIButton`) and a text field (`UITextField`), and we want to enable or disable the button based on the text field input. Let's see how we do that in imperative programming:

```
import UIKit

class ViewController: UIViewController {
    @IBOutlet weak var textField: UITextField!
    @IBOutlet weak var button: UIButton!
```

```
    override func viewDidLoad() {
        super.viewDidLoad()
        textField.addTarget(self, action: #selector
            (textFieldDidChange(_:)), for: .editingChanged)
        button.isEnabled = false
    }

    @objc private func textFieldDidChange(_ textField: UITextField) {
        button.isEnabled = textField.text?.isEmpty == false
    }
}
```

The code should be straightforward, as we wrote this pattern hundreds of times while working with imperative programming. Connecting a delegate to a test field is common in iOS development. But look how unclear it is – when we set up the text field, we define *what function will be called* when the user changes the text, not what will happen. It means we focus on the steps and implementation, not the final result.

In the text field delegate function, we indeed update the isEnabled property of the button, but that piece of code is called in another function in another place, perhaps even in another file.

Let's see a declarative approach to the problem:

```
import Combine
import UIKit

class ViewController: UIViewController {
    @IBOutlet weak var textField: UITextField!
    @IBOutlet weak var button: UIButton!

    private var subscriptions = Set<AnyCancellable>()

    override func viewDidLoad() {
        super.viewDidLoad()

textField.publisher(for: \.text)
        .map { $0?.isEmpty == false }
        .assign(to: \.isEnabled, on: button)
    .store(in: &subscriptions)
}
}
```

In the preceding code, we can see a much clearer solution to enable a button based on a text field input. We observe the text field "editing changed" event, map the `isEmpty` property to another Boolean, and assign it to the button's `isEnabled` property.

This means we declare what happens when a particular value is changed without any control flows or delegates.

The two coding paradigms contrast significantly when dealing with more complex workflows.

"How does declarative programming help handle state management in iOS apps?"

Why is this question important?

There's a strong relationship between declarative programming and state management. Before we answer that question, it is essential to understand what is considered a state and think about how you ever used a state in your apps.

Generally, a state is a condition of our app, screen, or view.

For example, a state can be a Boolean variable that represents whether the user is logged in to your app. Another example of a state is whether a button should be visible.

It is clear that a state is something we all used in our apps before, and in declarative programming, the state is a primary topic.

What is the answer?

Look at my last example – "whether a button should be visible." It seems like a great idea to have a state for button visibility. The problem is that every time we change the state value, we must also ensure that the button is updated.

One option is to use a `didSet` property observer:

```
var isTextEmpty: Bool = true {
    didSet {
        // Disable the button if the text is empty,
            enable it otherwise
        button.isEnabled = !isTextEmpty
    }
}
```

Even though a `didSet` property observer is a simple way to bind the state to button visibility, it's not the ideal solution for a few reasons:

- **Separation of concerns**: A variable can only have one property observer, meaning we cannot separate different concerns or responsibilities. For instance, we cannot have one `didSet` block for analytics and another `didSet` block for UI updates.

- **Not testable**: This relates to the previous point. Because the `didSet` block contains multiple actions, including possible UI changes, testing it can be challenging because it can have additional possible side effects.

- **Can't observe multiple variables**: It's nice to observe one property, but what if we want to observe changes in numerous properties and perform one action based on that change? `didSet` is not suitable for that.

Now, here's the Combine example version:

```
private var cancellables = Set<AnyCancellable>()
private var buttonVisible = PassthroughSubject<Bool,
    Never>()

override func viewDidLoad() {
    super.viewDidLoad()
    buttonVisible
        .assign(to: \.isEnabled, on: button)
        .store(in: &cancellables)
}
```

The Combine version is a much more elegant way of handling a state. We bind the state to button enablement just like we did with the `didSet` example. But this time, we also earn more benefits, such as the following:

- We can observe the `buttonVisible` variable in *multiple places* for different purposes

- We can use multiple instances of `buttonVisible` *along with more variables*

- We can perform *async operations* more efficiently and add sophisticated operators to the stream

Declarative programming is suitable for handling states because it lets us explain precisely what to do each time the state changes, and that's ideal for state management.

Speaking of states – let's dive in and go over states in SwiftUI, as they play a significant role in screen updates and layout.

Learning states and observable objects

"States" is a primary topic in SwiftUI and declarative programming. Unlike imperative programming, where we can directly update UI elements on the screen, declarative programming *works in the opposite way* – we update the state, and the UI is updated according to our changes.

In fact, using states is the only way to create dynamic views in SwiftUI.

SwiftUI uses something called a property wrapper to mark certain variables as states.

Here are some of them:

- `@State`: To manage simple UI state
- `@Binding`: To allow two directional updates between the view and its children
- `@ObservedObject`: To share data between views
- `@EnvironmentObject`: To share data between views across an app

When asked about SwiftUI, these different property wrappers play a significant role in understanding how SwiftUI works and building a full-featured app with SwiftUI.

If you want to read more about managing user interface state in SwiftUI, you can visit `https://developer.apple.com/documentation/swiftui/managing-user-interface-state`. For an overview of property wrappers, check out the link at `https://www.swift.org/blog/property-wrappers/`.

Now, let's look at two critical questions about that topic.

"Can you explain the differences and use cases for the @State and @Binding property wrappers in SwiftUI?"

Why is this question important?

These two property wrappers are fundamental to understanding how SwiftUI works. Going back to the *Understanding declarative programming* section, `@State` and `@Binding` are pure implementations of the concept of declarative programming.

`@State` and `@Binding` are essential wrappers to create complex and reusable views.

What is the answer?

`@State` is a property wrapper used to manage local states within a view. It's used for simple values managed by a single view, such as toggles or form data. When the value of a `@State` property changes, **SwiftUI** will automatically update the view to reflect the new state. Here's an example:

```
struct MyView: View {
    @State var toggleIsOn = false

    var body: some View {
        Toggle(isOn: $toggleIsOn) {
            Text("Toggle is on: \(toggleIsOn.description)")
        }
    }
}
```

The `toggleIsOn` variable is wrapped in `@State`, allowing the SwiftUI to observe and update `MyView` if needed. Within the view, there is `Toggle` that is linked to the `toggleIsOn` state. As the state value changes, a corresponding text is updated.

`@Binding` is a property wrapper that provides a two-way connection between the child's and parent's views. It's used to pass the state down the view hierarchy, allowing child views to modify values stored in a parent view. When the value of a `@Binding` property changes, both the child and parent views will be updated to reflect the new state. Here's an example:

```
struct MyParentView: View {
    @State var toggleIsOn = false

    var body: some View {
        VStack {
            MyChildView(toggleIsOn: $toggleIsOn)
            Text("Toggle is on: \(toggleIsOn.description)")
        }
    }
}

struct MyChildView: View {
    @Binding var toggleIsOn: Bool

    var body: some View {
        Toggle(isOn: $toggleIsOn) {
            Text("Toggle is on: \(toggleIsOn.description)")
        }
    }
}
```

In this example, `MyParentView` manages the `toggleIsOn` state and passes it down to `MyChildView` using a `@Binding` property. `MyChildView` can then modify the state by updating the `toggleIsOn` property. Both views are automatically updated to reflect the new state when this happens.

We can see that `@State` and `@Binding` have a strong relationship. `@State` is `@Binding` of its child view. If we compare this to imperative programming with UIKit, the `@Binding` feature is similar to the delegate pattern we know and love but much more powerful, simple, and mainly declarative.

"What is the purpose of @ObservedObject in SwiftUI, and in what situations would you use it instead of @State or @Binding?"

Why is this question important?

Now that we know what `@State` and `@Bining` roles are in SwiftUI, we must understand how `@ObservedObject` fits into our app architecture and how it differs from other view property wrappers.

What is the answer?

The @ObservedObject property wrapper in **SwiftUI** is used to share a reference to an object between multiple views. This is particularly useful when dealing with complex data models used by multiple app views. When a view is updated with new data, any other views that reference the same object via @ObservedObject will also automatically be updated.

Can the observed object be a singleton? Definitely. More importantly, it should be the same instance we inject into the different views.

Let's look at *Figure 8.1*:

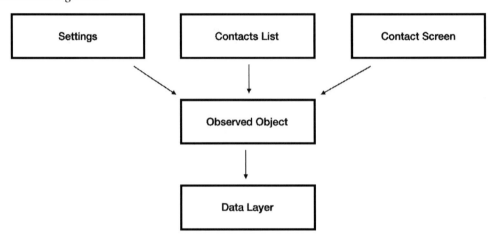

Figure 8.1: The role of an observed object in our app architecture

Figure 8.1 shows the different dependencies when using an observed object. It is an excellent practice to add more layers to our app that manage stuff such as persistent data and networking, and keep the observed object to share the data between the views.

Let's see a SwiftUI code example of a contacts list with the observed object.

First, the contacts list view:

```
import SwiftUI

struct ContactListView: View {
    @ObservedObject var viewModel : ContactViewModel
    var body: some View {
        List(viewModel.contacts) { contact in Text(contact.name ?? "")
        }
    }
}
```

We can see that the contacts list uses an observed object named `viewModel` that can be injected into the view or used as a **singleton**. What is unique about `@ObservedObject` is that SwiftUI doesn't recreate it whenever it needs to refresh the view, so it can safely store data.

Now, let's see what the `ContactViewModel` class looks like:

```
class ContactViewModel: ObservableObject {

    @Published var contacts = [Contact]()
    private let dataLayer: ContactDataLayer

    init(dataLayer: ContactDataLayer) {
        self.dataLayer = dataLayer
        loadContacts()
    }

    func loadContacts() {
        contacts = dataLayer.loadContacts()
    }
}
```

There are three important things to note in this code example:

- **Conforming to the** `ObservableObject` **protocol**: If we want the class to be an observed object, we need it to conform to the `ObservableObject` protocol.

- **Using** `@Published` **for the contacts list**: The contacts list variable has a `@Published` property wrapper, which lets the view observe changes in the contacts list.

- **DataLayer as a dependency**: To adhere to the separation of concerns principle, we separate the actual fetching and storing from the sharing class. The only responsibility of the `ContactViewModel` class is to share data between views. The `ContactDataLayer` class does the persistent operations.

To summarize, `ObservedObject` is a mechanism that facilitates data sharing among views. It is easy to grasp and incorporate and can help divide a project's structure into distinct layers.

Navigating SwiftUI views

Navigation in mobile apps was always a critical issue. UIKit supported navigation from day one, and SwiftUI launched with essential support from `NavigationView`.

Navigation in SwiftUI is quite different than UIKit. While in UIKit, we had to create a new view controller and push it to a stack using `UINavigationController`, in SwiftUI, it works slightly differently.

Remember we discussed declarative programming earlier in this chapter? This is how navigation works in SwiftUI. Instead of creating and pushing a new view, we use the state to present sheets, modals, and links to navigate to a new view.

Let's see how to present a modal view using state modification in SwiftUI:

```
struct ContentView: View {
    @State var isModalPresented = false

    var body: some View {
        VStack {
            Button("Present Modal") {
                isModalPresented = true
            }
        }
        .sheet(isPresented: $isModalPresented) {
            ModalView()
        }
    }
}
```

In this example, we have a state variable called `isModalPresented`. When a user taps the `Present Modal` button, we set `isModalPresented` to `true`, which triggers the view modifier **sheet** to present a view named `ModalView`.

Presenting a modal using a state may feel weird for developers who worked years with imperative programming, but this pattern fits naturally into declarative programming.

Now, let's move on to some interesting questions about SwiftUI navigation.

"How do you pass data between views using the SwiftUI navigation system?"

Why is this question important?

Passing data between views is critical to implementing an effective navigation pattern.

And this is not a trivial question – other patterns enable us to navigate to a new view without passing data. We can use the observed object pattern, which we reviewed in the previous section, or we can use some global state manager to understand what data to present.

However, it is considered a best practice to pass data to a new screen for better separation and modularity.

What is the answer?

The answer is that there are no tricks here that we don't already know from other patterns in UIKit.

The best way to pass data between views is to *inject the data when initiating the new view.*

Let's create a screen with a list of countries:

```
struct Country {
    let name: String
}

class DataStore {
    let countries = [
        Country(name: "USA"),
        Country(name: "Canada"),
        Country(name: "Mexico")
    ]
}

struct CountryListView: View {
    let dataStore = DataStore()

    var body: some View {
        NavigationView {
            List(dataStore.countries, id: \.name)
                { country in
                NavigationLink(destination:
                    CountryDetailView(country: country)) {
                    Text(country.name)
                }
            }
            .navigationTitle("Countries")
        }
    }
}
```

Now, let's create `CountryDetailView` with the `country` property:

```
struct CountryDetailView: View {
    let country: Country

    var body: some View {
        Text("Selected country: \(country.name)")
            .navigationTitle("Country Detail")
    }
}
```

The `CountryDetailView` struct has a property named `country`. In Swift, the compiler automatically generates a member-wise initializer for their properties. We use that to pass the `country` object when initializing `CountryDetailView`.

As we can see, it is straightforward to pass data between views just by using dependency injection. We can also evaluate that pattern and pass a state on one side and a binding on the next view to create a two-directional update between the two views, such as a delegate pattern in UIKit.

"Can you explain how to use @Environment(\.presentationMode) to dismiss a presented view in SwiftUI navigation?"

Why is this question important?

Using `NavigationLink` to move to a new place is easy, but how do we dismiss or navigate back?

This question tests our understanding of navigation and a property wrapper called `@Environment`, which can expose environment variables that provide more capabilities.

What is the answer?

`@Environment(\.presentationMode)` is a property wrapper that provides access to a view's presentation mode, allowing us to dismiss a presented view in SwiftUI navigation.

Here's an example of how to use `@Environment(\.presentationMode)` to dismiss a presented view:

```
struct DetailView: View {
    @Environment(\.presentationMode) var presentationMode

    var body: some View {
        VStack {
            Text("Detail View")

            Button("Dismiss") {
                presentationMode.wrappedValue.dismiss()
            }
        }
        .navigationTitle("Detail View")
    }
}
```

In this example, we have `DetailView` currently presented on the screen. We use the `@Environment(\.presentationMode)` property wrapper to access the view's presentation mode.

Once the user taps the **Dismiss** button, we call `presentationMode` to dismiss the function, which takes us back to the previous screen.

Note that if the view is not currently presented, we'll get a runtime error trying to do that. Therefore, if we are not sure whether the view is presented before we dismiss it, we can check using the same presentation mode:

```
if presentationMode.wrappedValue.isPresented {
    Button("Dismiss") {
        presentationMode.wrappedValue.dismiss()
    }
}
```

In this code example, the **Dismiss** button appears only if the view is presented, and since it's declarative, it will be hidden when it's not.

Navigation is a crucial component of any mobile app, and in a way, it becomes even more straightforward with SwiftUI. The preceding two questions should be enough for us to prepare for this part of the interview.

Expertise with the SwiftUI life cycle

We can't build UI screens without fully understanding the UI life cycle. States and modifiers such as `onChange` and `onAppear` are integral to the SwiftUI life cycle and essential to building a functional application.

We already went on some of the things related to the SwiftUI life cycle in the previous sections – for example, observed objects and states are part of the SwiftUI life cycle. Now, we must understand how they work when a view needs to reload, change, or move to a new screen.

"How does SwiftUI handle state changes during the view life cycle?"

Why is this question important?

SwiftUI's approach to state management differs from traditional UIKit or AppKit approaches, and it's crucial to understand how SwiftUI handles state changes and updates to avoid unexpected behavior in our app.

What is the answer?

SwiftUI generates the view hierarchy based on the current state. SwiftUI generates a new view hierarchy whenever the state changes and compares it to the current displayed hierarchy.

This means that all the variables are regenerated each time, except for the property wrappers such as `@State` and `@Binding`. The comparison to the current view tells SwiftUI what views it needs to update to reflect the new state. SwiftUI applies the changes to the user interface by adding, removing, or updating current views.

This process is very efficient because SwiftUI only updates the parts of the user interface that need to be changed.

Look at the following code:

```
struct ContentView: View {
    @State var labelText = "Hello, World!"

    var body: some View {
        VStack {
            Text(labelText)
                .padding()
            Button("Change Label Text") {
                labelText = "New Label Text"
            }
        }
    }
}
```

When the user taps the button, it changes the `labelText` state. In this case, SwiftUI generates a new view with a new value for the label (`Text`) and compares it to the current view hierarchy. Since only `Text` was changed and the button stayed the same, SwiftUI will only update `Text` and won't render the whole screen to keep it much more efficient.

"How do you use the onChange modifier in SwiftUI, and what state changes does it respond to?"

Why is this question important?

This question is important because it assesses our understanding of responding to state changes in SwiftUI. Responding to state changes is a fundamental aspect of building user interfaces in SwiftUI, and an onChange modifier is a key tool to accomplish this task.

What is the answer?

We use the onChange modifier to respond to changes in a specific state variable. When applied to a view, the onChange modifier will execute a closure when the specified state variable changes.

Look at the following syntax:

```
.onChange(of: stateVariable) { newValue in
    // Execute code here
}
```

In this syntax, `stateVariable` is the name of the state we want to observe, and `newValue` is the new value of that variable.

Here are some use cases we can think of for the preceding:

- Updating a view's layout in response to changes in a user's input

- Changing the button color when it is tapped

- Updating the layout in response to an environmental change

- Responding to changes in a data model and presenting a banner

- Navigating to a new screen when networking loading has finished

Here's an example of the last use case – navigating to a new screen when network loading has finished and the model updates:

```
struct ContentView: View {
    @StateObject var viewModel = ViewModel()
    @State private var navigateToDetail = false

    var body: some View {
        NavigationView {
            VStack {
                if viewModel.isLoading {
                    ProgressView("Loading...")
                } else {
                    Button("View Detail") {
                        viewModel.loadDetail()
                    }
                }
            }
            .onChange(of: viewModel.detail) { detail in
                if detail != nil {
                    navigateToDetail = true
                }
            }
            .sheet(isPresented: $navigateToDetail) {
                DetailView(detail: viewModel.detail!)
            }
            .navigationBarTitle("Content")
        }
    }
}
```

We can see that the code observes the `viewModel` detail property, and once it is populated, it navigates to a new view.

Expertise in Combine

We already discussed declarative programming throughout this chapter, so now, let's focus on the Combine framework for a second.

Apple introduced Combine in WWDC 2019 as part of the iOS 13 version. Combine is Apple's response to other popular reactive frameworks, such as React and **RxSwift**.

The Combine framework helps developers build reactive applications with robust async operations and data updates.

There are three main components in Combine:

- **Publishers**: A publisher is an object that emits a stream of values over time. Publishers can be thought of as a source of data, which can come from various sources, such as user input, network requests, or timers. Publishers can emit values of different types, such as integers, strings, or custom data types, and can emit an unlimited number of values or a finite number of values.

- **Operators**: Operators are functions that can be used to transform, filter, or combine streams of values emitted by publishers. Operators can take one or more publishers as input and return a new publisher that emits transformed values. Some examples of operators are `map`, `filter`, `flatMap`, and `zip`.

- **Subscribers**: A subscriber is an object that receives and processes values emitted by a publisher. Subscribers can be considered consumers of data, which can handle the values emitted by a publisher in various ways, such as printing to a console, updating a user interface, or storing in a database. A subscriber can receive values of different types, requesting a certain number of values or receiving an unlimited number.

By combining publishers, operators, and subscribers, we can create powerful data streams between the different parts of our app.

Let's see an example of Combine usage:

```
import Combine

let numbersPublisher = PassthroughSubject<Int, Never>()
let lettersPublisher = PassthroughSubject<String, Never>()

let cancellable = Publishers
    .combineLatest(numbersPublisher, lettersPublisher)
    .map { (number, letter) -> String in
        return "Number: \(number), Letter: \(letter)"
    }
    .filter { value in
        return value.count > 10
```

```
    }
    .sink { value in
        print(value)
    }

numbersPublisher.send(1)
lettersPublisher.send("A")
numbersPublisher.send(2)
lettersPublisher.send("B")
```

In this example, we will demonstrate the different components in Combine, as previously described:

1. We have two different publishers (`numbersPublisher` and `lettersPublisher`) that send different values over time.

2. We *combine* these two publishers using the `combineLatest` operator, which returns a publisher with the two most updated values each time one of the publishers is updated.

3. We then *map the values* to one string using the `map` operator, followed by a filter operator that returns only strings with more than 10 characters.

4. The `sink` method helps to *subscribe to the Combine stream* and print the output.

This complex yet interesting Combine stream demonstrates all the different Combine components effectively.

If you want to read more about Combine basics and principles, you can visit `https://developer.apple.com/documentation/combine#`.

Now, let's move on to some questions about Combine.

"Can you provide an example of how you would use Combine in an iOS app?"

Why is this question important?

The complex Combine example I just showed you is nice but not very practical, and it's there only to explain Combine framework principles.

The real challenge is understanding where to implement Combine in our app architecture in a real-world use case.

What is the answer?

Combine has many real-world use cases. Let's name some of them:

*   Performing *network requests* and handling data or errors
*   Updating UI elements with *data bindings* or state changes

- Validating *user input* and showing feedback
- Implementing *MVVM* or other architectural patterns
- Working with timers, notifications, *key-value observing*, and so on

Since we are requested to provide an example of where we would use Combine in our app, here's one where we bind data to UI.

In the following example, we observe the number of notifications and update the notifications button with the relevant image:

```
import UIKit
import Combine

class ViewController: UIViewController {
    @IBOutlet weak var notificationsButton: UIButton!
    private var cancellables = Set<AnyCancellable>()

    override func viewDidLoad() {
        super.viewDidLoad()

        let notificationsPublisher = NotificationsManager.
            shared.getNotificationsPublisher()

        notificationsPublisher
            .map { count -> UIImage? in
                if count > 0 {
                    return UIImage(systemName: "bell.
                        fill")?.withTintColor(.red)
                } else {
                    return UIImage(systemName: "bell")
                }
            }
            .assign(to: \.image, on: notificationsButton)
            .store(in: &cancellables)
    }
}
```

In our code example, we can see an excellent binding between data and a specific UI element. This example can also be used for other examples – title updates, color changes, button visibility, and so on.

Binding data as a UI element is also an excellent technique in the *MVVM design pattern*, where we can bind a state between the view model and the view.

Now, let's see a more complex example of how to use Combine – to fetch data from a network request and update a table view while using the MVVM design pattern:

```swift
import UIKit
import Combine

struct Article: Codable {
    let title: String
    let description: String
    let url: URL
}

class ArticlesViewModel {
    private let url = URL(string: "https://api.example.com/articles")!
    private let decoder = JSONDecoder()
    @Published private(set) var articles: [Article] = []

    init() {
        fetchArticles()
    }

    private func fetchArticles() {
        URLSession.shared.dataTaskPublisher(for: url)
            .map { $0.data }
            .decode(type: [Article].self, decoder: decoder)
            .replaceError(with: [])
            .receive(on: DispatchQueue.main)
            .assign(to: &$articles)
    }
}
```

The `fetchArticles()` function does most of the job while requesting data, mapping it, decoding it to the `articles` array, moving it to the main thread, and assigning the data to the `articles` `published` variable.

Now, let's look at the view controller:

```swift
class ArticlesTableViewController: UITableViewController {
    private let viewModel = ArticlesViewModel()
    private var cancellables = Set<AnyCancellable>()

    override func viewDidLoad() {
        super.viewDidLoad()
        viewModel.$articles
```

```
            .receive(on: DispatchQueue.main)
            .sink(receiveValue: { [weak self] _ in
                self?.tableView.reloadData()
            })
            .store(in: &cancellables)
    }

    override func tableView(_ tableView: UITableView,
        numberOfRowsInSection section: Int) -> Int {
        return viewModel.articles.count
    }

    override func tableView(_ tableView: UITableView,
        cellForRowAt indexPath: IndexPath) ->
            UITableViewCell {
        let cell = tableView.dequeueReusableCell
            (withIdentifier: "ArticleCell", for: indexPath)
        let article = viewModel.articles[indexPath.row]
        cell.textLabel?.text = article.title
        cell.detailTextLabel?.text = article.description
        return cell
    }
}
```

In the view controller, we bind the `articles` array to the table view by observing changes and reloading the data each time we get an update.

The last example shows how to use Combine to chain different operators to perform a network request, parsing, moving to the main thread, and handling errors in a few lines of code.

I think these two examples represent many widespread use cases with Combine. We should learn them thoroughly, which will help us answer this question efficiently.

"How do you debug a Combine stream?"

Why is this question important?

We already know that debugging is critical for developers, not only iOS developers.

Most of our experience with debugging as iOS developers revolves around imperative programming and standard code flows. On the other hand, Combine brings something different to the table, with new challenges in the debugging area.

In this question, the interviewer wants to hear how we handle Combine issues we may encounter in our job.

What is the answer?

We can debug Combine streams using Xcode built-in debugging tools, such as setting breakpoints, inspecting variables, and stepping through code execution.

However, the Combine framework offers additional tools to help us debug. Let's list two of them.

Reading the console with print() and handleEvents()

The print operator is a debugging tool that allows us to print the events that flow through a Combine pipeline. We can use it to visualize the data transformations and identify unexpected behavior or errors. The print operator can be placed at any point in the pipeline and will print all events that occur downstream of it.

Here's an example that demonstrates how to use the print operator:

```
import Combine

let numbers = [1, 2, 3, 4, 5]
let publisher = numbers.publisher

let pipeline = publisher
    .map { $0 * 2 }
    .print("Debug:")
    .filter { $0 % 3 == 0 }

let subscriber = Subscribers.Sink<Int, Never>(
    receiveCompletion: { completion in
        print("Completion: \(completion)")
    },
    receiveValue: { value in
        print("Value: \(value)")
    }
)
```

In this example, we use the print operator to label the debug output with "Debug:". This will help us distinguish the debug logs from any other output in the console. When we run this code, we will see the following output in the console:

```
Debug: receive subscription: (Sequence)
Debug: request unlimited
Debug: receive value: (2)
Debug: receive value: (6)
Debug: receive value: (10)
Completion: finished
```

The `handleEvents` operator is similar to the `print` operator, but instead of printing the events, it allows us to trigger side effects at specific points in the pipeline.

We can use it to perform actions such as logging, updating UI elements, or triggering notifications. The `handleEvents` operator can be placed at any point in the pipeline, and it will trigger the side effects for all events that occur downstream of it.

Here's an example that demonstrates how to use the `handleEvents` operator:

```
let pipeline = publisher
    .map { $0 * 2 }
    .handleEvents(
        receiveSubscription: { subscription in
            print("Subscription: \(subscription)")
        },
        receiveOutput: { output in
            print("Output: \(output)")
        },
        receiveCompletion: { completion in
            print("Completion: \(completion)")
        },
        receiveCancel: {
            print("Cancelled")
        }
    )
    .filter { $0 % 3 == 0 }
```

With the `handleEvents` operator, we can print each event separately and have complete control of our printing operations.

Including breakpoints in our stream

The Combine framework provides additional operators to generate breakpoints in our streams.

The first and primary operator is `breakpoint()`, which can help us pause a program at specific events, similar to `handleEvents()`:

```
let pipeline = publisher
    .map { $0 * 2 }
    .breakpoint(
        receiveSubscription: { subscription in
            return false
        },
        receiveOutput: { output in
            print("Output: \(output)")
```

```
            return output > 8
        },
        receiveCompletion: { completion in
            return true
        }
    )
    .filter { $0 % 3 == 0 }
```

In this code, we pause the program on completion or when the output is bigger than eight by returning true in the corresponding places.

The second breakpoint operator is `breakpointOnError()`, which pauses the program when any of the upstream publishers throws an error:

```
let pipeline = publisher
    .tryMap { value -> Int in
        if value == 4 {
            throw ExampleError.example
        }
        return value * 2
    }
    .breakpointOnError()
    .filter { $0 % 3 == 0 }
```

This example is simple – the `tryMap` operator throws an error. Therefore, the program will pause, thanks to the `breakpointOnError()` command.

Both `breakpoint()` and `breakpointOnError()` are great ways to pause a program when we need to perform deep Combine issue investigations.

Summary

In this chapter, we went over critical topics in declarative programming, SwiftUI, and Combine. We discussed the SwiftUI life cycle, debugging Combine, real-world examples, navigation, and states. By now, we should be fully covered for our interview when asked about SwiftUI and Combine.

The next chapter is a bit different. We will discuss a critical layer in our architecture – the data layer and, specifically, the persistent data layer.

9

Understanding Persistent Memory

While, as iOS developers, we primarily focus on UI-related topics such as UIKit and SwiftUI, there are other essential aspects of iOS development to consider, such as persistent memory. This topic is critical as it enables us to store and retrieve information even after an app is closed.

There are many benefits to managing persistent memory well, some of which are detailed here:

- **Improving user experience**: Apps that can save and retrieve user data later provide a better user experience. For instance, if the user has downloaded information from our backend server, we can show it to them the next time they enter the app without waiting for network requests to complete.

- **Providing offline access**: Offline access is a great feature allowing users to work with our app even when they are offline. For example, a messaging app may allow users to view their previous conversations even when they don't have an internet connection.

- **Keeping a local state**: With persistent memory, we can keep a local state even after the app is closed. For example, storing access tokens, user profile details, or continuing the user experience from the last time the user stopped are essential features we can add to our app.

Persistent memory is a critical component for iOS developers, involving user experience, security, and efficiency.

This chapter covers the following important topics in persistent memory:

- Mastering *Core Data* questions
- Handling persistent state with `UserDefaults`
- Storing sensitive information in the *Keychain*
- Working with the *filesystem*

Many young developers are often intimidated by a framework called Core Data. Let's begin by exploring this topic.

Mastering Core Data questions

Most interviewers don't ask about general frameworks (besides UIKit, SwiftUI, and Foundation), but Core Data is considered an exception. **Core Data** is a fundamental framework in iOS development because it's an optimized and simple solution for setting up our data layer and managing a persistent store.

Core Data evolved over the years and became a primary framework for many developers. It is integrated perfectly into the iOS development ecosystem, working perfectly with Xcode and other iOS frameworks.

There are several concepts to know about Core Data:

- **Data model**: Core Data is built around a data model, which defines the data structure stored in the app. The data model is typically determined using Xcode's data modeling tool and includes entities (which represent objects in the app), attributes (which describe properties of those objects), and relationships (which define how entities are related to each other).

- **Managed object context**: The managed object context is the heart of the Core Data framework. It is responsible for managing the life cycle of the app's data objects (known as "managed objects") and provides a way for the app to query, create, update, and delete those objects. It is also responsible for handling undo/redo operations and managing object relationships.

- **Persistent store coordinator**: The persistent store coordinator is responsible for managing the app's persistent store, where the data is stored on disk. It coordinates communication between the managed object context and the persistent store and ensures that changes made to the managed object context are properly persisted to disk.

- **Fetch requests**: We use Fetch requests to query the app's data model and retrieve specific objects from the managed object context. We can also customize Fetch requests with predicates (to filter results), sort descriptors (to order results), and fetch limits (to limit the number of results returned).

- **Relationships**: Core Data provides a powerful mechanism for defining relationships between entities in the data model. Relationships can be one-to-one, one-to-many, or many-to-many and can be uni-directional or bi-directional. Relationships can also be configured with delete rules, which define how objects should be deleted when a relationship is broken.

- **Migration**: Core Data includes tools for migrating data between different data model versions. This allows developers to change the data model over time while preserving existing data.

There's another important term we know about Core Data, and that's the **Core Data Stack**. The Core Data Stack is a layer set that allows our app to interact with the persistent store.

Here are the three Core Data Stack layers:

- **Managed object model**: This is the bottom layer containing the data model. Because everything is built around the data structure, we start with that layer.

- **Persistent store coordinator**: This is the persistent store coordinator built upon the object model. The coordinator uses the data model to define a corresponding persistent store that matches the data scheme. The store could be based on XML, SQLite, JSON, or a backend service. Core Data allows us to base the persistent store upon any technology we want. Another essential thing to remember about the persistent store is that it needs match the data model exactly. Any change in the data model will require a modification to the store and migration.

- **Managed object context**: This is the managed object context that manages the life cycle of the app's data objects (known as "managed objects"). It provides a way for the app to query, create, update, and delete those objects. It is also responsible for handling undo/redo operations and managing object relationships.

We need to set up the Core Data Stack to start using Core Data. This can be done quickly using NSPersistentContainer:

```
import CoreData

// 1. Create a persistent container
let container = NSPersistentContainer(name: "MyDataModel")

// 2. Load the persistent store
container.loadPersistentStores { (storeDescription, error)
    in
    if let error = error {
        fatalError("Failed to load persistent store: \(error)")
    }
}

// 3. Create a managed object context
let context = container.viewContext
```

In the code example, we use **NSPersistentContainer** to load a data model named MyDataModel. This line also creates the persistent store and returns a container object.

Afterward, we *load* the persistent store into the stack and create a managed object context so we can start working with Core Data.

Once we have the context, we can perform entity creation, fetching, updates, and deletion:

```
let newEmployee = Employee(context: context)
newEmployee.name = "John Doe"
newEmployee.title = "Software Engineer"
newEmployee.startDate = Date()
do {
```

```
    try context.save()
} catch {
    fatalError("Failed to save context: \(error)")
}
```

The code is so simple that it speaks for itself. We create a new `Employee` object based on the context we created earlier, set its properties, and save the new object using the `context` save method.

`Employee` is a subclass of `NSManagedObject`, and it allows us direct access to the entity's properties and an easy way to modify its data. The `context.save()` action commits the changes into the persistent store.

Generally speaking, the primary usage of Core Data is straightforward, and it has become even simpler over the years. While setting up a Core Data Stack is essential to using Core Data, it's not the only aspect developers need to master. Due to the challenges and complexities of working with Core Data, interviewers often ask about these challenges rather than just the basic setup.

Here are some challenges we may consider learning well before the interview:

- **Handling concurrency**: Concurrency is a complex topic not only in Core Data but in any persistent store or local data. Several techniques and patterns exist for performing concurrency jobs in Core Data and avoiding data loss and exceptions.

- **Designing a data model**: Technically, setting up a data model with entities and attributes is a simple job as we perform most of the work in a model editor, a built-in Xcode editor. But the real challenge is to *design* the data model in a way that serves our app's critical journeys and tasks. We need to master the primary terms such as **to-many** and **to-one** and fully understand the **deletion rules**.

- **Understanding data migrations**: We'll have to modify our data model, adding, editing, and removing entities and attributes over time. Changing the data model while there's data in the persistent store is called "data migrations," which is also a critical topic we, as iOS developers, need to understand and know how to perform. Mistakes in this area may lead to data corruption and even crashes.

Now, let's transition to some Core Data-related questions specifically addressing these topics.

"How do you design a Core Data Stack that supports concurrency while ensuring thread safety, and how can you use NSManagedObjectIDs in a multi-threaded environment to facilitate this?"

Why is this question important?

Concurrency is an important top in Core Data development, and handling concurrency well shows a deep understanding of how Core Data context works.

If we understand how Core Data context works, we should also answer the second part of this question – the NSManagedObjectID, which can help us identify an object in different contexts.

What is the answer?

First, let's talk about two principles that are related to Core Data concurrency:

- **Considering a context as a sandbox**: When working with contexts, we can create objects, update, and delete them. We do all that only in the context and not in the persistent store. When we call the save() method, Core Data pushes the changes to the parent context and, if there isn't any parent context, to the persistent store. We should think of context as a sandbox – we can perform changes and commit them only when ready.

- **Accessing a context from the same thread that created it**: In Core Data, a context belongs to a thread. Once we create a new background thread, we can't access an object created or fetched in another thread. Each thread needs to have its context to allow it.

After we understand these two principles, we can try to define the different patterns for setting up our Core Data Stack. These patterns rely on our application needs and requirements.

Let's go over them.

Working with multiple contexts

We have several private contexts in multiple context patterns, and each works directly with the persistent store. The multiple contexts are responsible for reading and writing and provide a flexible way to handle different concurrency operations across our app and do that even in a modular way.

Here's an example:

```
let persistentContainer = NSPersistentContainer(name: "MyApp")
persistentContainer.loadPersistentStores(completionHandler: {
(storeDescription, error) in
    if let error = error {
        fatalError("Failed to load persistent store: \(error)")
    }
})

let writeContext = NSManagedObjectContext(concurrencyType:
    .privateQueueConcurrencyType)
writeContext.persistentStoreCoordinator =
    persistentContainer.persistentStoreCoordinator

let readContext = NSManagedObjectContext(concurrencyType:
    .privateQueueConcurrencyType)
readContext.persistentStoreCoordinator =
    persistentContainer.persistentStoreCoordinator
```

In this example, we create two contexts for writing (`writeContext`) and reading (`readContext`). It is important to note that changes we make to the writing context don't reflect on the read context until we perform saving and re-fetching.

There are some significant drawbacks to multiple contexts patterns. For example, this pattern can add complexity to our database and requires us to manage changes between contexts.

Another drawback we may encounter is complexity with features such as batch changes and redo/undo, which can be critical in some application use cases.

However, we have a decent alternative: the parent-child context. Let's talk about it.

Working with parent-child context

If the multiple contexts pattern has a "flat" structure, the parent-child pattern is more hierarchical. The basic principle states that we have a root context (aka "parent") dedicated to writing operations and child contexts dedicated to reading operations. The parent context is private, and the child contexts work with the main queue. Every change we make in the writing context is reflected in the child's contexts.

The parent-child pattern is excellent for background updates, offline editing, and undo-redo use cases.

Here's a code example for the parent-child pattern:

```
let parentContext = NSManagedObjectContext(concurrencyType:
    .privateQueueConcurrencyType)
parentContext.persistentStoreCoordinator =
    persistentStoreCoordinator

let readContext1 = NSManagedObjectContext(concurrencyType:
    .mainQueueConcurrencyType)
readContext1.parent = parentContext

let readContext2 = NSManagedObjectContext(concurrencyType:
    .mainQueueConcurrencyType)
readContext2.parent = parentContext
```

We can see the parent context is private, and the children are the main ones. Also, we can see how we linked the children to their parent directly and not to the persistent store.

> **What does a "private context" mean?**
> A private context is typically used to perform background tasks such as importing or exporting data, allowing those tasks to be performed asynchronously without blocking the main thread.

Overall, both parent-child and multiple contexts serve different purposes and use cases. It is important to say they provide basic principles for managing concurrency with Core Data. Combining these patterns or even using their principles to create a new pattern is perfectly fine.

And what about using NSManagedObjectID?

When working with contexts, we cannot take a managed object fetched in one context and use it in another. We need to re-fetch it using NSManagedObjectID. That critical point may lead to an exception if not done right.

Here's a code example of re-fetching the same object in another context using NSManagedObjectID:

```
var object: MyEntity?
let fetchRequest: NSFetchRequest<MyEntity> = MyEntity.fetchRequest()
fetchRequest.predicate = NSPredicate (format: "id == %@", someID)
do {
    object = try mainContext.fetch(fetchRequest).first
} catch {
    print("Error fetching object: \(error)")
}

guard let objectID = object?.objectID else {
    return
}

Let backgroundContext = NSManagedObjectContext
    (concurrencyType: .privateQueueConcurrencyType)
backgroundContext.persistentStoreCoordinator =
    persistentStoreCoordinator
backgroundContext.perform {
    let backgroundObject = backgroundContext.object(with:objectID)
}
```

Each managed object has a property named objectID, which is identical to the same object across different contexts. Its primary purpose is precisely that – to ensure working with the same object when moving between contexts. NSManagedObjectID is an essential concept when performing concurrency operations in Core Data.

"What would your Core Data data model look like for a recipe app that includes ingredients, cooking instructions, and user ratings?"

Why is this question important?

We are iOS developers and not DBAs, but we have significant weight in designing a data model that fits our app business needs. A bad data model design directly influences the app's performance and stability. As developers, it is our responsibility to convert the requirements and workflows of an app into a technical design, and this question evaluates our proficiency in achieving that objective.

What is the answer?

Creating a data model for a specific app usage requires us to follow these steps:

1. Understand the *app's needs* and basic flows.
2. Define the *different entities and their attributes*, including the data types, default values, and more.
3. Create *indexes* for the relevant attributes.
4. Understand the *relationships* between the different entities – one-to-one or one-to-many.
5. Set the *deletion* rules.

These steps are always relevant when approaching a data model design, and the use case described in the question is no exception.

The first step is to identify the primary workflows of the app. It is important to remember that the data layer should support the business logic and UI and not exist independently. It's perfectly legitimate to ask the interviewer additional questions; it is even part of the task.

Second, we can define the basic entities:

-   `Recipe`: This holds the essential details for a single recipe. Attributes: title, date of creation, description, level, and category.
-   `Ingredient`: This can be shared across recipes. Attributes: name.
-   `Instruction`: This is part of the steps required when using a recipe. Attributes: description, title.
-   `User Rating`: This is a review of a single recipe. Attributes: name, rating (`int`), and description.

While entities are a crucial aspect of the data model, they are often ineffective without clearly defining the relationships between them.

So, let's understand how the entities are linked and the main challenges (because there are some!).

We understand that `Recipe` has a one-to-many relationship with `Instruction` and a one-to-many relationship with `User Rating`. That's easy. What do we do with the ingredients? The naïve approach would be to define a one-to-many relationship with `Ingredient`, just as we did with `Instruction` and `User Rating`. The thing about `Ingredient` is that we can share it across recipes. For example, let's say we have a feature that helps the user find all the recipes available based on ingredients.

In this case, a many-to-many relationship is required here. So, here's something we learn: to construct the data model effectively, it is important to communicate with the interviewer and evaluate the app's various features. We should also discuss potential use cases for the data to determine the best approach.

If we need to share ingredients between our recipes and create a many-to-many relationship, we will probably need to develop a different entity, and that's `IngredientUsage`.

`IngredientUsage` represents one usage of `Ingredient` for a recipe, and it links between `Recipe` and `Ingredient`. Besides that link, it also provides more information, such as the amount.

To explore this further, let's look at *Figure 9.1*:

Figure 9.1 – Relationships between Recipe, IngredientUsage, and Ingredient

The main issue we solve in *Figure 9.1* is that we cannot put additional information about relationships in Core Data. We can define a to-many relationship between `Recipe` and `Ingredient`, but we cannot tell the amount. The amount can't be part of `Ingredient` because we want to share the ingredient with other recipes, which probably have a different amount. That's the role of `IngredientUsage`.

Another helpful tip is to remember that a similar issue can arise during any many-to-many relationship. If it is necessary to load the relationship with more information, a dedicated entity for the relationship can effectively address this concern.

Now that we have defined the relationships between the data models, we need to consider the deletion rules. Core Data has several deletion rules, and it is important to pick the right one so we can maintain our data over time.

For example, if we delete `Recipe`, we want its `IngredientUsage`, `User Rating`, and `Instruction` data to be deleted. Therefore, we define the deletion rules between `Recipe` and the other entities as **Cascade**. Cascade is a deletion rule that deletes the related objects if the source object is being deleted.

However, that's not the case between `IngredientUsage` and `Ingredient`. If we delete `IngredientUsage`, we don't want to delete the ingredient as it is being shared with other `IngredientUsage` objects. In this case, we set the deletion rule for **Nullify**.

What about the inverse relationships? Do we need to delete a `Recipe` object if we delete one of its `User Rating` objects? Probably not. We want to keep `Recipe` if we delete a `User Rating` object. That's also the case with `Instruction`. In both cases, we set the deletion rule to *Nullify* as well.

To recap our approach, I started by outlining five fundamental steps that form the process of defining a data model. It's important to note that each step builds upon the previous one. To proceed with the answer, we can take a collaborative approach with our interviewer by walking through each step and discussing our thought process out loud. Doing that will ensure a great answer, even though the solution may not be perfect or ideal. Remember that the interviewer wants to see our thinking and not solve a real problem.

"How would you approach testing Core Data in an iOS app?"

Why is this question important?

Core Data is an essential framework that plays a significant role in the app's data layer. As such, it will be there when we are testing our app. But what does it mean? How can we test a persistent store? This question checks our understanding of the different tests we can perform with Core Data and the tools to perform them effectively and consistently.

What is the answer?

We can perform three different types of tests with Core Data, and we already discussed tests earlier in this book. If you need to refresh, go back to *Chapter 6* and ensure you are familiar with the different types of tests.

The first type of testing we can perform is the unit test – in this case, we want to simulate a Core Data Stack and not use an actual persistent store file. To do that, we can create an **in-memory** persistent store. The in-memory persistent store is lightweight, doesn't use an actual database file, and performs all the I/O operations in RAM.

Setting up an in-memory store is easy:

```
let managedObjectModel = NSManagedObjectModel.mergedModel
    (from: [Bundle.main])!
let persistentStoreCoordinator =NSPersistentStoreCoordinator
    (managedObjectModel: managedObjectModel)

do {
    try persistentStoreCoordinator.addPersistentStore(ofType:
    NSInMemoryStoreType, configurationName: nil, at: nil, options: nil)
} catch {
    fatalError("Failed to create in-memory persistent store
        coordinator: \(error)")
}
```

In the preceding code, we are adding a persistent store of type `NSInMemoryStoreType`, which only creates an in-memory store.

The second type of relevant test for Core Data is integration – in this case, we want to keep the Core Data store as it is and verify that actions we perform in the business logic or even the UI layers are being saved to the Core Data file. It is good practice to use a temporary database file or clean the data store before and after each test case.

The third test relevant to Core Data is the performance test. Core Data consists of I/O operations that can be heavy to perform, and it is a good idea to ensure we don't have any bottlenecks in our app. We can use the `measure` function in `XCTestCase` to check I/O operations:

```
func testFetchPerformance() {
    let context = persistentContainer.viewContext
    let request = NSFetchRequest<MyEntity>(entityName: "MyEntity")

    measure {
        do {
            for _ in 0..<200 {
                let result = try context.fetch(request)
            }
            let result = try context.fetch(request)
            XCTAssertEqual(result.count, 1000)
        } catch {
            XCTFail("Failed to fetch objects:
                \(error.localizedDescription)")
        }
    }
}
```

In the preceding example, we perform Core Data fetching and measure its duration. To simulate a workload, we perform the fetch operation `200` times. The test asserts when the duration exceeds a certain threshold.

To summarize – we can test Core Data in unit tests and eliminate any I/O operations, integration tests to ensure our system works as expected, and performance tests to check the impact Core Data has on our app performance.

Handling persistent state with UserDefaults

`UserDefaults` is a fundamental yet simple solution for iOS developers to store persistent information in a key-value format. We can easily store and fetch Boolean, int, string, arrays, and dictionary values with UserDefaults.

For example, this is how we store a Boolean in UserDefaults:

```
let defaults = UserDefaults.standard
defaults.set(true, forKey: "isUserLoggedIn")
```

And this is how we read it:

```
let defaults = UserDefaults.standard
let isUserLoggedIn = defaults.bool(forKey: "isUserLoggedIn")
```

The UserDefaults goal is not to store and retrieve large datasets – UserDefaults is a slow and unsecured solution for that use case. If we want to manage a local data store, we should use Core Data or SQLite for this purpose.

As mentioned earlier, UserDefaults is a very simple and straightforward tool. However, it still has some advanced capabilities we may need to know when preparing for our interview. Let's review some of them:

"Explain how an iOS app and its extensions can share data using UserDefaults. What steps are involved in setting up and using UserDefaults to share data between an app and its extensions?"

Why is this question important?

Many apps live happily isolated during their lifetime. But once we add an extension or another app, we will probably need to share some data between them. For example, we might need to share keys, tokens, or profile information.

Luckily, Apple provides us with a secure and easy way to do just that. Let's look at the answer.

What is the answer?

These are the steps we need to do to share data between an iOS app and its extension:

1. **Setting up an App Group**: The App Group feature allows us to combine and synchronize data between multiple extensions or apps. We create a new App Group using the Developer Portal and enable it for both our app and the extension.

2. **Configure the Xcode project settings**: Once we've set up the App Group in the Developer Portal, we'll need to configure the Xcode project settings for our app and extensions. We'll need to specify the App Group Identifier and enable the App Group entitlement for our app and extensions.

3. **Use UserDefaults to share data**: Once the Xcode project settings have been configured, we can use UserDefaults to share data between our app and extensions. To do this, we'll need to create a new `UserDefaults` object with the App Group Identifier as the suite name and then use the `set(_:forKey:)` method to save data and the `object(forKey:)` method to retrieve data.

Here's a code example of how to set and read data from shared `UserDefaults`:

```
let defaults = UserDefaults(suiteName: "group.com.yourcompany.
    yourapp")!

defaults.set(true, forKey: "myBoolValue")
let myBoolValue = defaults.bool(forKey: "myBoolValue")
```

In this code example, we are setting up a new `UserDefaults` and passing the App Group Identifier we defined in the Developer Portal.

The rest of the code stays as before in this section: reading and writing using a key-value mechanism.

As we can see – sharing data between an app and an extension is straightforward, but it is also something not many developers are familiar with. Sharing the Core Data store between the app and the extension is also a fundamental feature.

"Can you explain how to store a struct or a class in UserDefaults in an iOS app?"

Why is this question important?

Saving primitive dictionaries and arrays is probably the most common use case when working with `UserDefaults`. But there are many cases where we need to store an entire object or a class. For example, we sometimes need to save a user object that contains full details, and Core Data is like using a sledgehammer to crack a nut.

What is the answer?

UserDefaults has two popular ways to store an object or a struct:

- The first option is to use `NSKeyedArchiver`. One of the data types we can save in `UserDefaults` is Data. `NSKeyedArchiver` can take a struct or an object and convert it into a `Data` object, which can be saved directly to `NSKeyedArchiver`. To un-archive the object, we can use `NSKeyedUnarchiver`. Let's see a code example for that:

```
struct Person {
    var name: String
    var age: Int
}

let person = Person(name: "John Smith", age: 30)

let data = try? NSKeyedArchiver.archivedData(withRoot
    Object: person, requiringSecureCoding: false)
```

```
UserDefaults.standard.set(data, forKey: "person")

let storedData = UserDefaults.standard.data(forKey:"person")

if let storedPerson = try? NSKeyedUnarchiver.unarchivedObject
    (ofClass: Person.self, from:storedData!) {
}
```

In this code example, we converted a `Person` struct into a `Data` object using `NSKeyedArchiver`. The data can be set and restored easily, like any other data type saved to `UserDefaults`. After we fetch the data, we can convert it into a `Person` object again using `NSKeyedUnarchiver`.

- The second option is to use **JSONEncoder**. With `JSONEncoder`, we can convert to a `Data` object the same way we did with `NSKeyedArchiver`. Once we have a data object, we can set and restore the `Person` object from `UserDefaults`.

  Let's see how we save and restore the same `Person` struct, but now with `JSONEncoder`:

```
struct Person: Codable {
    var name: String
    var age: Int
}

let person = Person(name: "John Smith", age: 30)

let encoder = JSONEncoder()
if let encoded = try? encoder.encode(person) {
    UserDefaults.standard.set(encoded, forKey: "person")

    if let storedData = UserDefaults.standard.data
        (forKey: "person") {
        let decoder = JSONDecoder()
        if let storedPerson = try? decoder.decode
            (Person.self, from: storedData) {
        }
    }
}
```

We use `JSONEncoder` to convert the struct into data and `JSONDecoder` to restore the data back to `Person`. Notice that in this case, `Person` needs to *conform to Codable*, which requires its properties to also conform to Codable.

Which of the options is better? There's no clear answer. Generally, it is a best practice for our structs and classes to conform to **Codable** as it provides more capabilities such as automatic parsing and encoding.

On the other hand, `NSKeyedArchiver` is more efficient than `JSONEncoder` when working on large or complex datasets.

Both APIs are good enough for most cases, and it depends on our app structure and requirements.

Storing sensitive information in the Keychain

`UserDefaults` is an excellent storing mechanism, but it is unsuitable for storing data such as passwords or tokens. **Keychain** is Apple's solution for storing sensitive data, and it provides a higher level of security and is an essential tool for iOS developers to protect their data.

Storing data in the keychain is much more complex than using other solutions. The keychain provides a particular API, based on the C function, to prevent malicious hackers from reverse-engineering calls to that API. The keychain also requires more information when saving, so it can save and index it more efficiently.

Let's see how to store a simple token in the keychain while wrapping it with a class for convenience:

```
import UIKit
import Security

class KeychainManager {

    private let serviceName = "MyAppTokenService"

    func saveToken(token: String) -> Bool {
        guard let tokenData = token.data(using: .utf8) else {
            return false
        }

        let keychainItem = [
            kSecClass: kSecClassGenericPassword,
            kSecAttrService: serviceName,
            kSecAttrAccount: "MyAppToken",
            kSecValueData: tokenData
        ] as CFDictionary

        let status = SecItemAdd(keychainItem, nil)
        return status == errSecSuccess
    }
}
```

The first thing we notice from that code example is that we import the `Security` framework, which is also responsible for authentication, secure transport, and data protection.

We can also see that the code is much more complex than working with `UserDefaults`. Instead of storing a simple value, we need to create a keychain item with several properties:

- `kSecClass`: This key specifies the level of security of the item. We can choose from several constants, such as `kSecClassGenericPassword`, `kSecClassInternetPassword`, and `kSecClassIdentity`. Choosing the correct class ensures the right level of security for our data.

- `kSecAttrService`: `kSecAttrService` defines the service name for our item. We can group multiple items to increase security in case of compromising part of the app, to share part of the keychain items, and for better organization.

- `kSecAttrAccount`: This is used to add identification to the keychain item, such as a username or email.

- `kSecValueData`: This is the actual data we want to save. It can be either `Data` or `String`.

These four keys are not the only ones we can use for creating a keychain item, but they are the most common ones. Once we have `CFDictionary`, we can use `SecItemAdd` to push the keychain item into the keychain.

Here's how to read the token back from the keychain:

```swift
func readToken() -> String? {

    let query: [String: Any] = [
        kSecClass as String: kSecClassGenericPassword,
        kSecAttrService as String: service,
        kSecAttrAccount as String: account,
        kSecReturnData as String: true,
        kSecMatchLimit as String: kSecMatchLimitOne
    ]

    var result: AnyObject?
    let status = SecItemCopyMatching(query as
        CFDictionary, &result)

    if status == errSecSuccess, let tokenData =
        result as? Data, let token = String(data:
            tokenData, encoding: .utf8) {
        return token
    } else {
        return nil
    }
}
```

To read the token, we create `CFDictionary` once again and use `SecItemCopyMatching` to query the keychain and retrieve the token. Afterward, we examine the results – if the status is `success` and we have `tokenData`, we can extract the token by converting it into a string and return it.

As we can see, keychain management is not as trivial as other storage tools and a keychain wrapper is a good solution that can help us simplify the process.

"What is a Keychain Access Group, and how can it be used to securely share Keychain items between different components of an iOS app, such as the app and its extensions?"

Why is this question important?

In the previous section, we discussed UserDefaults and how to share information between our app and our extensions (or other apps, for that matter). Now we are moving forward with that question and being asked how to share sensitive information between the different components. This way, our app extensions can be much more powerful and independent.

What is the answer?

A **Keychain access group** is a unique identifier that specifies which Keychain items can be accessed by a particular app or extension.

Access groups are defined in the app's entitlements file and provide secure sharing of sensitive data between different components of an app, such as an app and its extensions.

By specifying the same access group for multiple components of an app, those components can securely share Keychain items without compromising their integrity. This feature is important for iOS app developers because it enables them to provide a secure and reliable storage mechanism for sensitive data that is accessible across multiple components of an app.

Here's how to set up a Keychain access group and use it.

First, we need to define a new access group in the app's entitlements file:

```
<key>com.example.myapp.shared-keychain</key>
<array>
    <string>$(AppIdentifierPrefix)com.example.myapp</string>
</array>
```

We must also define the same access group in the extension's entitlement file.

Now, we can use the access group we created in our code when saving and fetching keychain values:

```
func savePasswordToKeychain(password: String) -> Bool {
    guard let data = password.data(using: .utf8) else {
        return false
    }

    let query: [String: Any] = [
        kSecClass as String: kSecClassGenericPassword,
        kSecAttrAccessGroup as String:
            "com.example.myapp.shared-keychain",
        kSecAttrAccount as String: "myPassword",
        kSecValueData as String: data
    ]

    SecItemDelete(query as CFDictionary)

    let status = SecItemAdd(query as CFDictionary, nil)

    return status == errSecSuccess
}
```

Notice we added the kSecAttrAccessGroup key to our keychain item with our new keychain group.

When working with the keychain, we can see that most of our boilerplate is the different keychain values management, while setting up an access group is easy and simple.

Generally speaking – working with the iOS keychain is not as straightforward as the other tools we have – it requires more code, using C functions, and providing additional keys and information. But iOS development requires us to work with sensitive information and even share it between our apps. Therefore, we must understand how the keychain works and how to approach it with its API.

Working with the filesystem

There's a common assumption that iOS "doesn't have a filesystem." And even though there is a **Files** app, it is true that the filesystem is almost hidden for most standard users.

That's not the case for iOS developers.

iOS developers use the iOS filesystem to store documents, images, cache files, and even database files.

The filesystem allows us to store a large set of information, work with resources and even share data with other app components. Most interview questions focus on organizing our files and responding to different use cases. Understanding how the sandbox is built is crucial for us as developers.

So, let's review a question about our sandbox structure.

"Can you explain the purpose of each of the following folders in an iOS app: Documents, Library, Cache, and Temp? How would you decide which folder to use for storing different types of files in your app?"

Why is this question important?

File operations in iOS for reading and writing are generally straightforward from a technical perspective. However, the key is to grasp the methodological concept of properly organizing files in the appropriate folder. Each folder serves a distinct purpose and possesses different characteristics, and the iOS system distinctly manages each folder.

What is the answer?

As mentioned, each folder has its distinct purpose and characteristics, so let's go over them here:

- Documents: This folder is meant for storing data that can be created or edited by the user, such as documents, images, and videos. This folder is backed up by iCloud and is visible to the user through iTunes file sharing. We should use this folder for data that the user expects to be available even after the app is closed.

- Library: This folder is intended for storing app-specific data not created by the user, such as downloaded content, cache files, and preferences. This folder is backed up by iCloud but is not visible to the user through iTunes file sharing. We should use this folder for important data for the app's functionality, but it can be recreated if necessary.

- Cache: This folder is designed for storing temporary files that can be regenerated or downloaded again. This folder is not backed up by iCloud and can be emptied by the system when the device runs low on storage. We should use this folder for data that is not critical of the app's functionality and can be discarded if necessary.

- Temp: iOS also provides a temporary directory for storing temporary files, known as the Temp folder. This folder is intended to hold only needed temporary files and can be deleted when the app is closed.

The content type leads us to decide which folder to store our files. For example, we want to use the Documents folder for user-generated files. We can use the Temp folder if we need temporary files for generating information or calculations. The Library folder is suitable for storing the local data persistent store file.

Storing a file in the wrong folder may lead to unexpected behavior, such as data loss, performance issues, and increasing the user backup size for no reason.

Summary

In this chapter, we went over some critical topics in persistent memory. We discussed Core Data concurrency and data model design, advanced topics in `UserDefaults`, how to handle sensitive information with the Keychain, and the different folders in our app sandbox.

By now, we should ultimately be ready for that topic in our interview!

The next chapter will cover an essential topic that could hinder the scalability of an app for iOS developers who are unfamiliar with it: CocoaPods and the Swift Package Manager.

10
Libraries Management

So far, we have discussed the code *we write* – Swift, UIKit, and SwiftUI. But modern developers' work doesn't simply amount to writing code. Knowing how to integrate code can be a productivity multiplier, greatly enhancing our efficiency and allowing us to accomplish more in less time than simply knowing how to code.

CocoaPods and the *Swift Package Manager* are the leading solutions we have today for managing third-party and local dependencies. It is essential for any iOS developer to understand these tools thoroughly.

This chapter covers CocoaPods and the Swift Package Manager in terms of the following topics:

- Learning *how CocoaPods is built*, including different components such as `Podfile` and `Podspec` files

- Going over *CocoaPods' best practices* and use cases

- Covering the Swift Package Manager *creation process*

- Learning the Swift Package Manager's *common commands*

- Learning how to *use a Swift Package* in our projects

- Going over the *different advantages* the Swift Package Manager has compared to CocoaPods

- *Organizing our projects* with the Swift Package Manager

This is a "simple" chapter, yet it is a crucial topic in today's iOS development world. Let's start with CocoaPods as our first dependency manager.

Mastering CocoaPods

CocoaPods is one of the most popular dependency managers for iOS developers and has been maintained for many years as an open source project.

CocoaPods is often the first choice for many library developers and has a massive collection of frameworks that can be easily integrated with iOS projects.

Besides having a vast collection of frameworks, CocoaPods supports integration with local frameworks. It can help us modularize our project to different libraries and make it more flexible and organized.

Let's see how CocoaPods works and how it is built.

Learning how CocoaPods is built

When we use CocoaPods to manage dependencies in our Xcode project, CocoaPods creates a new workspace, which includes both our project and any dependencies we specified in our `Podfile` file. CocoaPods creates this workspace automatically when we run the `pod install` command.

> **Xcode Workspace**
>
> In Xcode, a workspace is a container for one or more Xcode projects and any other files and resources needed to build our app. Workspaces are used to organize and manage the different components of our app and make it easier to develop and test our code.

Using a workspace in CocoaPods has several benefits. It simplifies dependency management by including the project and its dependencies in the same workspace, simplifies integration, and follows the separation of concern principle by keeping the dependencies up to date, regardless of our main project.

Besides the workspace, CocoaPods comprises several different components, each of which plays a role in managing dependencies for iOS.

Here are some of the key components of CocoaPods.

Podfile

`Podfile` is a file that specifies which dependencies are required for our project. It uses a simple Ruby syntax to declare each pod's name and version number, as well as any options or configurations needed. `Podfile` is typically located in a project's root directory.

Here's an example of a `Podfile` file:

```
platform :ios, 16.0'

target 'MyApp' do
  use_frameworks!
  pod 'Alamofire', '~> 5.4'
  pod 'SwiftyJSON', '~> 4.0'
end
```

Now, let's understand how the file is built:

- The platform to target is iOS 16.0

- The target of `Podfile` is an Xcode project called **MyApp**

- The `use_frameworks!` directive tells CocoaPods to build the dependencies as **dynamic frameworks**

- The pod directives specify the two dependencies for the project, `Alamofire` and `SwiftyJSON`, along with their version requirements

The `~>` operator is an **optimistic operator**, which is used to specify a version for the pod and allows it to be updated to the next major version.

For example, look at the following row:

```
pod 'Alamofire', '~> 5.4'
```

In this case, CocoaPods will install and update the `Alamofire` pod up to version 6.0 (not including 6.0 itself). This allows us to enjoy hotfixes and minor versions without breaking backward compatibility.

`Podfile` is our project configuration file for all our dependencies and must be maintained carefully.

Podfile.lock

`Podfile.lock` is a file that stores information about the specific versions of the dependencies installed in our project. It ensures that the same dependencies' versions are installed on every machine, which helps prevent version conflicts and other issues.

Here's how it looks:

```
PODS:
    - AFNetworking (2.6.3)
    - Firebase/Analytics (7.6.0)
    - Firebase/CoreOnly (7.6.0)
    - FirebaseAnalytics (7.6.0)
    - FirebaseCore (7.6.0)
    - FirebaseCoreDiagnostics (7.6.0)
    - FirebaseInstallations (7.6.0)
    - GoogleAppMeasurement (7.6.0)

DEPENDENCIES:
    - AFNetworking (~> 2.6.3)
    - Firebase/Analytics
    - GoogleAppMeasurement (~> 7.6.0)
```

CocoaPods automatically generates `Podfile.lock` when we run `pod update` or `pod install`, and we shouldn't update it manually, as it can cause conflicts and issues.

The Pods directory

The `Pods` directory is a directory that contains all the dependencies installed by CocoaPods for our project. It includes each pod's source code, headers, and compiled binaries.

Podspec

A `Podspec` is a file that describes a single pod, including its name, version, source code location, dependencies, and other metadata. Podspecs are published to the CocoaPods repository and used by CocoaPods to download and install a pod.

Let's see an example of a podspec file:

```ruby
Pod::Spec.new do |s|
  s.name          = "MyLibrary"
  s.version       = "1.0.0"
  s.summary       = "A library for iOS and macOS
     development."
  s.description   = "MyLibrary provides a set of tools and
     utilities for iOS and macOS development."
  s.homepage      = "https://github.com/
     myusername/MyLibrary"
  s.license       = "MIT"
  s.author        = { "My Name" => "myemail@example.com" }
  s.platform      = :ios, '14.0'
  s.source        = { :git => "https://github.com/
     myusername/MyLibrary.git", :tag => "#{s.version}" }
  s.source_files = "Sources/**/*.{h,m,swift}"
  s.swift_version = '5.4'
  s.dependency    "Alamofire", "~> 5.4"
  s.dependency    "SwiftyJSON", "~> 4.0"
end
```

The podspec file is written in Ruby, a dynamic and object-oriented programming language. In fact, the `Podfile` file is also written in Ruby, as it is considered a convenient and popular way to write configuration files for frameworks.

The podspec file, in this example, describes a library named `MyLibrary` with a version of `1.0.0`. We can also see a summary, a description, and other general details, such as the home page, license, and author.

In the source and source files, we can see where the Git repository is located (in this case, in GitHub) and what files are included in the pod in the **wildcard pattern**.

> **The wildcard pattern**
>
> In Podfile, a wildcard pattern can be used to define directories where the pods should be installed.
>
> The wildcard pattern ("*") represents any character to match any file or directory. For example, if we want to specify all directories that start with "M," we can use the following:
>
> ```
> Pod "MyPod", :path => "M*"
> ```
>
> The wildcard pattern is not a Podfile-only pattern – it is used in many Unix-like command-line tools and terminals.

Finally, we add the dependencies our pod requires so that CocoaPods will know to manage its dependencies tree accordingly.

It is important to note that we can easily use a podspec file to create a local library and integrate it with our project. Here's a podspec file example for a local library:

```ruby
Pod::Spec.new do |s|
    s.name          = "MyFramework"
    s.version       = "1.0.0"
    s.summary       = "A framework that modularizes code from
        MyProject."
    s.homepage      = "https://github.com/
        myusername/MyFramework"
    s.license       = "MIT"
    s.author        = { "My Name" => "myemail@example.com" }
    s.platform      = :ios, '14.0'
    s.source        = { :path => "." }
    s.source_files = "MyFramework/**/*.{h,m,swift}"
    s.public_header_files = "MyFramework/**/*.h"
    s.frameworks    = "UIKit"
    s.dependency    "Alamofire", "~> 5.4"
    s.dependency    "SwiftyJSON", "~> 4.0"
    s.swift_version = '5.4'

    s.pod_target_xcconfig = {
      'SWIFT_INCLUDE_PATHS' => '$(SRCROOT)
          /MyProject/MyModule'
    }
end
```

Apart from modifying our `source` and `source_files` attributes, we can also see that we now have a `pod_target_xcconfig` attribute to specify the path to the source code for the module in our project.

`Podfile`, in this case, will look like this:

```
platform :ios, '14.0'

target 'MyApp' do
  use_frameworks!
  pod 'MyFramework', :path => '../MyFramework'
end
```

In `Podfile`, we direct `MyFramework` to its local path, where the source file exists.

Pod command-line tool

The pod command-line tool is the primary interface for working with CocoaPods. It provides a command set that allows us to install, update, and manage dependencies for our project.

These are some commonly used commands we can use:

- `pod install`: This command installs the dependencies specified in `Podfile` and generates an Xcode workspace, containing our project and the installed dependencies.
- `pod update`: This command updates the dependencies specified in `Podfile` to their latest versions and installs them. We can select a specific pod or a list of pods to update.
- `pod lib create`: This command generates a new CocoaPods library template. We can use it to quickly set up a new pod's directory structure, files, and configuration.
- `pod search`: This command searches the CocoaPods repository for pods that match a given query. We can search for pods by name, description, author, or other criteria.

Like many development tools, CocoaPods is based on command-line tools, configuration files, and a terminal, so "terminal-phobia" is not recommended in the case of CocoaPods!

We discussed five different CocoaPods components for managing and understanding CocoaPods. If you have never used CocoaPods before or didn't create your pod, it's a good idea to create a new project and play with it, followed by reading the CocoaPods documentation, which is clear and straightforward. I promise you that things will be much easier to understand after an hour.

Now, let's jump into two questions about CocoaPods that we may encounter in an interview.

"What best practices do you follow when working with CocoaPods, and why are they important?"

Why is this question important?

CocoaPods, or any other dependencies manager for that matter, is an essential part of a project.

In a way, we can even say *it's the vulnerable part of our project* for a few reasons:

- **It's not code we have written ourselves**: CocoaPods integrates thousands of lines of code that other developers wrote into our project. We have little control over the security, performance, and stability effect of adding code someone else writes. However, it will have probably gone through many fixes and testing cycles.

- **There's a potential for dependencies conflicts**: A poorly structured `Podfile` can cause conflicts between different versions of dependencies and may harm a project's stability.

- **Outdated frameworks can cause security breaches**: Developers often lock frameworks to specific versions to keep their project stability high. This can lead to obsolete code with security and stability issues.

Because of the reasons I just described, a well-structured `Podfile` tremendously affects our project quality.

What is the answer?

We can follow a few best practices when working with CocoaPods:

- **Keeping our frameworks up to date**: We need to ensure we get the latest bug fixes and features to keep our project stable. The `~>` operator I mentioned earlier is recommended to get the latest hotfixes and minor versions.

- **Understanding semantic versioning**: Keeping frameworks up to date is essential. However, we should understand how semantic versioning works. We want to ensure backward compatibility and avoid breaking changes.

- **Keeping dependencies at a minimum**: We should only include frameworks that we really need in our project and remove those that the Apple SDK can replace. Keeping our project light and simple is vital, avoiding potential issues such as conflicts and crashes.

- **Keeping our Podfile organized and readable**: We should treat our `Podfile` as part of our code base. Grouping dependencies in a logical way can provide us with flexibility and clarity. Another best practice here is to add comments next to each pod and explain why we added each pod. Pods can live in our app for years, and the comments we add can help us in the future.

- **Implementing the adapter pattern**: While the adapter pattern is not unique to CocoaPods, it is an excellent pattern for integrating a pod into our project seamlessly. Often, the pod's interface does not naturally align with our existing code base. By introducing a class that acts as an interface between our code base and the library, we can effectively connect these two components. Additionally, the adapter can assist in decoupling our code base from the pod and reducing dependencies.

We must remember something important – pods are part of our code. We should take care of our third-party frameworks with the same attention that we manage our project code base with, as they tremendously affect how our project performs.

"What is the difference between pod update and pod install?"

Why is this question important?

In the previous question, we talked about best practices for managing CocoaPods. One crucial aspect we covered was managing pods to prevent them from causing any issues or breaking our code.

Both the `pod update` and `pod install` commands help us to decide our strategy to update our pods, implementing a careful and responsible way to keep our third-party libraries up to date.

What is the answer?

`pod install` and `pod update` are commands used in the CocoaPods dependency manager for iOS projects. The main difference between them is how they handle dependency resolution.

`pod install` installs the dependencies specified in `Podfile.lock` and ensures that a pod won't receive unintended updates.

On the other hand, `pod update` updates the current pods to the latest minor version and, ultimately, updates `Podfile.lock` to the new version.

One thing to note is that if there is no `Podfile.lock`, *both commands behave similarly*.

The difference between the commands in day-to-day work is critical. `Podfile.lock` helps us control our framework's updates and keeps our pods in a specific version, as long as we use `pod install`, whereas `pod update` can bypass what's written in `Podfile.lock`.

I advise including `Podfile.lock` in a project's code base when discussing best practices. This is particularly crucial when collaborating with a team, as `Podfile.lock` guarantees that all team members use identical framework versions.

To summarize this section, by now, we should understand how CocoaPods works and how to use it to link third-party libraries and maintain a stable and robust project.

As an essential tool to manage dependencies in iOS projects, CocoaPods should be treated with the utmost importance. This applies to any dependency manager, including the Swift Package Manager, which we will now review.

Learning about the Swift Package Manager

CocoaPods and Carthage have played a significant part over the years in managing dependencies in iOS projects.

While CocoaPods and Carthage are terrific tools, every platform needs to have its in-house dependency manager, and Apple indeed developed a native dependency manager called the **Swift Package Manager (SPM)**.

So, what is the SPM?

The SPM is a dependency manager built right into Xcode and allows developers to easily create, manage, and share Swift packages, which are self-contained units of code that can be used in different projects. A package can contain one or more targets, each of which is a module that can be imported and used by other packages or projects.

Let's start creating a Swift package from scratch.

Creating a Swift package

Creating a new Swift package is simple. There are two ways to do it – using the *terminal* and *Xcode*:

- **Using the terminal**: Open the **Terminal** app, go to the project folder (or any other folder), and type the following command:

```
swift package init --type library
```

  This command will create a new folder with the relevant subfolders and files to set up a basic and empty Swift package.

- **Creating a Swift package with Xcode**: If you don't want to use the Terminal to create a Swift package, the other option is to use Xcode.

  Let's go over the steps required to create a new Swift package:

  I.   Open Xcode and select **File** | **New** | **Package** from the menu bar.

  II. In the **Create a new Swift Package** dialog, enter the package details, such as the package name, organization, and type. You can choose between a library or executable package and specify the package's platforms and products.

  III. Click **Create** to create the new Swift package. Xcode will generate a basic project structure with a `Sources` directory and a `Package.swift` manifest file.

Both options are simple and intuitive and take a few seconds to complete. Now, let's understand what we created.

Going over the package manifest and folders

The Swift package is built from three components:

- **The `Sources` directory**: This directory contains the Swift source files for our package. By default, it includes a single subdirectory with the same name as the package, and a single source file with the same name as the directory.

- **The** `Tests` **directory**: This directory contains the test files for our code. By default, it includes a single subdirectory, with a single test file with the same name as the directory.

- `Package.swift`: This file is the package manifest file. It contains information about the package, such as its name, version, and dependencies, and is used by the SPM to build and manage the package.

In the *Mastering CocoaPods* section, we discussed CocoaPods and mentioned the `podspec` file. In the SPM, `package.swift` serves a similar purpose to the `podspec` file in CocoaPods.

Here's a short example of standard `package.swift` file content:

```
// Package.swift

import PackageDescription

let package = Package(
    name: "MyPackage",
    platforms: [
        .macOS(.v10_12), .iOS(.v10), .watchOS(.v3), .tvOS(.v10)
    ],
    products: [
        .library(name: "MyPackage", targets: ["MyPackage"])
    ],
    dependencies: [
        .package(url: "https://github.com/
            Alamofire/Alamofire.git", from: "5.0.0")
    ],
    targets: [
        .target(name: "MyPackage", dependencies: ["Alamofire"]),
        .testTarget(name: "MyPackageTests", dependencies:
            ["MyPackage"])
    ]
)
```

We can see that the `package.swift` file is written in, well… *Swift*. Therefore, reading it should be simple for iOS developers. Let's understand what it says.

This `Package.swift` file specifies the details of a Swift package named `"MyPackage"`. The package targets multiple platforms – macOS, iOS, watchOS, and tvOS. It provides a single library product with the same name as the package.

The package depends on the `Alamofire` package, specified as a dependency with a minimum version of `5.0.0`. The package also contains two targets, one for the package itself and one for its tests. The package target depends on the `Alamofire` package, and the test target depends on the `MyPackage` target.

When the SPM installs our package, it also establishes the dependencies we define inside the `package.swift` file, just the way it works with CocoaPods.

Another interesting thing we should know is why it is called a "package" and not a "library." The reason is that a Swift package can contain *multiple libraries* (under "products") and various targets, and it is crucial to understand that hierarchy to create a flexible package.

How do we build and test the package? Let's see.

Swift package common commands

While it is possible to use the SPM from within Xcode, having a good understanding of the primary terminal commands is still essential. This is because user interfaces tend to change more frequently, while command-line tools remain more consistent over time.

However, a more significant reason is that terminal commands provide us with the ability to *integrate them into scripts and CI machines*, making them powerful and effective.

Here is the list of commands:

- `swift package init`: We saw this command earlier when we discussed Swift package creation. It initializes a new and empty Swift package in the current directory.
- `swift package update`: This updates the package's dependencies to their latest compatible versions. It's similar to `pod update` in CocoaPods.
- `swift build`: This builds the package and its dependencies, generating a binary or library product.
- `swift test`: This runs the package's unit tests, building the package if necessary.
- `swift package clean`: This deletes the build artifacts for the package, including the build directory.

In the context of an interview, think of this command list as a "features list." This list should show us how to operate and maintain a Swift package.

Using a Swift package

Using a Swift package library is like any other library we add to our project. Everything we know about access levels also applies in this case.

For example, an app can access only *public* and *open* functions, classes, and properties, while the *internal* level is reserved for the library.

Also, to use a library, we need to import it into our code. Here's an example:

```
import MyPackage

let myObject = MyClass()
myObject.myMethod()
```

In this example, we first import the `MyPackage` module into our code using the `import` statement. Then, we create an instance of the `MyClass` class and call its `myMethod` function. In this case, `MyClass` is part of `MyPackage`. This example is relevant for the app and the package when working with its dependencies.

Generally speaking, using the SPM is pretty simple and straightforward. Apple did a great job integrating it within Xcode while maintaining its ability to perform everything in terminal commands.

The goal here was to briefly explain the SPM before we move on to the next interview questions.

"What are the advantages and disadvantages of using the SPM compared to CocoaPods?"

Why is this question important?

Both tools are excellent to manage dependencies in iOS, but just like any other tool, they have their strengths and weaknesses.

Understanding the practical differences between the tools is perhaps even more important than using them, as the latter is straightforward and technical. Choosing the right tool significantly impacts our app's maintenance and stability.

What is the answer?

Like any cons and pros, the answer depends on a project's needs and requirements. However, there are some known differences between CocoaPods and the SPM.

These are the *SPM's advantages*:

- A *built-in* tool for Swift projects, so no need for third-party dependencies
- A simple and *easy-to-use* syntax
- *Integration with Swift and Xcode*, including support to generate Xcode projects
- *Automatic dependency resolution* and caching
- *Faster* build times for more minor projects

These are the *SPM's disadvantages*:

- Limited support for binary dependencies
- No support for Objective-C or mixed-language projects
- Limited customization options for build settings

This list suggests that the advantages and disadvantages of the SPM are inverse to the ones mentioned earlier in the *Mastering CocoaPods* section.

On one hand, CocoaPods is more used and flexible than the SPM. On the other hand, it is more complex and slow and performs as a foreign citizen in Apple's development ecosystem.

Before you start the interview, you should try each of the solutions to understand how they feel and what is possible.

"What are some best practices for organizing and structuring Swift packages to optimize build times and minimize dependency conflicts?"

Why is this question important?

This question is beyond technical. As we already saw, the technical part of handling Swift packages is simple, even for junior developers. However, organizing a project for packages effectively and efficiently is the real challenge.

The abundance of articles and research on code modularity and organization demonstrates the importance of this question. Most of them do not even mention the SPM.

Following even a tiny portion of the best practices here can significantly impact our project.

What is the answer?

There are some best practices for organizing our code to optimize build times and decouple our dependencies:

- **Keeping packages small**: Large packages with many dependencies can slow down build times and increase the risk of conflicts. To minimize these issues, keeping packages small and modular is a good practice. This makes it easier to manage dependencies and reduces the risk of conflicts.
- **Minimizing dependencies**: To reduce the risk of conflicts and improve build times, it's a good practice to minimize dependencies wherever possible. This can be achieved by using only the essential dependencies for the package and avoiding unnecessary or duplicate dependencies.

- **Using semantic versioning**: We can use semantic versioning to manage version numbers for a package and its dependencies. By using semantic versioning, we can communicate changes and compatibility requirements to other developers and users of the package.

- **Using incremental builds**: The SPM supports incremental builds, which means that only the necessary parts of the package are rebuilt when changes are made. This can help to improve build times and reduce unnecessary recompilation.

We can say that the best practices described here can be used to modularize any project or even any class. A flat hierarchy, minimum dependencies, and small libraries are all great tips for managing libraries in our projects.

Summary

Dependency managers are like double-edged swords. Both the SPM and CocoaPods can be time savers and great add-ons for our projects regarding modularity and separation. Conversely, they can have a devastating effect on our app's stability and architecture's simplicity if not handled correctly. That's why it's a topic we must master as iOS developers.

In this chapter, we learned the basics of CocoaPods and the SPM, including the best practices and their pros and cons. By now, we should have everything covered when asked about the most common third-party dependency managers for iOS.

In a way, our next chapter is linked to what we have discussed in this chapter. We will slowly move away from the standard Swift and UIKit topics into the world of design and architecture.

Our next chapter will be exciting!

Part 4:
Design and Architecture

This is the final part of this book, where we have unleashed the power of code design and architecture. We will cover different design patterns, such as MVVM and Dependency Injection, discuss architecture, and prepare for coding assessments. By the end of this part, we will be ready to successfully conclude the interview and receive our job proposal.

In this part, we have the following chapters:

- *Chapter 11, Design Patterns to Solve Complex Questions*
- *Chapter 12, Drilling into App Architecture*
- *Chapter 13, Acing the Coding Assessment*

11

Design Patterns to Solve Complex Questions

In previous chapters, we discussed different aspects of iOS development. We covered UIKit, Swift, reactive programming, SwiftUI, Core Data, and many more. These building blocks help us achieve our next level – design patterns.

Design patterns are like tools. Each one of them solves a different problem or a different need, such as the following:

- Do we need to change the behavior of a particular instance? We can use **dependency injection** (**DI**).

- Do we have a complex state to manage? We can use **Model-View-ViewModel** (**MVVM**).

- Do we need to define communication between objects? We can use delegation.

The more we expand our toolbox with design patterns, the more problems we can solve. We should remember that design patterns alone are not our goal – they are tools to accomplish our tasks. We should remember that we'll have to pick a particular design pattern or talk about it in our interviews.

In this chapter, we'll cover some commonly used design patterns in iOS development. We'll do the following:

- Discuss **Model-View-Controller** (**MVC**) and MVVM, including some interview questions

- Decouple our code using DI

- Improve communication with delegation

- Share a state with Singletons

- Improve performance using Concurrency

One of the most commonly asked topics in interviews is the first on the list – MVC and MVVM. So, let's dive right into it.

Building a UI with MVC/MVVM

Several known design patterns can help us build stable and complex screens, but MVC and MVVM are the most common and famous patterns.

Like many development areas, the topic of MVC and MVVM can be subject to personal preferences and opinions and may not always align with practical considerations. We always need to be careful with that, especially when interviewing for a job. Let me explain what I mean.

Solving different problems with MVC and MVVM

I want to go over several sentences I suggest avoiding when having a professional discussion with an interviewer or even colleagues:

- "My app is built with MVVM architecture."
- "MVC is antique and a horrible architecture. I never use it."
- "This is not how MVVM works. Let me show you."

Remember what I've said multiple times throughout the book – we should avoid dichotomous thinking as developers. MVC and MVVM solve different problems, and we should think of both patterns as different solutions to various issues.

In fact, we can use different design patterns in the same app, in the same feature, or even on the same screen.

Additionally, there is more than one way to implement MVC and MVVM. What's more important is to follow the different principles and explain them.

Let's start with the more straightforward pattern – MVC.

Learning MVC

MVC stands for Model-View-Controller. When the iOS development era started, Apple used MVC to demonstrate best practices for building UI screens, and it was the primary design pattern for building apps.

The basic principle of MVC is a separation between the *View,* which is what the user sees and interacts with, and the *Model,* which represents the business logic and the data layer.

In MVC, there's no direct connection between the View and the Model, and all the data flow is done using the *Controller*.

Let's have a look at a classic MVC pattern (*Figure 11.1*):

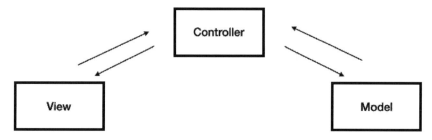

Figure 11.1 – MVC design pattern

In *Figure 11.1*, we can see that the View and the Model communicate with each other using the controller. This separation allows us to reuse each component in different use cases across our project.

How can we implement MVC in the iOS world? Let's see:

- **View**: The View represents the UI displayed on the screen. Therefore, we typically implement it with one of the UIKit view elements, such as buttons, labels, and text fields (we'll talk about SwiftUI in a second).

- **Model**: The Model is our data and business logic. We implement it using data structures, persistent storage, different algorithms, and network requests.

- **Controller**: The controller in iOS development is mostly `UIViewController` and its different subclasses, such as `UITableViewController` and `UIAlertController`.

One thing to notice is how Apple implements the MVC pattern in iOS. `UIViewController` is not really a pure controller like we saw in *Figure 11.1*. It has a view of its own and is responsible for user interaction. In a way, `UIViewController` is part of the UI, not just a controller.

Things are a little different with SwiftUI – the SwiftUI pattern resembles MVVM rather than MVC. We'll examine this more closely when we get to MVVM.

Let's see how to implement MVC in iOS. Here is the Model part:

```
class Person {
    var name: String
    var age: Int

    init(name: String, age: Int) {
        self.name = name
        self.age = age
    }

    func canVote() -> Bool {
```

```
            return age >= 18
        }
    }
```

`Person` represents the data structure and has a logic function (`canVote()`). It doesn't have any reference to the view or even to the controller.

And here's the View:

```
class PersonView: UIView {
    var nameLabel: UILabel
    var ageLabel: UILabel
    var canVoteLabel: UILabel

    init(frame: CGRect) {
        super.init(frame: frame)
        nameLabel = UILabel()
        ageLabel = UILabel()
        canVoteLabel = UILabel()
    }

    func configure(with person: Person) {
        nameLabel.text = person.name
        ageLabel.text = "\(person.age)"
        canVoteLabel.text = person.canVote() ? "Can vote" :
            "Can't vote"
    }
}
```

We can see that the `PersonView` class has nothing to do with logic and focuses purely on UI presentation. This allows it to be reusable with other logic and models.

Notice that `PersonView` has a `configure(with person:Person)` function. This common practice helps us load the view with a specific model. We can move this code to an extension and increase the code separation.

Now, let's move on to the controller:

```
class PersonViewController: UIViewController {
    var person: Person
    var personView: PersonView

    init(person: Person) {
        self.person = person
        personView = PersonView()
```

```
            super.init(nibName: nil, bundle: nil)
    }

    override func viewDidLoad() {
        super.viewDidLoad()
        view.addSubview(personView)
        personView.configure(with: person)
    }

    required init?(coder aDecoder: NSCoder) {
        fatalError("init(coder:) has not been implemented")
    }
}
```

PersonViewController has a reference to both Person and PersonView and is responsible for linking between them and loading the view with data from Person. Notice that PersonView and Person don't have a reference to each other – PersonViewController acts as the controller and sets up what is needed in the viewDidLoad function.

Earlier, we discussed how MVC improves our code to make it reusable, as we can reuse the Model and View components. In iOS development, we should also consider MVC as a self-contained unit we can reuse.

For example, we can have a screen that is built upon two embedded view controllers, each one of which is an MVC unit. Look at *Figure 11.2*:

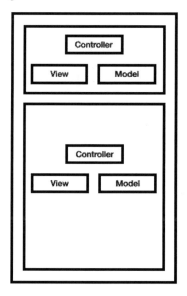

Figure 11.2 – Two embedded MVC units

An MVC unit doesn't have to be a whole screen – this approach can help us reuse part of the screen and extend our project's flexibility.

The MVC pattern is excellent for simple screens that don't require complex state and data manipulation. In this case, we must move to a more complex pattern – MVVM.

Exploring MVVM

I believe this is a critical checkpoint in the chapter (and maybe even in the whole book). Developers tend to be attached to a specific pattern, especially related to the UI. MVVM is not "better" than "MVC" and vice versa. They are both patterns for different use cases, which is crucial to explain in an interview. We should never be tied to a specific technology or pattern, especially not in interviews.

We said that MVC is not the best pattern for complex state and data management. But why?

Complex screens require state management – to show/hide certain UI elements, update text, change colors, and present dynamic information on the screen. All of this can make our view controller bloated.

That's why iOS developers used to rely on MVC in the first era of the App Store but quickly moved on to a more suitable pattern – MVVM.

MVVM stands for Model-View-ViewModel. The idea is that the View is connected to the Model using a **ViewModel** – another component that can help us manage the state and manipulate data.

Look at *Figure 11.3*:

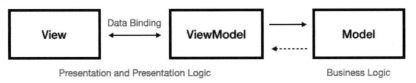

Figure 11.3 – The MVVM design pattern

In *Figure 11.3*, we can see that the ViewModel stands between the View and Model like the controller in the MVC pattern.

But in MVVM, the responsibilities of the different components are much more transparent and intuiitive.

Let's go over the different components now:

- **View**: The View is responsible for presenting the information and responding to user interaction. It's the only component with access to the UIKit framework (we'll talk about SwiftUI shortly), which is a significant difference from the MVC pattern we discussed earlier.

- **ViewModel**: The ViewModel handles the state and prepares data for presentation. Also, the ViewModel decides on user interaction and moves the requests forward to the Model layer.

- **Model**: The Model layer is the actual business logic and is responsible for accessing the persistent store and performing network requests.

Notice that the View and the ViewModel communicate using **data binding**, which connects the input field to the corresponding data model. In fact, the ViewModel doesn't even have a reference to the view – the view observes changes in the ViewModel and refreshes itself accordingly.

That's where SwiftUI and Combine come in handy. In SwiftUI, for example, the ViewModel is usually derived from the `@ObservableObject` class with `@Published` properties.

> **Forgot about SwiftUI and Combine?**
>
> Now is a good time to return to *Chapter 8* and refresh your memory regarding SwiftUI and Combine. It looks like Apple took a close look at how developers develop screens and built a dedicated framework for MVVM.

Now, let's see MVVM in practice.

Going over some code examples

Let's see a code example of the MVVM design pattern. In our example, we have a screen with a label that shows the status of a loading request (**Loading…**, **Ready**, or **Error**). The label is bound to a specific ViewModel that communicates with the Model and updates its View.

Let's start with the ViewModel:

```
import Foundation
import Combine

class StatusViewModel {
    private let networkService: NetworkService
    private var cancellables = Set<AnyCancellable>()
    private let statusDidChange = PassthroughSubject
        <String, Never>()
    var status: String = "Loading..." {
        didSet {
            statusDidChange.send(status)
        }
    }

    init(networkService: NetworkService) {
        self.networkService = networkService
    }

    func fetchStatus() {
        networkService.fetchStatus()
            .sink { completion in
                switch completion {
```

```
                        case .failure(let error):
                            self.status = "Error: \
                                (error.localizedDescription)"
                        case .finished:
                            break
                        }
                    } receiveValue: { isReady in
                        self.status = isReady ? "Ready" : "Not ready"
                    }
                    .store(in: &cancellables)
            }
```

And now, let's observe the status change:

```
        func observeStatusChange(handler: @escaping (String) ->
            Void) {
            statusDidChange
                .receive(on: RunLoop.main)
                .sink { status in
                    handler(status)
                }
                .store(in: &cancellables)
        }
    }
```

The code example is a bit long, yet simple to understand. The ViewModel observes a network request-response and updates its values using a Combine pattern. The combine stream starts with the network service and forwards the results to the `status` property, which can be observed by the view. Notice that the ViewModel doesn't deal with any UI elements – that's the View's job.

Now, let's see the View:

```
import UIKit

class StatusLabel: UILabel {
    var viewModel: StatusViewModel? {
        didSet {
            viewModel?.observeStatusChange { [weak self]
                status in
                self?.text = status
            }
            viewModel?.fetchStatus()
        }
    }
}
```

The `StatusLabel` class has a direct reference to the ViewModel, and it observes changes to refresh itself.

The only thing left to do is to connect the view with the ViewModel, and that's the only job of the view controller in this case:

```
import UIKit

class ViewController: UIViewController {
    let networkService = NetworkService()
    let statusViewModel = StatusViewModel(networkService:
        NetworkService())
    let statusLabel = StatusLabel()

    override func viewDidLoad() {
        super.viewDidLoad()

        statusLabel.frame = CGRect(x: 50, y: 50, width:
            200, height: 50)
        statusLabel.textAlignment = .center
        view.addSubview(statusLabel)

        statusLabel.viewModel = statusViewModel
    }
}
```

`ViewController` injects the ViewModel into the view and `NetworkService` into the ViewModel. Imagine doing that with MVC, with several components and complex data manipulation; you'd get 3,000 lines of code with a view controller.

MVVM is a modern design pattern compared to MVC and can help us separate our concerns more efficiently and handle much more complex state management and data manipulation. We can create a ViewModel for each view that we think needs one and organize our presentation logic however we want.

Now let's move on to some questions about MVC/MVVM design patterns.

"How would you implement navigation in an MVVM architecture, considering that the ViewModel should not have knowledge of the View?"

Why is this question important?

Learning MVVM is easy in theory. Binding ViewModel properties to UI elements is simple, but applying it to *real-world problems is the real challenge*. One of the most common real-world problems in iOS and mobile is navigation combined with state and logic.

What is the solution to the navigation problem when the ViewModel lacks a direct reference to the View and the View cannot handle navigation on its own?

What is the answer?

When discussing navigation, we need to decide on three things:

- How to *trigger* the navigation action
- How to *choose* where to navigate
- How to *navigate*

These are three different responsibilities that can be separated into various components. For example, we can decide that the ViewModel can trigger the navigation action and also choose where to go, while the View can handle the navigation action itself.

Another option is to decide that the ViewModel triggers the navigation. Still, where to go can be part of the View or another object explicitly dedicated to that.

Let's look at *Figure 11.4*:

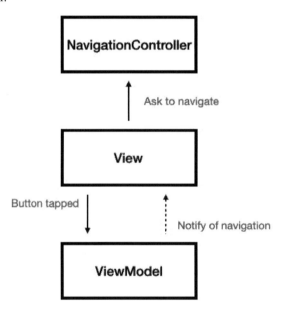

Figure 11.4 – Simple navigation pattern using MVVM

In *Figure 11.4*, the ViewModel triggers the navigations and notifies the View using a delegate pattern or **Combine**. The View then asks the navigation controller to navigate to a specific destination, which is part of the reason view controllers have a reference to the navigation controller. This simple navigation pattern puts the navigation responsibility on the View.

Here's how to implement that in code. This is what the ViewModel looks like:

```
import Foundation
import Combine

class MyViewModel {
    private let navigationSubject = PassthroughSubject
        <Void, Never>()

    var navigation: AnyPublisher<Void, Never> {
        return navigationSubject.eraseToAnyPublisher()
    }

    func didTapButton() {
        navigationSubject.send(())
    }
}
```

We can see that the ViewModel has a `didTapButton()` method and decides to send a message using `navigationSubject`.

Now, let's go over the view controller:

```
import UIKit
import Combine

class MyViewController: UIViewController {
    var viewModel: MyViewModel!

    private var cancellables = Set<AnyCancellable>()

    let button = UIButton()

    override func viewDidLoad() {
        super.viewDidLoad()

        setupUI()

        viewModel.navigation
            .sink { [weak self] in
                self?.navigateToDetails()
            }
            .store(in: &cancellables)
    }
```

```
    private func setupUI() {
        button.addTarget(self, action: #selector
            (didTapButton), for: .touchUpInside)
    }

    @objc private func didTapButton() {
        viewModel.didTapButton()
    }

    private func navigateToDetails() {
        let detailsViewController = DetailsViewController()
        navigationController?.pushViewController
        (detailsViewController, animated: true)
    }
}
```

The ViewModel navigation subject triggers the navigation according to its own logic, which in this case is tapping the button.

`ViewController` observes the ViewModel navigation publishers and pushes `detailsViewcontroller` using the navigation controller.

As mentioned, this pattern is simple and puts a lot of responsibility on the view controller. If we want to separate our code, we can delegate the navigation responsibility to another class (**Coordinator**). See *Figure 11.5*:

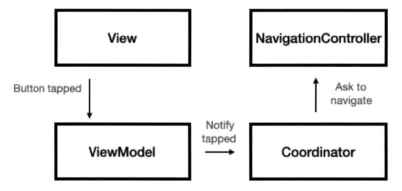

Figure 11.5 – MVVM and coordinator pattern

In the coordinator pattern, the ViewModel notifies the coordinator about a navigation intent, which pushes a new screen. See how the ViewModel looks now:

```
import Foundation
import Combine
```

```
class MyViewModel {
    private let didTapButtonSubject = PassthroughSubject
        <Void, Never>()

    var didTapButtonPublisher: AnyPublisher<Void, Never> {
        return didTapButtonSubject.eraseToAnyPublisher()
    }

    func didTapButton() {
        didTapButtonSubject.send(())
    }
}
```

The ViewModel sends a message with the button tap, and the coordinator can subscribe to it and respond. This is what the coordinator looks like:

```
class MyMainCoordinator: MyCoordinator {
    private var cancellables = Set<AnyCancellable>()

    func start() {
        let viewModel = MyViewModel()
        viewModel.didTapButtonPublisher
            .sink { [weak self] _ in self?.didTapButton()
            }
            .store(in: &cancellables)

        let viewController = MyViewController()
        viewController.viewModel = viewModel

        navigationController.pushViewController
            (viewController, animated: true)
    }

    func didTapButton() {
        let detailsViewController = DetailsViewController()
        navigationController.pushViewController
            (detailsViewController, animated: true)
    }
}
```

We can see that the coordinator creates the ViewModel and the view, then wires everything together. In the previous example, the view controller observed the ViewModel events and pushed a new view controller. Similarly, in this case, the coordinator observes `didTapButtonPublisher` and decides to push a new view controller – `DetailsViewController`. The view and ViewModel are unaware of this transition as it is managed entirely by the coordinator.

In general, both ways have their pros and cons. Using a coordinator is a powerful and complex pattern. Still, there is little overhead for simpler cases, where we can connect the navigation controller to the view controller. What's important is to understand the navigation principles and balance the responsibilities.

"Why is the MVVM architecture considered good for testability in iOS app development?"

Why is this question important?

When designing code, tests have become increasingly important in recent years. It's not just about being able to test the code but also about writing high-quality code that is well structured and easy to maintain. With this in mind, the interviewer wants us to consider the importance of writing testable code in our response.

What is the answer?

The MVVM design pattern is suitable for testing because it separates the concerns in an easy way. The state and the data manipulation code, which is the most important part we want to test, is part of the ViewModel. We can set up the ViewModel easily without handling the UI and simply test it by mocking the View.

We can also test an MVC unit, but since the state management is part of the View Controller or the View, it is more complex than testing an MVVM pattern.

Here's a code example of how to test a ViewModel. Let's start with defining a standard ViewModel:

```
import Foundation
import Combine

class MyViewModel {
    let didTapButton = PassthroughSubject<Void, Never>()
    @Published var labelValue: String = ""

    private var cancellables = Set<AnyCancellable>()

    init() {
        didTapButton
            .map { "Ready" }
            .assign(to: \.labelValue, on: self)
```

```
                .store(in: &cancellables)
        }
    }
```

We created a ViewModel that handles a tap button and updates a label. Notice that there is no UIKit-related code here, so it should be reasonably easy to test. Now, let's see the test itself:

```
import XCTest
import Combine
@testable import MyProject

class MyViewModelTests: XCTestCase {

    func testLabelValue() {
        let viewModel = MyViewModel()

        let labelValueExpectation = viewModel.$labelValue
            .dropFirst() // Ignore initial value
            .sink { labelValue in XCTAssertEqual(labelValue, "Ready")
            }

        viewModel.didTapButton.send(())
        labelValueExpectation.cancel()
    }
}
```

The `testLabelValue()` function observes the ViewModel's `labelValue` to see whether it equals `"Ready"` when tapping the button. We did all that without setting up the View, which only handles UI logic in this case.

Decoupling with Dependency Injection

DI is a powerful pattern that helps us to create modular and testable code. It's another tool in our toolbox that can help us make our code flexible and decoupled.

There are several ways to implement DI in iOS, which are discussed next.

Using constructor injection

This is the most common form of DI in iOS. In constructor injection, dependencies are passed into an object through its initializer. For example, if we have a view controller that depends on a data manager, we can inject the data manager into the view controller's initializer.

In the following code example, we created a custom `init()` function and a private variable to hold the injected data manager:

```
class MyViewController: UIViewController {
    private let dataManager: DataManager

    init(dataManager: DataManager) {
        self.dataManager = dataManager
        super.init(nibName: nil, bundle: nil)
    }
}

let viewController = MyViewController
    (dataManager: dataManager)
```

The main advantage of constructor DI is that we have a clear interface with the required dependencies for the class, as we must pass them in our `init()` method.

Simplifying things with setter injection

In setter injection, setter methods pass dependencies into the object. The object declares its dependencies as public properties, and the DI framework sets those properties with the appropriate dependencies. Setter injection is less common than constructor injection but can be helpful when changing the object's dependencies at runtime.

Here's a code example of setter injection:

```
// Define a view controller that depends on a data manager
class MyViewController: UIViewController {
    var dataManager: DataManager?
    }
}
let dataManager = ConcreteDataManager()
let viewController = MyViewController()
viewController.dataManager = dataManager
```

In this example, we haven't changed the `init` function of the view controller. After we created the view controller, we passed `dataManager` using the built-in setter property method.

The primary advantage of using setter injection is simplicity; we don't have to modify the `init` function and decoupling. On the other hand, this approach is not suitable for the required dependencies.

Using pure functions with method injection

In method injection, dependencies are passed into an object's methods as parameters. This is similar to constructor injection but allows for more fine-grained control over when and how dependencies are injected.

The `fetchData()` method is an example of a pure function:

```
// Define a view controller that depends on a data manager
class MyViewController: UIViewController {
    func fetchData(dataManager: DataManager) {
        let data = dataManager.fetchData()
    }
}
let dataManager = ConcreteDataManager()
let viewController = MyViewController()
viewController.fetchData(dataManager: dataManager)
```

In this code example, we have the same view controller and data manager, but this time we don't have an instance variable for the data manager. We pass the data manager as part of the `fetchData` method and make the function pure.

> **What is a pure function?**
>
> A pure function is a function that does not rely on instance variables or any state outside of its scope and only operates on its input parameters. It produces the same output for the same input and has no side effects on the program or environment. A pure function can rely on method injection to use external dependencies, where dependencies are passed in as parameters rather than depending on global or instance variables.

Method injection is excellent for testability as it increases the decoupling of the class from the dependency. It also decouples the class from the method (that's part of the "pure" definition we discussed), but it also requires our method signatures to be more complex and manage states outside the class.

These three ways of DI are great to improve decoupling and testability. But we can make all these ways much more decoupled. How? Easily, using protocols.

Decoupling our code using protocols

We discussed protocols in *Chapter 5* when we talked about the Swift language features. Protocols play a significant role in design patterns, especially in DI.

We can inject different objects with different behavior using protocols as long as they conform to the protocol interface.

Here's an example of using a protocol to inject a different object with a different implementation:

```swift
protocol DataManager {
    func fetchData() -> [String]
}

class ConcreteDataManager: DataManager {
    func fetchData() -> [String] {
        return ["Item 1", "Item 2", "Item 3"]
    }
}

class OtherDataManager: DataManager {
    func fetchData() -> [String] {
        return ["Item A", "Item B", "Item C"]
    }
}

class MyViewController: UIViewController {
    let dataManager: DataManager

    init(dataManager: DataManager) {
        self.dataManager = dataManager
        super.init(nibName: nil, bundle: nil)
    }
}

let concreteDataManager = ConcreteDataManager()

let viewController1 = MyViewController
    (dataManager: concreteDataManager)
let otherDataManager = OtherDataManager()
let viewController2 = MyViewController
    (dataManager: otherDataManager)
```

In this example, we have two instances of MyViewController. We inject concreteDataManager, an instance of the DataManager protocol, into the first instance, and we inject otherDataManager, another instance of the DataManager protocol, into the second MyViewController instance. They both have the same interface but different implementations. In this case, they return other elements in their fetchData() method. This technique allows us to inject whatever implementation we want with any object. It is especially powerful with testing and helps us to use mocks in our code.

To summarize DI, we can pick any pattern we want out of the three I mentioned – constructor, setter, or method – and expand its capabilities with a protocol. It all depends on the level of simplicity and coupling we want.

Communicating using delegation

Delegation is a simple pattern that allows objects to communicate with each other in a loosely coupled interface. Delegation is also based on a protocol that allows classes to communicate with different types of objects.

Let's see a small example of delegation:

```swift
protocol MyViewDelegate: AnyObject {
    func didTapButton()
}

class MyView: UIView {
    weak var delegate: MyViewDelegate?
    private let button = UIButton(type: .system)

    override init(frame: CGRect) {
        super.init(frame: frame)
        button.addTarget(self, action: #selector
            (buttonTapped), for: .touchUpInside)
        addSubview(button)
    }

    override func layoutSubviews() {
        super.layoutSubviews()
        button.frame = bounds
    }

    @objc private func buttonTapped() {
        delegate?.didTapButton()
    }
}

class MyViewController: UIViewController, MyViewDelegate {
    private let myView = MyView()

    override func viewDidLoad() {
        super.viewDidLoad()
        myView.delegate = self
        view.addSubview(myView)
```

```
    }

    func didTapButton() {
        print("Button tapped!")
    }
}
```

The `MyViewController` class has a view named `MyView` and conforms to a protocol named `MyViewDelegate`. This protocol has a method called `didTapButton()`.

`MyView` needs to communicate with `MyViewController` but doesn't have a direct reference. Instead, it has a delegate property of the `MyViewDelegate` type. This delegate property creates a loosely coupled interface between the view and its view controller (its "delegate").

Here are two takeaways from this code sample:

- *We need to create a delegate property*: The object that communicates with the delegate needs to have a delegate property, and the delegate property is obtained from the type of the protocol we just declared. This ensures a loosely coupled relationship; every object can conform to that protocol, even mocks for testing purposes.

- *We must mark the delegate as weak*: This is a critical point. Based on our code, the view controller has a strong reference to the view, and the view has a reference to the view controller through the delegate property. This means that the delegate property must be weak, and that's a common mistake many developers make. In fact, the weak reference to the delegate property is a common topic in interviews, and we should remember that when asked about it.

Even though delegation is a widely used pattern, it has some drawbacks compared to modern patterns such as Combine, and many developers consider it a little bit outdated.

To begin with, when using delegation to pass a message between multiple objects, the code can become cumbersome and difficult to read. This is especially true when each object must act as the delegate of the previous object, as it requires the creation of multiple protocols and delegates properties. As a result, the code can become boilerplate and challenging to follow and maintain.

Creating protocols can decrease our coupling, but our delegate must conform to a specific interface. With reactive programming, the subscriber observes updates without being tied to a particular interface, making the communication even more loosely coupled.

So, what can be a reason to choose delegation over Combine? With delegation, we can define a clear interface and even a complex one, which is not always true with Combine. But more than that – delegation clearly separates concerns and helps us keep our code modular and easy to maintain.

Let's go over a common interview question about the delegate design pattern.

"How does the delegation pattern differ from other communication patterns, such as notifications or closures, in Swift?"

Why is this question important?

A delegate design pattern is just one way for an object to communicate with another object. Over the years, new ways of communication have been added – notifications, closures, and, of course, reactive approaches such as Combine and RxSwift.

Each of these options has its pros and cons and we should match the pattern to the problem we are trying to solve. Therefore, it is important to understand the practical differences between these options.

What is the answer?

The delegate design pattern is different from notifications, closures, and Combine in several key ways:

- *One-to-one communication relationship*: While the notifications pattern and a Combine publisher can send a message to an unlimited number of instances, the delegate pattern typically communicates with a single object. This might initially seem like a disadvantage, but it also simplifies complex situations where we need more control over our code coupling.

- *Formalized protocol*: In a delegate pattern, there's a clear interface to work with the delegate, thanks to the use of protocols. The protocol formalizes the communication and provides clear expectations for both the delegate and the owner. This is extremely important when the communication becomes complex – for example, several functions to implement with multiple parameters.

- *More complex to set up*: Using the delegate pattern becomes more complex to set up when we want to pass a value or an event between different layers and components of our app. But it's not just the setup – following the data flow becomes cumbersome, as you have to jump between one protocol implementation and another. It's another example of a flexibility versus simplicity use case.

Overall, the delegate pattern is great for certain use cases and choosing the right communication option depends on the specific requirements of our problem.

As for interview questions, especially related to design patterns, we must remember that "better" relies on the context.

I think the next topic describes that perfectly.

Sharing a state using Singleton

There are two questions that interviewers love to ask:

- "How do we create a Singleton?"
- "Is it good to have singletons in our app?"

The first question is technical, but the second one is tricky.

Let's start with the definition of a Singleton.

What is a Singleton?

In the Singleton design pattern, there is only one instance of a class that can be globally accessed through a `static` property. It is often used to manage shared resources or states in a program where multiple instances could cause issues with synchronization or consistency. To implement a Singleton, a class typically has a private constructor and a static method or property that returns the single instance of the class.

In Swift, it is simple to create a Singleton. We use a static property for that task:

```
final class MySingleton {
    static let shared = MySingleton()
    private init() {}

    func doSomething() {
        print("Doing something...")
    }
}

MySingleton.shared.doSomething()
```

Note that the Singleton is defined with one line only:

```
static let shared = Singleton()
```

The critical thing is to always access the Singleton using the `shared` property, as seen in the preceding code example. To prevent creating another instance of the `MySingleton` class, we can mark the `init()` method as private and ensure there is only one instance.

But that was the easy question. The real question is – should we use a Singleton in our projects? Is it considered a legit pattern or an anti-pattern?

There are a couple of reasons why a Singleton can be an anti-pattern for many developers. Let's discuss some of them:

- *Having a global state*: Singletons provide a global state for the app, and multiple app components can manipulate this global state. As a result, it can be hard to track down where and when these changes are made. In a way, the main problem of having a global state that can be accessed from everywhere in the code, is when the app gets more extensive.

- *Coupling increasing*: We build a modular app with great code separations. But once our different app components access a shared instance (aka Singleton), the coupling between these components increases. Tight coupling becomes more of a concern as the number of Singletons in a program increases.

- *Challenge multithreading*: Because the Singleton can be accessed from everywhere, it also means that we can modify and read values from a shared instance from different threads. This can lead to race conditions and other synchronization issues.

So, what is the answer? Well, there are cases where having a Singleton is perfectly legit. For example, there should be only one instance of a particular object in the app – a configuration manager or database connection.

But we should try to avoid using a Singleton whenever possible. How? Let's answer that with an interview question.

"How would you avoid using a Singleton in your code? Can you describe some of the alternative approaches you might consider?"

Why is this question important?

At this point, we should already be familiar with the different design patterns and can come up with a suitable alternative. And that's the goal of the question – to test the ability to take your experience and knowledge and provide a good, acceptable solution.

If finding an alternative is possible, the general guideline regarding Singletons is to avoid them.

What is the answer?

The most common way to avoid a Singleton is using DI to inject services used within the class or the function.

Instead of creating a static constant (Singleton), we can approach the `Service` instance from the `Client` class:

```
class Service {
    static let shared = Service()
```

```
    func doSomething() {}
}
class Client {
    func useService() {
        Service.shared.doSomething()
    }
}
```

We can create an instance and inject it into the `Client` class:

```
class Service {
    func doSomething() {}
}

class Client {
    let service: Service

    init(service: Service) {
        self.service = service
    }

    func useService() {
        service.doSomething()
    }
}

let service = Service()
let client = Client(service: service)
```

If a global state is not required, injecting a new instance (or passing an existing instance) instead of using a Singleton is better.

We can improve that example by converting `Service` into a protocol:

```
protocol Service {
    func doSomething()
}

class ServiceImpl: Service {
    func doSomething() {}
}

let service = ServiceImpl()
let client = Client(service: service)
```

Now that `Service` is a protocol, it makes our coupling even looser. That's a nice code modification we can make.

"Can you describe the potential issues with using Singletons in a multithreaded environment, and how can these be addressed?"

Why is this question important?

We briefly mentioned multi-threading issues when we discussed Singleton's disadvantages earlier in this section. A Singleton is a shared resource, and as such, we must understand how it fits in a multithreaded environment.

What is the answer?

Here are some of the potential issues we can encounter with Singleton in a multithreaded environment:

- *Having race conditions*: If multiple threads try to access and modify the same Singleton instance simultaneously, it can result in race conditions that can cause unpredictable behavior and data corruption

- *Encountering deadlocks*: If multiple threads try to access a Singleton instance in a different order, it can lead to deadlocks where one thread waits for another to release a lock on the Singleton

- *Having an inconsistent state*: If a Singleton instance is modified by one thread while another thread is reading or using it, it can result in an unstable state and unexpected behavior

As developers, unpredictable behavior is one of the most challenging things to encounter, making debugging and investigation more difficult.

The simplest solution is to assume the Singleton is not a thread-safe object and can be accessed only from the same thread. Take the following example:

```
MySingleton.shared.doSomething()

DispatchQueue.global().async {
    DispatchQueue.main.async {
        MySingleton.shared.doSomething()
    }
}
```

In this example, we assume the Singleton can only be accessed from the main thread. We're using the **Grand Central Dispatch** (GCD) API to move to the main thread to ensure the Singleton is always accessed from the main thread.

Another option is to make the Singleton a thread-safe object by locking access using **NSLock**:

```
class MySingleton {
    static private var privateShared: MySingleton?
    static private let lock = NSLock()

    private init() {
        // Perform any necessary setup or initialization
    }

    static func threadSafeShared() -> MySingleton {
        lock.lock()
        defer {
            lock.unlock()
        }

        if privateShared == nil {
            privateShared = MySingleton()
        }

        return privateShared!
    }

    func doSomething() {
        // Perform some action or logic
    }
}
```

In this example, we make the shared instance a private property and add a static method that ensures locking and unlocking before returning the Singleton instance. This is a common practice to lock an object and make it thread-safe.

To summarize the topic – there is an ongoing debate and discussion in the iOS developer community. Some developers find Singleton a helpful tool that simplifies sharing states and resources, while others see Singleton as an anti-pattern that has the potential to cause problems. The truth, as always, is somewhere in the middle.

Improving performance with Concurrency

Concurrency is a complex computer science topic, not only in iOS development. A bad design can lead to crashes, race conditions, deadlocks, and lags.

But don't worry – do you remember what we said about design patterns in this chapter's introduction? They are here to solve our problems. So, let's review some of the design patterns and best practices for concurrency to see what tools we can add to our toolbox.

Working with GCD

GCD is a powerful concurrency framework that enables the efficient and scalable execution of tasks. GCD provides a simple way to create queues of tasks and schedule them for execution without managing threads manually. This makes it easy to write efficient and responsive code that takes full advantage of the available system resources.

Here is an example of how to use GCD to download an image asynchronously in the background:

```
func downloadImage(url: URL, completion: @escaping
    (UIImage?) -> Void) {
    let queue = DispatchQueue.global(qos: .background)
    queue.async {
        if let data = try? Data(contentsOf: url),
            let image = UIImage(data: data) {completion(image)
        } else {
            completion(nil)
        }
    }
}
```

In this example, we define a function, `downloadImage`, which takes a URL and a completion handler as parameters. The function creates a global background queue using the `DispatchQueue.global` method and then calls the async method to add a task to the queue. The task downloads the image data from the URL, converts it into a an image, and then calls the completion handler with the result. Because the task is executed asynchronously in the background, it does not block the main thread and allows the app to remain responsive.

Creating advanced queues with OperationQueue

An operation queue is a higher-level concurrency mechanism that manages tasks and executes them concurrently, like the GCD API we just discussed. **OperationQueue** provides advanced features and a simple interface for managing queues.

The basic unit of `OperationQueue` is `Operation`, which can perform a specific task. The operation queue's job is to take an operation and perform it simultaneously or one after the other.

We simply subclass the `Operation` class and implement the `main()` function to create an operation.

Here's an example of how to download multiple images using Operation Queue:

```
class ImageDownloadOperation: Operation {
    let url: URL
    var result: UIImage?

    init(url: URL) {
        self.url = url
    }

    override func main() {
        if let data = try? Data(contentsOf: url),
            let image = UIImage(data: data) {
            result = image
        }
    }
}

let urls: [URL] = // an array of image URLs
let queue = OperationQueue()

let downloadOperations = urls.map { url in
    ImageDownloadOperation(url: url)
}

queue.addOperations(downloadOperations,
    waitUntilFinished: true)

let images = downloadOperations.compactMap { $0.result }
```

In this example, we subclassed `Operation` by creating the `ImageDownloadOperation` class, which has a `url` property and performs a download operation in its main method.

Right after that, we create an operation queue called `queue` and an array of download operations. We add the operations array to our created queue and collect them by calling the `result` property.

One of Operation Queue's best features is the ability to configure how it works. If we want the queue to perform a maximum of three operations at the same time, we can set its `maxConcurrentOperationCount` value:

```
queue.maxConcurrentOperationCount = 3
```

If we set that property to `1`, our queue will perform the operations one after the other.

Another exciting option is *adding dependencies between the queue operations* – we can define that a specific operation cannot start before another operation ends.

Here's an example:

```
let downloadOp1 = ImageDownloadOperation(url: url1)
let downloadOp2 = ImageDownloadOperation(url: url2)
downloadOp2.addDependency(downloadOp1)
```

In this example, `downloadOp2` cannot start before `downloadOp1` ends.

Operation Queue generally provides advanced capabilities and patterns to perform complex background operations with more control.

Blocking threads with NSLock

`NSLock` is a synchronization mechanism for managing access to shared resources in a multi-threaded environment. `NSLock` provides a simple way to block threads that attempt to access a locked resource, allowing only one thread to access the resource at a time.

Here's an example of how to use `NSLock` to protect a shared resource:

```
class SharedResource {
    private var count = 0
    private let lock = NSLock()

    func increment() {
        lock.lock()
        count += 1
        lock.unlock()
    }

    func getCount() -> Int {
        lock.lock()
        let result = count
        lock.unlock()
        return result
    }
}
```

Let's assume that `SharedResource` can be used in different threads. This can cause race conditions and deadlocks in trying to access and modify the `count` variable simultaneously.

To handle that, we "lock" the read and write access with `NSLock` – we call `lock()` before the read/write operation and release it by calling `unlock()` afterward.

Using the Combine Future publisher to implement async operations

We already discussed Combine earlier in *Chapter 8*, but now let's discuss integrating async operations into the Combine stream.

The **Future** publisher is not only for concurrency operations – we use the `Future` publisher for any action whose value is not received immediately. For example, the `Future` type can include opening a modal, selecting an item, and dismissing it.

But let's see how we can use `Future` for async operations.

The `Future` publisher has a closure with a **promise** parameter that contains an output and a success/failure. Inside that closure, we call the `promise` parameter with either success or failure depending on the operation result.

Let's see an example:

```
func loadJSONFile() -> Future<Data, Error> {
    return Future { promise in
        DispatchQueue.global().async {
            let fileURL = FileManager.default.urls(for:
                .libraryDirectory, in: .userDomainMask)[0].
                    appendingPathComponent("articles.json")
            do {
                let data = try Data(contentsOf: fileURL)
                promise(.success(data))
            } catch {
                promise(.failure(error))
            }
        }
    }
}
```

In this example, the `loadJSONFile` function returns a `Future` publisher. Inside, it creates a background queue and loads a big JSON file. It calls the promise type with success and data if everything works fine. If not, it sends a failure and an error.

Now let's see how to use that function in a Combine stream:

```
let newArticles = loadJSONFile()
    .decode(type: [Article].self, decoder: JSONDecoder())
    .map { articles -> [Article] in
        let lastUpdate = UserDefaults.standard.object(
```

```
        forKey: "lastUpdate") as? Date ?? Date.distantPast
      return articles.filter { $0.publishedAt > lastUpdate }
  }
  .eraseToAnyPublisher()
```

Now, we can integrate the JSON loading operation in one line, decode its data, and map and filter it, as part of a Combine stream.

We can see how the `Future` publisher makes it very easy to integrate async operations in the Combine stream. We can also include more complex async operations in Combine by combining `OperationQueue` and `Future`.

Going over concurrency development best practices

Regardless of the different techniques we just learned, there are some best practices we should follow to keep our code safe from race conditions and deadlocks.

Some of them are derived from what we've learned till now. Also, these best practices are excellent for interview discussions about concurrency:

- *Avoid blocking the main thread*: The main thread handles UI updates, so blocking it can cause the app to become unresponsive. To avoid blocking the main thread, use background threads or operation queues to perform long-running or CPU-intensive tasks.

- *Use structs for safety*: Structs are value types, which means they're thread-safe by default. If we need to pass data between threads or queues, using structs can help prevent race conditions and other concurrency issues.

- *Avoid shared state*: Shared state between threads or queues can lead to race conditions and other concurrency issues. Instead, try to keep the state local to each thread or queue and use message passing or other communication mechanisms to share data between them.

- *Use Combine*: Combine is a robust framework for reactive programming in iOS and can help simplify concurrency by allowing you to define data streams and transformations that operate on those streams. By using Combine, you can avoid complex thread management and synchronization issues.

- *Always return a closure in the same thread*: When performing asynchronous operations, it's essential to ensure that any closures or callbacks are executed in the same thread or queue where they were initially created. This helps avoid race conditions and other concurrency issues when executing code across multiple threads.

Summary

This chapter was long, and this topic could be a book of its own. In fact, many books focus solely on design patterns, and it's obvious why – design patterns are our toolbox for everything we do in iOS development.

This chapter taught us about MVC/MVVM, DI, delegation, singletons, and concurrency patterns and tools. By now, we should have a great understanding of the primary design patterns in iOS.

This knowledge of design patterns is a great foundation to prepare us for the next chapter, which will focus on app architecture and development.

12
Drilling into App Architecture

In the last chapter, we discussed an important topic – design patterns. We said that design patterns are repeatable solutions that solve common problems. We can also say that design patterns are the building blocks of our code. Before looking at design patterns in this book, we went over Swift, then built upon it with the design patterns. Now we are at the top level – the app architecture.

App architecture is a critical topic in interviews, not just in the architecture design interview. Architecture discussions can happen *earlier*, even in the first stage. For example, the interviewer can ask about our previous projects and how we built them. Understanding the basic terminology and having the skills to use them in our interview is essential.

But don't worry because in this chapter, we will go over the most fundamental principles of mobile architecture:

- We'll go over the **Separation of Concerns (SoC)** principle
- We'll cover some *great tips* for separation in our code
- We'll learn how to *break our app into layers* and how data flows between them
- We'll talk about the *design interview*, how to approach it, and how to communicate with the interviewer

We've almost reached the end of the book, and as you'll have learned by now, I like to start with the basics, as it helps me to explain complex topics much better. The basics of app architecture is the SoC principle.

All about the Separation of Concerns principle

I have mentioned the **SoC principle** in the book several times. In fact, I mentioned this principle many times in my previous books and articles as well. In a way, the SoC principle sits at the heart of many design patterns and architectural decisions, and for a pretty good reason. Before we dive into understanding why, let's try to understand what SoC means.

Defining the Separation of Concerns principle

We'll begin with defining what SoC is. SoC refers to organizing code to separate different functionalities into different objects and owners. It means that a class or a module must have one and only one responsibility.

Look at the following example:

```
func processUserData(userData: [String: Any]) {
    // Responsibility 1: Validate the data
    guard let name = userData["name"] as? String,
        !name.isEmpty,
            let age = userData["age"] as? Int, age > 0,
            let email = userData["email"] as? String,
                !email.isEmpty else {
        print("Invalid user data")
        return
    }


    // Responsibility 2: Save the data to a file
    let documentsDirectory = FileManager.
        default.urls(for: .documentDirectory, in:
            .userDomainMask).first!
    let fileURL = documentsDirectory.
        appendingPathComponent("userData.txt")


    let userDataString = "Name: \(name)\nAge:
        \(age)\nEmail: \(email)\n"
    do {
        try userDataString.write(to: fileURL,
            atomically: true, encoding: .utf8)
        print("User data saved to file.")
    } catch {
        print("Error saving user data to file: \(error)")
    }


    // Responsibility 3: Send a welcome email
    print("Sending welcome email to: \(email)")
    }
}
```

In our code example, we can see that the `processUserData` function has three different responsibilities:

- *Validate* the user data
- *Save* the user data to a file
- *Send* a welcome email to the user

Notice that the problem starts earlier – the name `processUserData` indicates that the function has an unclear responsibility.

Separating the function into three different functions – `validateUserData`, `saveUserDataToFile`, and `sendWelcomeEmail` – would be an excellent solution to fix the problem of unclearness.

The SoC principle applies to functions and variables – a variable should have its own responsibility, just like functions and classes.

Take the following example:

```swift
class BadSoCExample {
    var name: String

    init(name: String) {
        self.name = name
    }

    func printFullName(firstName: String, lastName: String) {
        name = firstName
        print("First name: \(name)")

        name = lastName
        print("Last name: \(name)")

        print("Full name: \(firstName) \(name)")
    }
}

let example = BadSoCExample(name: "John Doe")
example.printFullName(firstName: "John", lastName: "Doe")
```

In this example, we use `name` to store both first and last names instead of creating two dedicated variables – `firstName` and `lastName`. These bad practices often happen when trying to save time, but they are error-prone and can lead to issues.

We can see that the SoC principle is a relevant factor in all levels of development, from variables, functions, and classes up to modules.

But…why is it so important? Let's see.

Explaining the importance of SoC

Now that we know what the SoC principle is, it is time to understand why it is important when designing and writing code.

There are a few reasons why we want to have a single responsibility for every part of our app and every variable. Let's name some of them:

- *Making our code more explicit*: When each part focuses on a single task, it is easier for us (and others) to understand what's happening. Clarity is also critical with debugging and code investigation – here's a quote from Brian Kernighan: "*Debugging is twice as hard as writing the code in the first place. Therefore if you write the code as cleverly as possible, you are, by definition, not smart enough to debug it.*" The only way to reduce the gap between writing and debugging is clarity.

- *Maintaining the code becomes easier*: We all know writing code is easier than maintaining it. One of the reasons is that every code modification we perform can create a new bug. Moreover, modifications often change the code structure to something we hadn't planned when writing it. We are reducing both risks when isolating tasks to specific functions or classes.

- *Increase our code reusability*: This is another important benefit of the SoC principle. When a view, a controller, or a module has a specific task and responsibility, it makes it easier to reuse. Let's take, for instance, a library that handles text manipulation. Adding more features and capabilities to that library may increase its dependencies and side effects. It also makes it bigger and more error-prone since it now handles more responsibilities irrelevant to what we need and may collide with another library we want to link. Separating part of the library from another is smarter and allows us to work with different libraries like LEGO pieces.

- *Improve our code testability*: One of the critical aspects of testing is ensuring that the outcomes are predictable. When a method is responsible for multiple tasks, it might reduce its predictability over time. Think of a function that returns a computed value and updates user defaults. Testing the function's returned value can have side effects we don't want in our test use case. It is better to separate that calculation into another function and test it separately.

These benefits are the foundation of any design pattern or architectural decision we make when working on our projects. Moreover, SoC is an essential principle to follow when approaching an architectural task in an interview. It is the basis for any professional discussion we may have during our interviews.

Now, let's dive a bit deeper and look at some practical tips for the SoC principle.

Going practical with the Separation of Concerns principle

This chapter aims to prepare us for the architectural interview, which may contain whiteboard tasks and professional discussions. We understand the SoC principle's importance, but how do we transform it into practical tools?

The good news is that we reviewed these tools in previous chapters. Let's list them now and add some more.

Having a clear understanding of using UI design patterns

I do not doubt that the topic of MVVM or MVC will be central in your interviews. What's important here is to really understand the different components and their responsibility. If we decide to use MVVM for our screen, we must ensure that we do it because we need to manage a complex state and not because "this is how things are done today." We must ensure we use the right tool for the right job and that each component performs its role.

To help understand this, look at *Figure 12.1*:

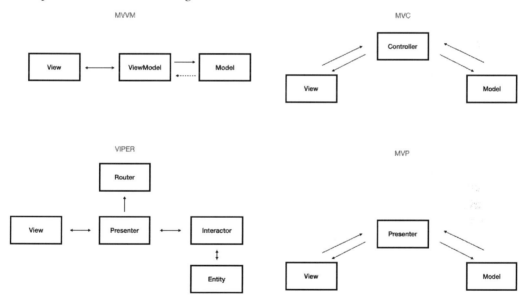

Figure 12.1 – The most popular UI design patterns in iOS

In *Figure 12.1*, we can see that our selection of design patterns is broader than just MVC and MVVM. Furthermore, there are no rules here, just best practices. Choosing the correct design pattern while considering the different responsibilities and separations is essential to implementing the SoC principle.

For example, VIPER can be incredible for screens that work with many services and data entities, and MVP is suitable for a UI that focuses on formatting and presentation tweaks.

VIPER and MVP?

I won't go over VIPER and MVP because they are less common design patterns in iOS development than MVC and MVVM. I recommended reading about these patterns and learning the pros and cons, so you have broader knowledge for your interview.

Here are some great reads on VIPER and MVP:

- VIPER: `https://www.kodeco.com/8440907-getting-started-with-the-viper-architecture-pattern`

- MVP: `https://www.javatpoint.com/ios-model-view-presenter`

Using Clean Architecture

Later, in the *Designing app architecture* section, we will discuss app architecture, but for now, we are just laying the groundwork, and **Clean Architecture** serves as a great foundation. So, what is Clean Architecture?

Clean Architecture is an architectural approach emphasizing the SoC principle when developing a full-blown app. It involves dividing our project into layers – the data layer, presentation layer, business logic layer, and network layer – and pushes for clean SoC between the different layers and components. If we take that even further, we're discussing creating various libraries for other parts of the project and trying to make our app feel like a giant puzzle. Notice that breaking our app into modules has a price – maintaining different modules can be difficult and requires planning and sometimes complex interface decisions. We must always consider the trade-off between a stable structure and a complicated interface.

Writing small functions

This is a tip most of us have heard several times before. They say a function length should be "less than a screen," but if we want to go extreme, we can say that functions should be *as small as possible*. Breaking a long function into two/three functions is a good idea to make our code cleaner, less error-prone, and easier to maintain.

Look at the following code example:

```
func calculateTotalPrice(itemPrices: [Double],
    itemQuantities: [Int]) -> Double {
    var totalPrice = 0.0
    for i in 0..<itemPrices.count {
        totalPrice += itemPrices[i] * Double(itemQuantities[i])
    }
    return totalPrice
}
```

While this function works, it has multiple responsibilities – it iterates the list of items and calculates their prices. To improve the SoC, we can separate this code into another function that calculates a single item's price:

```swift
func calculateItemPrice(price: Double, quantity: Int) -> Double {
    return price * Double(quantity)
}

func calculateTotalPrice(itemPrices: [Double],
    itemQuantities: [Int]) -> Double {
    var totalPrice = 0.0
    for i in 0..<itemPrices.count {
        totalPrice += calculateItemPrice(price:
            itemPrices[i], quantity: itemQuantities[i])
    }
    return totalPrice
}
```

Now we have a dedicated function to calculate a specific item price, and we use it in the original `calculateTotalPrice()` function. Small modification? Well, regarding code design, that's a dramatic change – we can test the calculation separately and reuse it in other places in our code. Also, the code is more readable, and the `calculateItemPrice()` function name also saves us from explaining what `price*Double(quantity)` does and even avoids unneeded comments.

It's interesting to see that even though the original function was small and worked well, we can still break it and improve our code in several aspects. That's why the phrase "as small as possible" is much more accurate.

Using descriptive names

Descriptive names are always a good idea, but how does naming help us have good, clean, and separated code?

Naming has a secret power – it forces us to think about the responsibility of our function and describe precisely what it does. The attention we give it can help us make the right design decisions.

Here's an example – look at the next function interface:

```swift
func getProducts() -> [Product] {}
```

It's clear that `getProducts()` is supposed to fetch and return products. But what exactly does it do? Does it load the products from local data storage or use a network request?

Let's improve the function name:

```swift
func retrieveProductsFromServer() -> [Product] {}
```

Now, things have become more apparent. We understand exactly what the function does. But the issue is unclear – our question about the function's job helped us think deeply about its responsibility. Maybe originally, we came up with the following name:

```
func retrieveProductsFromServerAndSaveThemToDB() -> [Proudct] {}
```

That's a great indication we need to break the function since describing its responsibility becomes long and cumbersome.

Here are some more examples of good naming:

```
fetchData() -> fetchUserDataFromServer()
calculate() -> calculateAvrageSalary()
validate() -> validatePasswordStrength()
add() -> addItemToCart()
load() -> loadDataFromCache()
```

Coming to the interview process with naming conventions in mind is a good idea. And you know what? You'll have written hundreds (if not more) functions in your life. You just need to think back and reflect on them. Maybe we'll learn something using our code.

> **Here's a disclaimer!**
>
> I know some tips here are not about "architecture." But these principles and recommendations are relevant at any level.

SoC lays the groundwork for designing a scalable, modular, and maintainable app architecture. We can move on to designing app architecture now that we understand that.

Designing app architecture

One of the most common mistakes candidates make when asked about app architecture is replying, "MVVM, of course!"

So, I want to remind you – MVVM is a design pattern, not an architecture, and I want to emphasize the difference.

A design pattern is a reusable solution to a common problem. Dependency Injection, Singletons, and MVVM are examples of design patterns. On the other hand, architecture is the general structure of our project that represents our app idea.

An excellent real-world example is a building. In this case, the architecture describes the number of floors, where the parking lot and the entry door are, or what type of roof we have. Design patterns describe *how each apartment is built* – the number of rooms in each apartment, the kitchen's location, and the electrical wiring.

We can say that each apartment and floor could be designed differently – meaning we can use different design patterns for various problems and needs.

Valuable insights can be gained by drawing parallels with the building industry, as there are many similarities between constructing an application and building structures.

Instead of apartments, we have application screens; instead of a roof and lobby, we have application layers.

So, let's talk about application layers for a second.

Breaking the architecture into application layers

The different layers of an app can be a good starting point for describing an app architecture. But what are layers?

Layers are different components or sets of components that have different concerns and app responsibilities. Most apps work with three primary layers:

- **Presentation layer**: Responsible for presenting information using a UI. We can find here the different screens and UI components.

- **Business logic layer**: Responsible for the app logic, rules, and calculations.

- **Data layer**: Responsible for storing and retrieving data from local databases or other sources.

Layers or tiers?

One common mistake people make when discussing layers is calling them "tiers." The term "tiers" refer to the physical component of an application, while "layers" refers to the software component. For example, a tier can be a different computer or server responsible for a specific concern. In the case of an iOS app architecture, the term "tiers" is irrelevant unless we include the backend side.

For a quick reminder, we'll review design patterns – MVVM is an example of implementing a screen as part of the presentation layer. A Singleton is a design pattern that can help us to implement a Core Data handler as part of the data layer.

Let's see a typical application architecture (*Figure 12.2*):

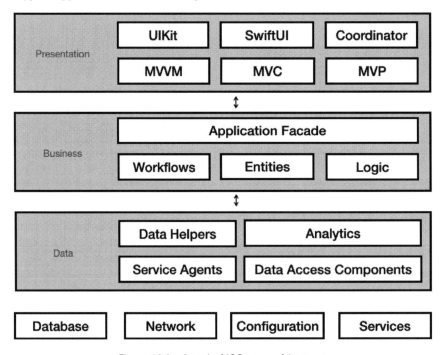

Figure 12.2 – A typical iOS app architecture

Don't be intimidated by the diagram in *Figure 12.2* – remember, *we already know* that things need to be reorganized in our heads.

We can see that the architecture in *Figure 12.2* is separated into the three different layers we discussed earlier in this section:

- We can see that the *presentation* layer has various technologies and design patterns.

- In the *business logic* layer, we have another design pattern – Façade, which is a design pattern that provides a simplified interface to a complex and large code block. This is our entry point to the app logic. We can also see the different entities we work with in the business layer, the logic of the workflow, and the general app logic.

- In the *data layer*, we can see different service agents (connectors) that can help us connect to various services. We can also see analytics and helper services.

Underneath the diagram, we have external services, such as the database, network, and configuration. These services are data sources for the data layer.

The architecture diagram illustrates another aspect: how the data flows between the different layers, which we will see next.

Learning about data flow

We understand that if the presentation layer needs to show information to the user, we need it to fetch the information from the business layer all the way to the data layer and the database. There are cases where we can have an app with more layers, such as notification, security, and persistence layers. In that case, the data flow gets a little more complex.

One interesting question that may arise is whether it's feasible for a layer to bypass another layer while retrieving data.

Let's try to answer that briefly.

When designing a layered system, there are two terms that we need to learn – closed and open layers:

- **Closed layer**: A closed layer means the given layer cannot be bypassed to one of the layers below it
- **Open layer**: An open layer means the given layer can be passed to any layer below it

It is considered a best practice for a system to be fully closed or open, but in most cases, systems have a mixture of open and closed layers.

So, what are the benefits of having a closed or open layer?

Look at *Figure 12.3*:

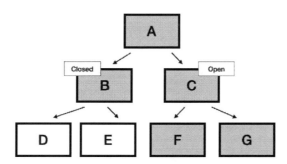

Figure 12.3 – Open and closed layers

In *Figure 12.3*, we can see a system architecture with different layers and their dependencies. Layer B is closed, meaning layer A can't access layers D and E. On the other hand, layer C is open, meaning that layer A can access layers F and G.

The gray-filled layers are those layer A has access to, but it also means that these are dependencies.

What the open layer does is increase coupling by exposing the top layers to more layers. On the other hand, closed layers are harder to maintain and require designing an excellent and flexible interface ahead of time. We already know that reducing the number of dependencies creates a loose and flexible system, but it doesn't mean we need to create an overly complex design. This is an excellent example of a trade-off between simplicity and flexibility.

What's more important is to understand these terms when designing architecture and making decisions. Building a layered system without thinking at all is probably the worst thing we can do.

Architecture concepts combined with design patterns are the ground for designing good architecture for our projects.

Let's take a real-world example and review its design together.

Designing an offline-first system architecture

An **offline-first** system architecture is a typical design many interviewers like to discuss. The reason is that this use case involves working with different data sources and design patterns to achieve what seems to be an important advantage of having a mobile-native app instead of a web app.

The way an offline-first system works is by having two data sources – a *persistent store* and *network* communication. On top of that, we have a *sync service* that is responsible for updating the persistent store with data from the network. The business logic layer that connects the UI to the data layer works directly with the persistent store, regardless of the network status.

Let's see a diagram of such a system (*Figure 12.4*):

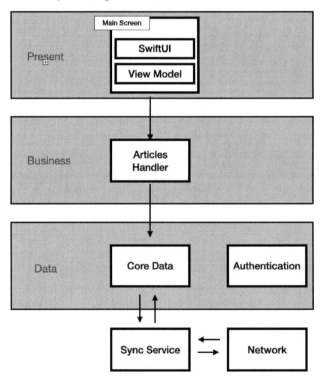

Figure 12.4: Offline-first system architecture

Looking at *Figure 12.4*, we can see that **Articles Handler** on the business layer works directly with Core Data *without being aware* of the network layer. The sync service is the only component that links the Core Data store and the network.

We provide a superb user experience to our users by adding offline loading. Besides that, we have an excellent implementation of the SoC principle with a decoupled system that makes its components totally disconnected.

A typical implementation option candidates love to answer with in interviews is doing all the sync work in one class in the business logic or even as part of the view model. Sure, that option can work great, but this is a very narrow point of view when designing a system that can scale and be maintained over time. Having a dedicated service that can handle sync logic and maintain it separately is perfectly fine.

It is always important to remind ourselves of the responsibility of every component in our system and how it communicates with other components. That can lead us to a better and clearer design.

The architecture design interview

The architecture design interview is a crucial step toward our proposal, and it requires skills that are much softer and communication oriented.

Unlike Swift, Combine, and Core Data questions, the architecture design interview requires us to step forward and come up with a more holistic point of view – product requirements, backend, scale, analytics, and user experience are all factors we need to consider when trying to design a complete system.

The architecture interview, perhaps even more than the other steps in the hiring process, is based on communication and meeting expectations. Therefore, we'll start with understanding the interviewer's point of view.

Entering the head of our interviewer

So, what does our interviewer want from us? What are their expectations?

The most important thing to understand here is that the interviewer doesn't care whether your answer is the most optimized solution, or even whether it's right or wrong. The architecture design interview is definitely in another field, and the interviewer is looking for something else – they want to see how we *think*, approach problems, *manage trade-offs*, and find a path to a decent solution based on the product requirements.

Let's take, for example, the following interview question:

"Design the Messages app that comes with iOS."

Obviously, the top app feature would be the messaging screen ("chat"). Here is a list of issues we need to tackle when we approach that problem:

- What would the UI components we will use be?

- What is the data model? What will the properties of each message be?

- What endpoints do we need? Are we going to implement pagination? If not, how do we handle an endless number of messages?

- Do we support offline use? How are we going to do that?

- Do we support attachments? How is it going to work?

- What if we want to have a group chat?

- Are we going to support real-time updates?

These are just some of the questions that arise when approaching this task, and none are straightforward. It's our job to find the answers.

So, how do we start?

Approaching the mission

I've interviewed hundreds of candidates in my life, and many of them struggled to understand how to approach an architecture interview.

It's not that they didn't know how to design an app or explain their ideas – they didn't know two things:

- What the starting point for the task was

- What their boundaries were

These two topics are critical to understand for the interview to warm up and get on track to a great solution.

Let's begin with the starting point – understanding the problem and the scope.

Understanding the problem and the scope

The first thing we need to do when approaching a design question is to stop, breathe, and try to understand what the interviewer expects from us. Most candidates fail at this point because they know they have limited time to answer a question, so they rush up to scribble boxes on the whiteboard.

But the design interview represents a real-life task. The interviewer expects us to understand the problem before describing what we do.

Let's return to our problem – designing a messages app similar to the one that comes with iOS. Several questions we can ask the interviewer are as follows:

- Do we have a UI wireframe or must we produce it ourselves?

- How many screens do we have?

- Does the design need to contain the backend services as well?

- Is it cross-platform (including Android or web) or iOS only?

- Do we have a given database scheme, or do we need to plan it ourselves?

These are just a few examples, but they can help us understand what we must do.

Once we understand the problem and what to do, we can retrieve the product requirements.

Getting the product requirements

Unlike with conventional development tasks, we don't have a **Product Requirements Document (PRD)** or a kickoff meeting with our product manager in the architecture design interview. Instead, we must understand the product requirements and ask our interviewers for more information. In fact – this is what the interviewer is looking for!

Imagine the interview is like a dark maze where we navigate with a flashlight and unveil more areas, rooms, and paths. Sometimes even the interviewer doesn't know where we will take the interview!

Going back to the messages app task, there are some questions we can think of when starting to design the app. Take the following examples:

- Do we support offline reading and writing?

- Do we have an integration with the device contacts?

- Do we need to support notifications and real-time chat?

- Can the user edit or delete messages?

- Do we need to support landscape mode?

These questions weren't posed out of curiosity. They impact the design and technical decisions we'll need to make. For example, offline support is crucial to understand our data source's behavior and sync mechanism. Integration with the device contacts influences our data model. Real-time chat defines our network methods, and edit and delete features affect how we sync information back to the backend.

It is perfectly fine not to ask all the questions at first – sometimes we just need to start designing to understand what we need to ask, but having a good start is a good idea.

But how do we start the design? With wireframes? Or entities? That's a good question, so let's see.

Starting the design

The design part is dynamic. No one expects us to have the final answers when we start to draw, and we should expect things to change during the interview according to new findings and conclusions. Presenting things clearly and in detail can help us communicate better with the interviewer and express our thoughts better.

Going to the whiteboard – wireframes

We are not product designers, and no one expects us to be. But knowing how to present our ideas on a whiteboard is crucial for that process. We already discussed that in *Chapter 1* when we discussed technical preparations, and now, we understand exactly why.

So, how do we start? Some developers like to start with basic UML that describes the different entities or classes. But in my opinion, it is better to start with wireframing the different screens when it comes to app architecture. Let's start with the messages screen (*Figure 12.5*):

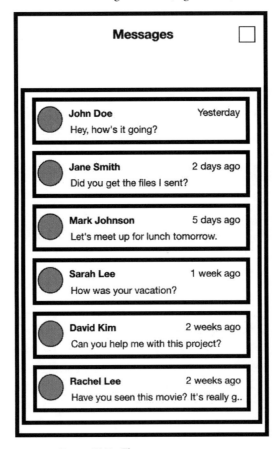

Figure 12.5 – The messages screen

Looking at *Figure 12.5*, we can understand why starting from the UI is better. Ignoring the font size and the layout (I'm not a good designer, I know), it looks like there are many things we can learn from this wireframe. Let's list them:

- We're starting to understand the *different entities*. For example, we see a full name and an avatar – that describes the `Contact` entity. We can also see that the list shows the contact's last message, which contains text property, so we have another entity here – `Message`.

- We see that the list is being sorted by time. That's maybe the place to dig a little bit deeper – do we want to sort it according to the most updated message for each contact, or do we want to have an `updatedTime` property of the `Contact` entity? This is a classic *trade-off between performance and simplicity*; we should discuss it with our interviewer.

- How about the *UI*? We know we are supposed to have some sort of `UITableView` here. But do we want to load all the messages into the table view, or do we want to support pagination? What design pattern are we going to use here, MVC or MVVM? We should decide on the app's scale, the first-time experience, and common user usage.

Before we continue, I want you to notice something – there are no clear answers, just considerations and trade-offs. I asked questions but haven't given you any answers because the questions we ask ourselves and the interviewer are part of the process. That's the place to show that we understand there are gray areas where we need to make the decisions.

So, are we just using the whiteboard to draw a UI? Not necessarily – let's continue.

Adding entities and backend services

It's *Chapter 12*, and we know that an app is more than just the UI. But is one screen enough to start designing the other parts? Definitely, yes!

Let's add entities (*Figure 12.6*):

Contact

Name	Type
id	UUID
First name	String
Last name	String
Avatar	Url

Message

Name	Type
Id	UUID
Text	String
Sender	String
Time	Date

Figure 12.6 – Initial entities for the message's app

Writing the entities on the whiteboard sounds like a technical task, but similar to wireframing, it can help us find more exciting things about our app.

For example, we mentioned a URL for a contact avatar – this means we need to create some kind of image downloader service and a caching mechanism based on that URL. As a result, the *image downloader* can be added to our drawing on the whiteboard.

Look what we've achieved based on a single entity's property!

But the actual value of drawing the entities is when we start thinking about their relationships. We have `Contact` and `Message`. But what describes a conversation with a contact? Maybe we need to create another entity named `MessagesThread`. And if we have a `MessagesThread` entity, what would its properties be?

At this stage, things become a little bit more complex, because thinking about the connections brings up more questions – for example, do we support group messaging? The answer sets the relation type between `MessageThread` and `Contact`.

Drawing the entities next to our wireframes creates a back-and-forth process that helps us shape our design and make it more complete. Each decision leads to more questions, leading to more design decisions. It also sets the path to our next task: designing the interaction with our backend.

Adding network calls

Now that we have the basic UI wireframes and entities, planning how we will work with our backend service should be easier. Remember that the UI and entities are still part of our app learning stage – now we understand better what we need to do. The different endpoints define the user experience and the design patterns we will use, and that's where we can really work on our app architecture, as we learned in this chapter.

Let's see what endpoints we need for the main screen:

- `GET/threads`: To retrieve the list of all the threads
- `POST/thread`: To create a new messages thread

Generally, when working with a list of information, it is common to include these two endpoints as a part of our design. But there are more things to consider here:

- How are the threads sorted? Do we get them sorted from the server, or do we sort them by a specific property?
- Do we have a pagination mechanism? Or do we fetch all threads and use an incremental update sync?
- Do we need the `POST` request at this stage? Or can we do that only after the first message we send?

The endpoints also help us to define the app architecture. They answer important questions about the UI layer and its design patterns (MVC/MVVM). But they also help us understand our data layer and the different services we will need. The following are examples:

- Core Data handler

- Image downloader

- Sync service

- Network service and real-time management

If we continue adding more endpoints to the rest of the screens, we will learn more about our app and get more answers.

Designing an app architecture is a discovery process. Nothing is clear at the beginning, and communicating the process to find the answers is essential. That's why our next topic is extremely important – our communication with the interviewer.

Communicating with the interviewer

As mentioned earlier in this section, many candidates believe their primary goal in the architecture design interview is to provide the most optimal solution to the problem they just received. But the truth is that the goal is for the interviewer to see how we think and offer a decent solution to problems that might come up.

Therefore, effective communication with the interviewer is crucial to be successful in this kind of interview. Some of our most critical soft skills are being tested here!

Let's go over some tips to help us focus on what matters:

- *Listen to the interviewer*: That's obvious, right? Of course we are going to listen to the interviewer! But I mean, *really* listen to them. First, because the task requirements and the scope are very important to be precise on what we do. Moreover, there are valuable tips our interviewer will give us that can help us with our goal.

- *Clarify doubts*: If you are uncertain about your decision, you must communicate this to the interviewer. Interviewers need to see that candidates see things in shades of gray and not just black and white, but it is also a way to get clues or discuss things with the interviewer.

- *Be confident*: I know it sounds like it contradicts the previous point, but it doesn't. It's true that when we have doubts, we need to communicate them, but when we are confident about something, we must show it. Self-confidence is an essential factor in these interviews.

- *Think out loud*: We know what we want to achieve with our design, and we even drew it on the whiteboard. But what is clear to us is not always apparent to the other person in the room. Thinking out loud can help us explain what we're doing more clearly and help the interviewer understand the fantastic architecture we've just designed.

- *Use the correct terminology*: In this book, I have been strict about the different terms used – method versus function, design pattern versus architecture, and more. Using the correct terminology in these interviews is essential, not just to appear professional; it also makes our explanations much more evident to our interviewer. Not all interviewers are strict about it – but that doesn't mean we shouldn't be.

- *Be open to feedback*: The interviewer may provide feedback or suggestions during the interview. Sometimes it is a clue for the direction we can take, or sometimes it's because we went out of scope. What happens many times, in this case, is that candidates lose their self-confidence and close themselves off, finding it difficult to accept that feedback. We should put our egos aside when we enter the design interview (actually, we should put our egos aside all the time) and use the interviewer's feedback to improve our answers. Feedback during the interview doesn't mean we failed – it means that we have a chance to provide a better solution.

It seems like we are being tested on how we communicate and express ourselves, but that's the reality! The interviewer wants to see what it is like working with us, discussing design issues, and having architecture debates. That's where our personality stands out.

Summary

The architecture design interview is the highlight of the hiring process. It incorporates extensive knowledge of design patterns, architectures, iOS user experience, and critical soft skills such as planning, communication, and presentation.

However, at this point, we should be in a position where we know how to crack the interview with several primary steps.

In this chapter, we've learned about the SoC and how it applies to iOS architecture, including function size and naming. We've learned about application layers and data flows and even discussed an excellent example of an architecture for offline working. And finally, we discussed the architecture design interview – how to approach it and communicate with the interviewer.

In the next (and final!) chapter, we will discuss the most practical step in the interview: the live coding interview and the home assessment. All hiring processes now include this step, and it's our job to be ready for the unknown.

13
Acing the Coding Assessment

In the previous chapter, we discussed architecture in depth. Architecture discussions tend to be very theoretical and methodological; the same can be said for design pattern discussions.

In this chapter, we will get to the meat – to the code, working with Xcode, and playing with algorithms. We will cover everything related to coding interview tasks, such as the following:

- How to succeed in a live coding interview, the different tests, and how to code like a pro
- How to excel in home assessments by discussing different skills to use and reviewing home assessment examples
- How to avoid mistakes that may raise red flags in our interviews

This is the final chapter! You will be fully prepared for your first interview by the end of it. Now, let's dive straight into tips for the live coding interview.

Succeeding in live coding

The live coding interview is probably the most intimidating in the process.

It's easy to understand why – for most developers, it's a stage that is an uncomfortable situation in any case.

For a start, in most cases, we aren't working in our beloved (to some of us) Xcode. We are required to handle tasks that we usually don't face in our day-to-day work, and we're doing that under pressure while someone is watching us at every step.

The reason why I said "probably" and "most developers" at the start of this section is that it doesn't have to be intimidating. Sure, live coding is a stressful interview, but we can make it exciting and much more joyful with the right approach.

Skeptical? Don't be! Throughout the preceding 12 chapters, we have observed that proper preparation can make anything achievable.

Before we rush into the interview itself, let's learn about the different environments we will work in and the different types of tests.

Learning about the different live coding tests

Unlike the other interview stages, the live coding interview usually has different shapes and forms that dramatically affect how the whole interview feels and looks.

There are three types of live coding interviews – whiteboard, online, and in-person. We call them live coding here, but each provides different experiences and challenges. Let's start with the whiteboard interview.

The whiteboard interview

If I recall correctly, this is the third time we're mentioning the importance of the whiteboard. The first time was in *Chapter 2*, when we discussed preparing for the interview process (in the *Getting ready for the screening interview* section). The second time was in *Chapter 12* (in the *The architecture design interview* section) when we discussed the architecture interview, and now, we're mentioning it in approaching the live coding stage.

Why is the whiteboard such an essential tool in interviews? What makes interviewers highly value the whiteboard, and how can we maximize it for our benefit?

Well, the whiteboard has one significant advantage – it promotes clarity and communication between people and allows us to visualize our thinking when explaining an idea. That's the reason why most meeting rooms include a whiteboard.

Now, as candidates, it is sometimes difficult to use the whiteboard if we are not used to it. And the fact that we're standing there struggling with a coding question doesn't help that situation either.

But it can also be a good tool for communicating with our interviewer, as we did in the previous chapter.

If you think that communication is not a big deal in interviews, let's get into the online interview, and you'll understand why it is critical.

The online interview

The online interview is a session that takes place via a **video conference** using a platform such as Zoom, FaceTime, or Google Meet.

You might think the online interview's significant advantage would be using an **integrated development environment** (**IDE**). But in most cases, the session happens on a dedicated website without indentation, code completion, or syntax highlighting.

In addition, the online coding interview has another drawback that we didn't have in the whiteboard interview: communication.

I have observed, on multiple occasions, that interaction with the interviewer plays a vital role in the success of an interview. It is undeniable that communication is more challenging in online sessions compared to in-person meetings.

However, complaining is not the path to success.

We need to look for other advantages of an online coding session. For example, the fact that we are coding on a computer allows us to edit and push rows down if needed. Whiteboard editing is much more difficult and forces us to plan what we are going to write.

Furthermore, scheduling and preparing for an online coding interview is comparatively more straightforward. Remote meetings and using computers are likely within our comfort zone, as the Covid-19 era has taught us how to navigate these aspects effectively.

Combining both worlds – the in-person coding interview

The "in-person" coding interview takes place on a laptop in front of our interviewer. This is a unique approach compared to the previous two methods (whiteboard and remote), and there's an excellent reason for that. The in-person coding interview has an advantage in terms of personal interaction. Still, this advantage is often not strong enough when considering the logistical efforts that come with it.

Therefore, the whiteboard coding interview is preferable when discussing in-person sessions.

Having said that, the in-person coding interview usually happens in companies that wish to see us coding in a natural working environment. In some instances, the interviewer accompanies us while we code, while in other cases, we are given privacy to code in a room on our own, with the interviewer checking in periodically to assess our progress. Both cases can be stressful for developers, having to code while someone is watching them. But sometimes, that's part of the test – to see how we perform complex tasks under slight pressure.

All three ways (whiteboard, in-person, and remote coding) are common, and all of them can be stressful experiences. The best way to decrease the pressure level is to practice and be prepared for this challenge.

Preparing ourselves for the coding interview

I know you might be thinking that the fact that we are veteran developers means that we are ready for a coding interview since coding is what we do almost every day. But you can't be more wrong on that – the coding interview requires new skills and techniques to pass it successfully.

We have already reviewed the different coding test types – whiteboard, in-person, and remote. We will see that some skills need to be sharpened to pass these tests. We'll start with the first and primary one – writing code in a plain text editor.

Working with a plain text editor

In most coding interviews, we will work with a **plain text editor**. A whiteboard, for that matter, is a plain text editor.

A plain text editor lacks syntax highlighting, indentation, and code completion, creating an unfamiliar environment for us.

It might be easy to declare a function without any problems in a plain text editor, as you can see in the following code:

```
func foo() { print("foo") }
```

But that's the easy part! Let's see what the challenges are and how we deal with them.

Spotting syntax errors

Syntax highlighting helps us spot keywords and expressions, but it also helps us find syntax errors, such as missing parentheses, brackets, or semicolons. In a text editor, there's a best practice of typing both open and closed brackets or parentheses and only then writing the expression inside.

However, on a whiteboard, we can't use that technique. One option is to *highlight delimiters* ourselves and write them in a different color. Sure, doing that can slow us down, but it will make our code much clearer and more aesthetic. Another option is to *draw the delimiter bigger*, which is another way of highlighting.

Avoiding typos

While syntax is just one aspect of an IDE, code completion is another crucial feature. We are used to writing extended descriptive functions and variable names, relying on the code editor to handle them through code completion. However, that's not the case with a plain text editor. Without code completion, typos can break our code. Although typos can be more acceptable in whiteboard coding interviews than in in-person or remote interviews, they still look bad and unprofessional.

A way to help us avoid typos is to use clear and short names for functions and variables. That can speed up the coding and help us organize our writing on the whiteboard.

Mastering complex Swift expressions

I mentioned earlier how simple it is to declare a function in Swift. But Swift is much more than functions and variables declarations. So, to master Swift, we need to have complete knowledge of more complex expressions and functions, such as the following:

- Collections functions – `filter`, `map`, and `reduce`
- Closures

- Advanced type system features – generics and protocols
- Tuples and enums

This list contains features prone to mistakes, and when I say mistakes, I don't mean just cosmetic ones. The closure format, for example, has critical components that directly affect our code flow. The same goes for generics and protocols.

We should practice Swift's complex expressions and ensure we master them.

Maintaining code organization

Code organization is a critical topic because it's a real challenge when working with a plain editor. As you know, a plain editor doesn't have indentation, which usually helps us to create a readable and organized code. Remember closures and filtering? Trying to read these Swift features without indentation is complex, and code readability affects our chances of success.

Indentation becomes even more critical when coding on a whiteboard. On a laptop, at least, we can use tabs, something that doesn't exist on whiteboards.

We understand now that many of the challenges we face in plain text editor coding become even more prominent on a whiteboard. Don't worry! There's still time to manage that.

Practicing on a whiteboard

For most of us, coding on a whiteboard is not natural. Consider developers who have spent nearly 10,000 hours coding in front of a computer; the transition to coding on a whiteboard can be challenging.

When it comes to coding on a whiteboard as opposed to a laptop, there are several challenges that we should bear in mind. For example, whiteboards don't have scroll capabilities, it is much more difficult to edit or insert new rows, there are no straight lines or font sizes, and our canvas is just one big white surface without a grid.

Having said that, some tips can help us improve our whiteboarding skills. Let's go over them:

- *Visualize our code structure*: As I said, whiteboards don't have any built-in scrolling mechanism, and their coding area is fixed. Therefore, before coding on a whiteboard, we should visualize our answer structure. Notice I wrote *answer* and not *code*. The reason for that is that our answer is much more than just the function we were supposed to implement – there are tests, diagrams, and perhaps even notes we need to consider. We should divide the whiteboard into zones and allocate space for each answer's component. Of course, the same goes for the coding area itself – try to imagine how long your answer will be and choose your font size accordingly. Look at *Figure 13.1*:

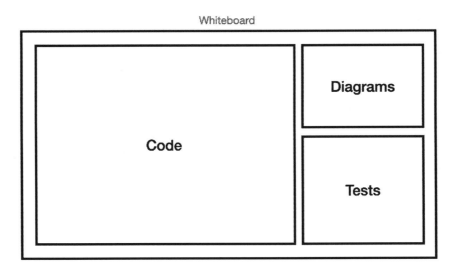

Figure 13.1 – Dividing the whiteboard into spaces

Figure 13.1 shows how we set a different space for each part of our answer. Organizing your whiteboard is the key to presenting a clear answer.

- *Use diagrams*: We talked about allocating a specific space for diagrams. However, diagrams are not a limitation of whiteboards at all – drawing diagrams is a significant advantage we don't have on a laptop, especially when working remotely. Diagrams let us visualize our algorithms, ideas, and thoughts and communicate them to our interviewer much better. When practicing coding questions, we should try to illustrate our thinking and answers. The best way to learn how to do that is to watch videos on the internet that explain how to solve different algorithms and focus on the visual part. We should know how to describe flows, arrays, trees, and database schemes on a whiteboard.

- *Practice out loud*: A common challenge many developers face is solving a coding question on a whiteboard while effectively explaining it. Why? Because most developers are not used to writing code down on a whiteboard and then explaining it at the same time. We shouldn't just practice writing on a whiteboard – we should also practice presenting our solutions while thinking out loud, whether to ourselves or others.

Few developers have good whiteboard drawing skills, but practicing is an effective way to improve dramatically. These small tips can raise the bar and provide us with more skills.

Now, let's move on to the actual coding. How do we start?

Starting to code

Now that we understand the different interview options, we can start with the real fun – coding. Can you guess what tip I have when facing a coding question unrelated to iOS, Swift, or coding in general?

Take your time

We first need to relax, step back, and analyze our task. It is a common mistake to start coding immediately even if we (think that we) already know the answer.

First, sure, you might know the answer or at least know how to approach the question. But take one or two minutes to rethink what you will do. Maybe find a more effective way to solve the question or a more engaging way to present the answer. If you have the time, why not use it?

Furthermore, taking your time is not a bad sign for the interviewer. The opposite is the truth. The fact that you are not rushing to code is a sign that you are thinking before you act and want to focus on planning and researching. In the previous chapter, we said interviewers are searching for soft skills during the architecture interview. However, soft skills are tested everywhere, including in the coding interview. Planning and critical thinking, essential soft skills, are also evaluated during the interview process.

Start with testing

Are we doing **test-driven development** (**TDD**)? Well, not exactly. One of the most noticeable differences between the coding and the architecture interview is that in the coding interview, we must understand all our constraints and guidelines from the beginning. We can't discover them as the interview proceeds.

In coding interviews, the session begins when we ask our interviewer for all the necessary information to accomplish our task.

But how do we know what to ask?

The best way is to *write down the tests for the function* we will code.

Look at the following coding question:

> *Write a function in Swift that takes an array of integers as input and returns the maximum difference between any two elements in the array. The maximum difference should be calculated by subtracting the smallest element from the largest element.*

Now, let's write down our test cases:

```
Input: [1, 2, 3, 4, 5] | Expected Output: 4
Input: [7, 2, 9, 5, 1] | Expected Output: 8
Input: [10, 3, 5, 2, 8] | Expected Output: 8
Input: [6, 5] | Expected Output: 1
Input: [6] | Expected Output: 0
Input: [] | Expected Output: 0
Input: [-10, -5] | Expected Output: -5
```

These test cases are crucial for us to provide a good answer. First, they answer all our questions – what if we have negative numbers? What if the input has one element or no elements at all?

Not only can the test cases lead us to the algorithm we need to write, but they also behave as a checklist throughout the session. If we want to ensure we've finished our coding and covered all our cases, we can review the list and check our code.

Start strong – don't be afraid of brute force

One thing that rings in our heads during interviews is that we need to provide an optimized solution in terms of space and time complexity.

And this is true – providing an efficient solution is one of the things we are tested on. But, as a starting point, we need to focus on accomplishing the task and only then optimize it. In other words, we should start with **brute force**.

> **What is brute force?**
>
> The term *brute force* refers to a straightforward approach to solving a problem involving basic algorithms without thinking of optimizations and efficiency. Brute-force solutions are impractical in real-world scenarios due to their high space and time complexity.

If brute force is not practical in real-life scenarios, why have I suggested starting with it?

When we receive a task to do, we first want to provide a working solution. A working solution proves that we understand the problem and is a great starting point for optimization. We can start measuring the time and space complexity and perform incremental updates.

In other words, brute force is an anchor for further changes we want to make, providing us the flexibility to revert and find an alternate path if something goes wrong.

Let's go over an example:

Find the maximum sum of a subarray within an array of integers.

The brute-force solution would be to iterate an array with two nested loops while maintaining a maxSum variable:

```
func maxSubarraySum(_ nums: [Int]) -> Int {
    var maxSum = Int.min

    for i in 0..<nums.count {
        var currentSum = 0

        for j in i..<nums.count {
            currentSum += nums[j]
```

```
            maxSum = max(maxSum, currentSum)
        }
    }

    return maxSum
}
```

In the first loop, we iterate all the elements in the array, and for each iteration, we create another loop that starts from the current element until the end of the same array. In this approach, we cover all the different subarray combinations and try to find the maximum sum by using the maxSum array.

This solution works! But we understand that using nested arrays makes our algorithm inefficient with a time complexity of O(n^2).

So, how can we improve it?

We said a brute-force solution is a great starting point for optimization. Having two nested loops should raise a concern – we understand that our time complexity is too high. Usually, the trade-off for time is space. In this case, we can have one array iteration and preserve the current sum in a specific variable.

Let's see an optimized version of the code:

```
func maxSubarraySum(_ nums: [Int]) -> Int {
    var maxSum = nums[0]
    var currentSum = nums[0]

    for i in 1..<nums.count {
        currentSum = max(nums[i], currentSum + nums[i])
        maxSum = max(maxSum, currentSum)
    }

    return maxSum
}
```

The preceding algorithm is called **Kadane's algorithm**, and it is an efficient way to solve that problem. In Kadane's algorithm, we calculate the maximum subarray that ends in a specific index using the previous index's subarray calculation.

Confused? Let's test it on a random array:

```
[2, -3, 5, -1, 6]
Iteration 1: currentSum = 2, maxSum = 2
Iteration 2: currentSum = -1, maxSum = 2
Iteration 3: currentSum = 5, maxSum = 5
Iteration 4: currentSum = 4, maxSum = 5
Iteration 5: currentSum = 10, maxSum = 10
```

Kadane's algorithm is a clever algorithm that provides an efficient and straightforward solution to a complex problem. You would not be expected to be able to use this algorithm if you haven't come across it before. But the point here is that we have two versions for our answer, and unless the optimal solution pops into our mind, we should start with the brute-force method and then continue solving the problem.

Coding like a pro

So, how do we code like a pro? We already know that our chances to succeed in the coding interview have much to do with how much we practice and solve algorithm problems at home. But practicing is only part of the solution. There are some key factors that we should follow during the session.

Let's start with two critical key factors – time and space complexities.

Use the terms "time complexity" and "space complexity"

We've mentioned time and space complexities in this chapter several times for a good reason. We know that effective communication with the interviewer is essential, and it should be done with proper terms.

After we finish the brute-force solution (as soon as possible), we need to optimize it and use the correct terms. This is so important because time and space complexities are objective ways to evaluate our code's efficiency.

For example, saying something such as "*It's not efficient to have a nested loop*" is not a professional way of describing an algorithm. The proper way would be, "*This algorithm has a time complexity of $O(N^2)$, but I think we can improve it to $O(N)$.*"

So, what is time complexity? The following information box provides a definition.

> **What is time complexity?**
> Time complexity refers to the time an algorithm requires to run as the input size grows. We describe the input size as N and express the complexity with big-O notation.

There are several use cases for time complexity:

- *Constant time complexity, "O(1)"*: Accessing a specific index in an array or performing basic arithmetic operations

- *Linear time complexity, "O(n)"*: Iterating an array or a linked list with the size of n

- *Quadratic time complexity, "O(n^2)"*: Using nested loops or bubble sort

- *Logarithmic time complexity, "O(log n)"*: Binary search

I don't want to get into too many details about time and space complexity, but there are two things to keep in mind when discussing complexity in an interview:

- *Complexity calculation*: This is a topic we should address before starting the interview, and it's broader than we think. First, we should count the different operations in our code and define each's complexity. Then, we need to sum it up and, in the end, determine the complexity of different inputs – best, worst, and average cases.

- *Understand logarithmic time complexity*: Most of the use cases I mentioned earlier are straightforward, but O(log n) is the one that confuses many developers. This complexity describes an algorithm whose runtime grows nonlinearly (**logarithmically**) with the input size. The increase is slower than O(n) and O(n^2), making it more efficient.

Let's have a look at the following findElement function and try to calculate its time complexity:

```
func findElement(_ array: [Int], target: Int) -> Bool {
    for element in array {
        if element == target {
            return true
        }
    }
    return false
}
```

The algorithm is simple – we iterate in an array and check each element to see whether it's equal to the target function parameter. If we find an element with the same value, we return true. Otherwise, we return false.

To calculate the function time complexity, we need to list our operations and describe their complexity individually. We have a for loop with a time complexity of O(n) and an if statement with a time complexity of O(1).

In this case, the overall time complexity of the function is O(n), and it is determined by the linear dominant operation.

And what about **space complexity**?

What is space complexity?

Space complexity refers to the memory or storage an algorithm requires to run as the input size grows. We describe the input size as N and express the complexity with big-O notation.

Space complexity is usually the trade-off of time complexity. When we optimize an algorithm, we need to consider the balance between the amount of memory it consumes and the time taken to execute the algorithm.

We measure space complexity in a similar way as we do for time complexity. For instance, let's look at the following code:

```
func printNumbers(n: Int) {
    var numbers = [Int]()   // Array to store numbers

    for i in 1...n {
        numbers.append(i)   // Adding numbers to the array
    }

    for number in numbers {
        print(number)   // Printing each number
    }
}
```

The printNumbers() function takes n as input and creates an array to store the numbers from 1 to n. The space complexity of this function is O(n) as the size of the numbers grows linearly with the input n.

The main goal of using time and space complexities is to not only communicate with the interviewer professionally, but also to be able to evaluate our solutions so we can provide an optimized answer.

Come with a set of tools

Never enter a combat field without a weapon or ammo – the same goes for a coding interview and a suitable set of tools. Every interview question or challenge can be addressed if we come prepared with a list of techniques to help us.

For example, we can have a complex question about linked lists. To solve that question, we must master the basics of a linked list – how to traverse a list, remove/add an element, or convert a list into an array and vice versa. We should know how to do these things before we come to the interview.

Knowing the basic data structures well can help us focus on the real challenge, which is the algorithm itself. In the previous chapter, we discussed app architectures and said that design patterns are the building blocks of architecture. Here, we also have building blocks. We start with data structures, then go over the fundamental design patterns that manipulate these data structures, and then the algorithms that are based upon these patterns.

Leave time for testing

Not testing is a common mistake many candidates make in coding interviews. When we discussed how to start the coding interview, we discussed testing as a key to understanding the problem. Eventually, the coding interview evolves around the tests – they are the key to understanding the problem, but they are also our checklist that ensures our answers fulfill the interviewer's requirements.

But it's not just leaving time for testing – presume that your tests will fail and you'll have to fix them, so you'll also need to leave time to fix bugs, similar to a real-world deployment process.

In this book, I've aimed to guide you through solving complex interview challenges by accompanying you every step of the way. The architecture interview (discussed in *Chapter 12*) and the coding interview are separate interviews that target your development skills from different angles. The home assessment is the interview that combines most of your skills.

Excelling in a home assessment

A **home assessment** is a common interview task many companies use to check a candidate's skills in dealing with a real-world problem. Home assessments require us to plan, architect, code, test, and deploy, sometimes with unfamiliar iOS topics we have no experience with.

Let's start with analyzing what a home assessment is.

What does a home assessment look like?

The framework for a regular home assessment won't come to you as a surprise. However, it is still worth going over it so we can be aligned on the process:

1. *Assignment*: This is the initial phase where we receive the task, including the requirements and instructions.

2. *Understanding*: In this stage, we carefully read the instructions and analyze the requirements. This is also the phase where we ask the interviewer anything we are unclear about and clarify what we must do.

3. *Execution*: This is the current assignment implementation, which typically takes place remotely. However, there are instances where it may be carried out at the hiring company's office. This step involves planning and writing our task, and if carried out at home, the execution phase may span several days.

4. *Testing*: Once the implementation is complete, we test our solution. That includes running test cases and addressing bugs and issues.

5. *Submission*: After the testing, we must submit the assignment to the interviewer. In most cases, the submission is done using Git for convenience.

6. *Post-delivery discussion*: In many companies, the interview is followed by a discussion or another interview where the interviewer will review the assessment with you to understand the different decisions and approaches taken while doing the home assessment.

The exact structure may vary between companies and assessments, but this framework provides an understanding of the significant steps involved in the process.

Now that we know what a home assessment looks like, let's understand why companies choose to spend their and our time on this type of task.

The different skills being tested in a home assessment

The home assessment examines some skills that are hard to test in the other interview stages, primarily the ability to develop an end-to-end app.

The skills required for a home assessment are both soft and hard, representing what is needed from an iOS developer in real-world situations.

Most of the skills are what we've discussed in previous chapters, but let's list them here so we can be aligned on what the interviewer expects from us:

- *Technical proficiency*: We are being tested for our technical skills – Swift, frameworks, Xcode, and other tools are all part of the skills we need to master as part of the test.

- *Problem solving*: Home assessments check our ability to solve problems and break them into smaller, more manageable steps while using our experience and creativity. Architecture and app design are part of those skills, which are crucial in these kinds of tests.

- *Algorithm design:* This may not be as superior a skill as the coding test, but it is part of the home assessment. Notice that we have a project, probably a tiny app, to develop. Being able to choose suitable data structures and write efficient algorithms may be required to solve complex problems and demonstrate our knowledge.

- *Attention to detail*: Unlike the other interview steps, in the home assessment, we have time. How much time? Enough to provide a good, accurate, and error-free solution. So, you see, more time means more expectations of us, and we are tested on being able to handle edge cases and complete code.

- *Code quality*: Our approach to the home assessment needs to resemble a complete project in terms of code quality. It means we need to document our code using comments, perform testing and QA, choose proper naming conventions, and have an organized file structure. Yes, I know it's a *small* project for an interview. But here's a secret – at this stage, the interviewer already knows we can build a table view and set up a Singleton. The quality of the implementation is what is important.

- *Independence*: One of the best things about home assessments is that they allow us to showcase our ability to fulfill a task from end to end, including project setup, coding, testing, and deployment, while being observed.

Having said that, the different skills required depend on the specific role and the company we are interviewing for. At this stage, we should already know what the company culture is and what is expected from us.

Now, let's go over some common examples of projects you may encounter in a home assessment.

Going over examples

Before moving on, a quick note on how to read these examples. You probably won't encounter one of these examples in an interview, and that's perfectly fine because that is not my intention. The goal of providing these examples is to strengthen your skills and make you prepared for the unknown. Unlike iOS interview questions, where knowledge matters, a home assessment concerns skills and techniques. That's why I'm trying to emphasize the list of skills and the home assessment process.

Each example can teach us a different aspect of the home assessment, and the ability to quickly build a small app with a short explanation is crucial for that task.

Let's go over the examples and pay attention to what's essential:

- *Build a to-do list app*: A home assessment focuses on table views, local data storage, and state management. Also, typical to-do apps usually support offline work and provide a streamlined user experience.

- *Build a weather app with an engaging user interface and reactive API updates*: It's important to integrate Combine frameworks in this kind of app to provide updated information to the user in an elegant design pattern.

- *Build a photo gallery app*: Photo gallery apps require close work with **PhotoKit** (the iOS SDK's photos framework), working with a collection view while optimizing it for fast loading and caching. Also, memory management capabilities are essential to handle large amounts of data.

- *Create a social media feed*: A social media feed usually works with a table view combined with a pagination pattern. It is vital to provide efficient memory management, user interactions such as likes and comments, and image loading as part of the feed.

- *Build a calendar app*: A calendar app requires managing an events list with tight integration to the **EventKit** framework (Apple's framework that helps us connect to the calendar), including a table view with a pagination design pattern.

Each of these assessments requires us to face different challenges, implement various design patterns, and tweak the architecture to create an organized project. It's a great mental exercise for your brain, trying to think about the different solutions and architectures, and is something that can improve your chances of succeeding in the test.

Even though our code results are extremely important, it is important to understand that our interviewer is looking at additional aspects of our work – red flags.

Avoiding red flags

Now that we understand what live coding interviews and home assessments are, let's briefly discuss perfection. Do we have to provide a perfect solution to pass the interview? What is the interviewer looking for?

That's not an easy question as it may differ for various interviewers and companies.

But there's something that all interviewers will look out for: red flags. The fact that we didn't provide an optimized solution or didn't know a particular Swift feature can be accepted by many interviewers – in most cases, they are looking for signals of something unhealthy in the way we approach, think, and code.

There are red flags we should avoid, even if they may initially seem insignificant to the interview process. Let's go over some of them now.

Inability to explain or defend a solution

This is a red flag that incorporates two crucial missing skills. The first one is *deep thinking and code/design understanding*. Many developers use their memory to regurgitate solutions without understanding why and how they work. Passing an interview question is not enough; we should also understand why we have done what we have done. Now that we are at the end of the book, it is essential to go back and validate that we fully understand the different answers and solutions.

The second skill is *communication and the ability to explain* ourselves. Sometimes it is hard to find the right words to describe why we made certain decisions, which can be translated into communication skills. But that is what this book is for – to help you verbalize your knowledge and get you ready for the interview.

Dichotomic thinking

Many interview questions, especially the design, architecture, and coding questions, require trade-offs and multiple approaches to be considered. There's no room for black-and-white thinking without explaining the alternative solutions. We should always be flexible and understand that there is not always a single correct answer.

Limited error handling

While it may sound trivial, ignoring error handling can be perceived as a red flag by interviewers, indicating a potentially unhealthy approach. Focusing on happy flows suggests a lack of attention to detail and a very shallow level of development. Handling code flows that may produce errors and unexpected results is significant.

Poor code quality

Our code is our artwork, and it should look good and express our expertise and capabilities as developers. But what does this mean? It means we should make structured and organized code with clear naming conventions, including comments and documentation. Try to avoid too short and unclear names and add indentations and spaces to your code.

Also, good separations, short functions, and folder organization can greatly help with our code appearance and clarity. The basics do matter at this stage.

Summary

That's it! We have reached the finale of the book, and what an exciting journey it has been!

In this concluding chapter, we delved into live coding, home assessments, and avoiding red flags. We learned how to tackle a whiteboard task, what to focus on when coding, and how to approach this important stage in the process. At this point, you should feel prepared to tackle the most experimental stage of the interview process: the coding assessment.

While the book may have ended, our journey of practice and hard work is just beginning. The world of iOS development is vast, and there is always more to learn and explore. Each chapter, section, and question has opened the door to numerous topics that can help you improve.

So, don't stop now; you're just getting started. Embrace continuous learning and strive for excellence in your iOS development career.

Index

Symbols

P

Package.swift 206, 207
pagination
    challenges 141, 142
pagination, in UITableView
    implementing, to load and display
        large amount of data 141
performance testing
    performing, in iOS applications 113
performance, with Concurrency
    advanced queues, creating with
        OperationQueue 239-241
    Combine Future publisher, used for
        implementing async operations 242, 243
    improving 238
    threads, blocking with NSLock 241
    working, with GCD 239
persistent memory
    benefits 177
persistent state
    handling, with UserDefaults 187-190
PhotoKit 279
plain text editor
    code organization, maintaining 269
    master complex Swift expressions 268, 269
    syntax errors, spotting 268
    typos, avoiding 268
    working with 268
planning 107, 108
    task development time, estimating 109, 110
    technical design document, creating
        for iOS task 110, 111
pod command-line tool 202
Podfile 198, 199
Podfile.lock 199
Pods directory 200

Podspec 200-202
pod update
    versus pod install 204
post notification 139
presentation layer 254
preset options
    for presenting, UIViewController in iOS 145
print() operator
    used, for reading console 173, 174
private context 182
Product Requirements
    Document (PRD) 259
profile scanning 42
programming paradigm 153, 154
    versus imperative programming 154-156
project planning process
    standard framework 109
project timeline and plan
    creating, for iOS app's development
        process 108, 109
promise parameter 242
Proof of Concept (POC) 108
Protocol Oriented Programming
    (POP) 102, 114
protocols
    questions, solving 101, 103
    used, for decoupling code 229-231
public GitHub repository, maintaining 45
    gists, adding 46
    showcase projects, adding 46
    side project, creating 45, 46
    solutions, sharing with Swift
        Package or pods 45
public Git repository 45
pure functions
    using, with method injection 229

`Packtpub.com`

Subscribe to our online digital library for full access to over 7,000 books and videos, as well as industry leading tools to help you plan your personal development and advance your career. For more information, please visit our website.

Why subscribe?

- Spend less time learning and more time coding with practical eBooks and Videos from over 4,000 industry professionals

- Improve your learning with Skill Plans built especially for you

- Get a free eBook or video every month

- Fully searchable for easy access to vital information

- Copy and paste, print, and bookmark content

Did you know that Packt offers eBook versions of every book published, with PDF and ePub files available? You can upgrade to the eBook version at `packtpub.com` and as a print book customer, you are entitled to a discount on the eBook copy. Get in touch with us at `customercare@packtpub.com` for more details.

At `www.packtpub.com`, you can also read a collection of free technical articles, sign up for a range of free newsletters, and receive exclusive discounts and offers on Packt books and eBooks.

Other Books You May Enjoy

If you enjoyed this book, you may be interested in these other books by Packt:

iOS 16 Programming for Beginners

Ahmad Sahar | Craig Clayton

ISBN: 9781803237046

- Get to grips with the fundamentals of Xcode 14 and Swift 5.7, the building blocks of iOS development.

- Understand how to prototype an app using storyboards.

- Discover the Model-View-Controller design pattern and how to implement the desired functionality within an app.

- Implement the latest iOS 16 features such as SwiftUI, Lock screen widgets, and WeatherKit.

- Convert an existing iPad app into a Mac app with Mac Catalyst.

Test-Driven iOS Development with Swift

Dr. Dominik Hauser

ISBN: 9781803232485

- Navigate Filmora's interface with ease.
- Add and manipulate audio using audio tracks.
- Create high-quality professional videos with advanced features in Filmora.
- Use split screens and Chroma keys to create movie magic.
- Create a gaming video and add humor to it.
- Understand career prospects in the world of video editing.

Packt is searching for authors like you

If you're interested in becoming an author for Packt, please visit authors.packtpub.com and apply today. We have worked with thousands of developers and tech professionals, just like you, to help them share their insight with the global tech community. You can make a general application, apply for a specific hot topic that we are recruiting an author for, or submit your own idea.

Hi!

I'm Avi Tsadok, the author of The Ultimate iOS Interview Playbook. I really hope you enjoyed reading this book and found it useful for increasing your productivity and efficiency in iOS Interview.

It would really help me (and other potential readers!) if you could leave a review on Amazon sharing your thoughts on The Ultimate iOS Interview Playbook here.

Go to the link below or scan the QR code to leave your review:

`https://packt.link/r/1803246316`

Your review will help me to understand what's worked well in this book, and what could be improved upon for future editions, so it really is appreciated.

Best Wishes,

Avi Tsadok

Download a free PDF copy of this book

Thanks for purchasing this book!

Do you like to read on the go but are unable to carry your print books everywhere?

Is your eBook purchase not compatible with the device of your choice?

Don't worry, now with every Packt book you get a DRM-free PDF version of that book at no cost.

Read anywhere, any place, on any device. Search, copy, and paste code from your favorite technical books directly into your application.

The perks don't stop there, you can get exclusive access to discounts, newsletters, and great free content in your inbox daily

Follow these simple steps to get the benefits:

1. Scan the QR code or visit the link below

https://packt.link/free-ebook/9781803246314

2. Submit your proof of purchase
3. That's it! We'll send your free PDF and other benefits to your email directly

Made in United States
Troutdale, OR
12/06/2023

15460536R00179